Praise for *The Bedrock of Christianity*

"Was there ever a real Jesus? If so, who was he, and what did he do and say? Since much disagreement about Jesus exists even among scholars, is it possible for non-experts to make an informed decision? In this book, Dr. Justin Bass serves as your expert guide through the maze. And he does so in a manner that's easy to understand. For what more could the serious inquirer reasonably ask? This book is unique and is an enjoyable read!"

—**Michael Licona,** associate professor of theology,
Houston Baptist University

"Justin Bass offers a delightful excavation of the historical foundations of the Christian faith pertaining to the life, death, and resurrection of Jesus. A terrific exposition of early Christian testimony about Jesus. Wisely researched and artfully written."

— **Michael F. Bird,** academic dean and lecturer of theology,
Ridley College, Melbourne, Australia

"Another exposition of the bedrock historical facts surrounding the most crucial origins of Christianity is always welcomed. The data are certainly available, firm, and very widely acknowledged by scholars across the landscape. Justin Bass's volume is the latest effort in this direction and presents a readable and very well-documented example, viewed from a variety of research perspectives. Very highly recommended."

— **Gary R. Habermas,** Distinguished Research Professor and chair,
philosophy department, Liberty University

"*The Bedrock of Christianity* stands unique in that it focuses its scope on the bedrock facts that are upheld by 99 percent of scholars—Jewish, Protestant, Catholic, agnostic, atheist, liberal, and conservative. The book not only challenges the unbeliever, but it also takes the believer to a new depth of realization of the bedrock truth: he has risen indeed!"

—**Imad N. Shehadeh,** president,
Jordan Evangelical Theological Seminary

"Jesus directed his disciples to build on the rock. In this exciting new volume, Justin Bass does precisely that as he carefully demonstrates how Christian faith is founded on the bedrock of powerful historical evidence. The result is exhilarating, faith-affirming, and just plain fun."

— **Randal Rauser,** professor of historical theology at Taylor Seminary; author of *Is the Atheist My Neighbor?*

"This is an excellent defense of the essential, historical foundation of Christianity. It is brief enough to edify the layperson and thorough enough—with excellent research from ancient and modern sources—to satisfy the scholar. I highly recommend it!"

— **Trent Horn,** staff apologist, Catholic Answers; author of *Counterfeit Christs*

"In a culture full of skepticism, cynicism, and doubt—particularly about the claims of Christianity—Justin Bass has provided a clear, cogent, and rock-solid defense of the foundational claims of the Christian faith. This book will cause the skeptics to doubt their own skepticism and Christian believers to grow deeper in their faith in Christ and their trust in the truthfulness and authority of Scripture."

— **Matthew Y. Emerson,** Dickinson Associate Professor of Religion and director of MACS and MAIS programs, Oklahoma Baptist University

"The resurrection is the make-or-break doctrine of Christianity. In this brief, fair, and thoughtful book, Justin Bass takes us down to the core historical facts that have to be explained, surveys the best historical scholarship on each, and shows why, ultimately, they point toward a risen Lord."

— **Andrew Wilson,** teaching pastor, King's Church London; author of *If God, Then What*

"Justin Bass, through proof and argument, gives clear and compelling evidence that the historical Jesus indeed came down to Earth, died on the cross, was buried, and was resurrected on the third day. This powerful book will not only encourage and build your faith, but inspire you in your journey of life."

— **Hanna Massad,** author and pastor from Gaza; founder and president of Christian Mission to Gaza

"Before anyone pursues any depth of the faith, the death and resurrection of Christ—as a fulfillment of the Old Testament and as the fount of the New Testament—must be believed. This Justin Bass sets forth clearly and forcefully."

— **Tommy Nelson,** senior pastor, Denton Bible Church, Texas

"Bass's accessible yet rigorous study shows how a crucified Jewish carpenter came to be acknowledged as the promised Messiah, galvanizing his followers to travel widely and spread the good news of repentance and forgiveness of sins. For apologists and open-minded skeptics, *The Bedrock of Christianity* demonstrates conclusively that Jesus is worthy to be worshiped as Lord and Christ."

— **Max McLean,** artistic director, Fellowship for Performing Arts

"This is the most helpful book for unbelievers I've seen that argues the evidence for the resurrection of Christ. Bass takes a conservative approach in selecting evidence that virtually all scholars accept, showing that even this minimal bedrock evidence is best explained—or only *can* be explained—if Jesus really rose from the dead two thousand years ago."

— **Allen Hainline,** Reasonable Faith chapter director; artificial intelligence researcher and owner of Omega Software; contributing author of *The Story of the Cosmos: How the Heavens Declare the Glory of God*

"After reading this book, I believe that you, too, will affirm the claims and creed about Jesus Christ: that he died for our sins, was buried, and on the third day rose from the dead."

— **Trog Trogdon,** urban missionary; author of *A Walk to Wisdom*

"Layer by layer, *The Bedrock of Christianity* provides substantive, thoughtful, and accessible clarity to the source facts of Jesus and early Christianity. Whether the reader is a skeptic or a growing disciple, agreement can be found in the basic 'givens' of a history and faith that have withstood the test of time and criticism. Accessible to the lay reader but written with the acuity of a New Testament scholar, Justin Bass informs all."

— **Mark Penick,** senior pastor, Metro East Baptist Church, Wichita, Kansas

"If you have any doubts that Christian faith and religion are based on facts—or if you are exploring faith—read this book. Justin addresses why Jesus, even two thousand years later, still possesses a 'mysterious sway' over humanity today. As I was reading this book, many of my own questions regarding my faith were answered."

—**Jeff Scruggs,** cofounder, Hope Matters Marriage Ministries

"Tim Keller recounts how, as a Christian pastor, he believed in the resurrection of Jesus, but reading N. T. Wright's *The Resurrection of the Son of God* made him sit up and say, 'Oh my gosh, it really did happen!' That's how I felt reading this book. Some Christians may not like it that Bass plays by so many of the broader scholarly guild's rules (restricting himself to Paul's seven 'undisputed' letters, for example). But rather than criticize him for his methodology, we should thank him for showing Christians how much solid evidence for the resurrection we can produce even when fighting with one hand tied behind our backs."

—**Justin Dillehay,** pastor, Grace Baptist Church, Hartsville, Tennessee; contributing editor for The Gospel Coalition

THE

BEDROCK

OF CHRISTIANITY

Foreword by Darrell L. Bock

THE
BEDROCK
OF CHRISTIANITY

The Unalterable Facts of
Jesus' Death and Resurrection

JUSTIN W. BASS

LEXHAM PRESS

The Bedrock of Christianity: The Unalterable Facts of Jesus' Death and Resurrection

Print ISBN 978-1-68-359360-7
Digital ISBN 978-1-68-359361-4
Library of Congress Control Number: 2019957133

Lexham Editorial Team: Elliot Ritzema, Claire Brubaker
Cover Design: Owen Craft
Typesetting: Danielle Thevenaz

*This book is dedicated to my wonderful children,
Arianna and Christian.
May their generation and generations after stand firm
on the bedrock of Jesus' death and resurrection.*

Contents

Abbreviations

AB	Anchor Yale Bible Commentary
Ag. Ap.	Josephus, *Against Apion*
Ant.	Josephus, *Jewish Antiquities*
CBQ	*Catholic Biblical Quarterly*
COQG	Christian Origins and the Question of God
ICC	International Critical Commentary
JBL	*Journal of Biblical Literature*
J.W.	Josephus, *Jewish War*
LCL	Loeb Classical Library
1 Macc	1 Maccabees
2 Macc	2 Maccabees
NIGTC	New International Greek Testament Commentary
NPNF	*The Nicene and Post-Nicene Fathers*, Series 1. Edited by Philip Schaff. 1886–1889. 14 vols. Repr., Peabody, MA: Hendrickson, 1994
NT	New Testament
OT	Old Testament
Sir	Sirach/Ecclesiasticus
WUNT	Wissenschaftliche Untersuchungen zum Neuen Testament

Foreword

T here are many things said about Jesus, just as there are many,
often conflicting, views about him. So where should one
start in thinking about him and his significance? How do we sort
out the range of things claimed about him: a myth, a religious
great, a misguided revolutionary, a model of piety, a deceiver, a
blasphemer, a Christ, or a Son of God? That is where this work
comes in. Justin Bass has asked, Why not start with what is
not so debated and what we know about him? Christianity has
uniquely been a religion about core events and claims centered
in a singular person. Bass explores what that view means, where
it came from, how far back it can be traced, and what that could
well mean. It is a helpful starting point to sort out the cacophony
of claims about Jesus.

The Bedrock of Christianity takes you on a journey. You will
learn much about what we know about Jesus and central claims
coming from the earliest Christian faith. It involves travel
through ideas, history, and archaeology. It also is more. It asks
basic questions about how far back these ideas go. Were they late
ideas, fabricated to bring hope to a sad tragedy of an untimely
death of a curious, distant, ancient figure? Do they parallel anything else we have seen in history? How did this core history
change the direction of the way our world sees life? How do we
even know what was core and early? How did such a backwater

movement emerge from a handful of "believers" with no social or political power to become such a global presence? Above all, why do any of these questions matter?

The question about the bedrock of Christianity is really a query about the nature of our lives and their purpose. So this history ultimately entails a deeply personal story, a claim that the Creator God intentionally entered our world as one of us to show us the way to life and meaning. Heaven came down to earth and left footprints on the ground, laying a bedrock we can trace. In that bedrock are the core early claims of Christian faith. And the personal story claiming to come from God aims to become our story as well, giving sense and direction to how we see life. It is in the history treated here that we start to see our own story. To get there we need to take a careful look at the basis for whether Jesus' story matters or not. We need to know whether that account is merely a story or something more solid. With Justin Bass as a qualified guide, you might not only get answers to such questions, but you might find yourself in the middle of God's story, just as have many others throughout history.

Darrell L. Bock
Senior Research Professor of New Testament Studies
Dallas Theological Seminary

Horatio: O day and night, but this is wondrous strange!
Hamlet: And therefore as a stranger give it welcome.
There are more things in heaven and earth, Horatio,
    Than are dreamt of in your philosophy.

William Shakespeare, *Hamlet*, act 1, scene 5

Introduction

Suppose that a Catholic, a Protestant, a Jew, and an agnostic—all honest historians cognizant of 1st-century religious movements—were locked up in the bowels of the Harvard Divinity School library ...

John P. Meier, *A Marginal Jew*

This sounds like the beginning of a joke, but it is actually a thought experiment from New Testament scholar John Meier. He begins the first of his multivolume work on the historical Jesus asking his audience to imagine this group of learned scholars, from a wide range of diverse backgrounds in worldviews and religions, trying to hammer out an agreement on who the historical Jesus was, what he said, and what he did.[1]

The goal of this book, *The Bedrock of Christianity*, is similar, but even bolder. Instead of just a few scholars from different backgrounds, imagine *all* scholars alive today who are teaching in the relevant fields of ancient history, classics, and biblical studies from universities and seminaries across the world, locked up in the Harvard Divinity School library until they

---

1. Meier writes, "By the 'historical Jesus' I mean the Jesus whom we can recover, recapture, or reconstruct by using the scientific tools of modern historical research" (*Marginal Jew*, 1). This is also the definition I will use when I refer to the historical Jesus throughout this book.

can form a consensus on the facts concerning Jesus and early Christianity. Could they find agreement? Yes!

This book will show you where they all agree.

To illustrate how incredible this agreement among scholars is, we only need to look at the myriads on myriads of facts and stories about Jesus and early Christianity they do not agree on. The annual meeting of the Society of Biblical Literature contains the largest gathering of such scholars in the world. There are currently over eighty-five hundred members from over eighty countries. These members are from a widely diverse group of backgrounds and worldviews: Jewish, Protestant, Catholic, agnostic, atheist, liberal, and conservative. To paraphrase John 21:25, if all that they disagreed on were written down in detail, I suppose that even the whole world would not be able to contain the books that would be written!

And yet, the bedrock facts laid out in this book concerning Jesus and early Christianity have virtually unanimous consensus among the thousands of scholars who are associated with the Society of Biblical Literature, and who teach and publish in the relevant fields.

This is truly extraordinary.

AN ABSURD ABERRATION

Before I get into the main argument of the book, though, let me illustrate how nearly unanimous scholars are in affirming these bedrock facts by dealing with the first and most foundational fact: Jesus existed. Establishing this bedrock fact from the outset is key, since if Jesus did not exist, he probably would not be able to do anything else in history either.

That Jesus existed is virtually undisputed among scholars teaching in the relevant fields of ancient history, classics, and

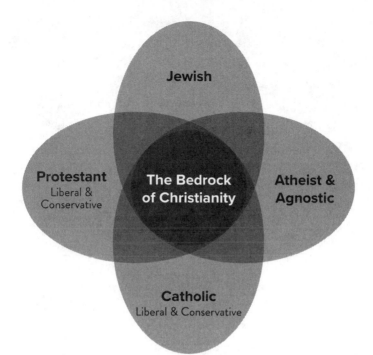

biblical studies. In conversation, I prefer to say all scholars believe Jesus existed, but in order to be precise I say here "virtually all" (99 percent). For an analogy, it is right to say that the historical fact that over six million Jews were murdered in the Holocaust of World War II is agreed on by *all* scholars of history today, even if a handful of Holocaust deniers happen to have scholarly credentials. If we are being precise, however, we must say that 99 percent of scholars agree that the Holocaust occurred because of the existence of Holocaust deniers. If we ignore the Holocaust deniers, which I believe historians should, then it could be said that *all* historians agree that the Holocaust occurred during World War II.

Those who deny Jesus' existence are in a similar category. New Testament scholar and historian Robert Van Voorst has discovered that "many books and essays—by my count, over one hundred—in the past two hundred years have fervently denied the very existence of Jesus." Van Voorst goes on, "Contemporary New Testament scholars have typically viewed their arguments as so weak or bizarre that they relegate them to footnotes, or often ignore them completely."[2] Considering that there have been tens of thousands of scholars publishing books and articles about Jesus and early Christianity during the past two hundred years, this means that over 99 percent of scholars have consistently affirmed the historicity of Jesus of Nazareth. Additionally, we have no record of anyone denying the historicity of Jesus *before* a little over two hundred years ago.

These handful of scholars—the less than 1 percent—who have doubted Jesus' existence are known as mythicists. Just as historians of World War II have to deal with (or ignore) Holocaust deniers and NASA has to deal with (or ignore) moon-landing deniers, so also biblical scholars and ancient historians have to deal with (but usually ignore) mythicists. Meier, for example, dismisses G. A. Wells, who was a professor of German and the leading mythicist proponent in the twentieth century, in a single footnote, saying, "Wells's book, which builds its arguments on … unsubstantiated claims, may be allowed to stand as a representative of a whole type of popular Jesus book that I do not bother to consider in detail."[3]

New Testament scholar (and an agnostic himself) Bart Ehrman has rightly noted that virtually all mythicists identify as atheist or agnostic.[4] In 2014, at a meeting for the Freedom

---

2. Van Voorst, *Jesus Outside the New Testament*, 6.

3. Meier, *Marginal Jew*, 87n59.

4. Ehrman: "It is no accident that virtually all mythicists (in fact, all of them, to my knowledge) are either atheists or agnostics. The ones I know anything about are quite virulently, even militantly, atheist" (*Did Jesus Exist?*, 337–38).

from Religion Foundation, Ehrman delivered an intellectual spanking to a mythicist after he challenged the historical existence of Jesus:

> Once you get out of your conclave, there's nobody who thinks this. This is not even an issue for scholars of antiquity. ... There is no scholar of any college or university in the Western world who teaches classics, ancient history, New Testament, early Christianity, any related field who doubts that Jesus existed. ... I think atheists have done themselves a disservice by jumping on the bandwagon of mythicism because frankly it makes you look foolish to the outside world. If that's what you're going to believe, you just look foolish.[5]

You just look foolish.

Ehrman also wrote a book called *Did Jesus Exist?* that hurt a lot of mythicist feelings. In it he wrote about mythicism's modern origins: "The idea that Jesus did not exist is a modern notion. It has no ancient precedents. It was made up in the eighteenth century. One might well call it a modern myth, the myth of the mythical Jesus."[6] He concludes, "Jesus existed, and those vocal persons who deny it do so not because they have considered the evidence with the dispassionate eye of the historian, but because they have some other agenda that this denial serves. From a dispassionate point of view there was a Jesus of Nazareth. ... Jesus *certainly* did exist."[7]

Even mid-twentieth-century German scholar Rudolf Bultmann, who is famous for his attempt to "demythologize"

---

5. Abrahamic Faith, "The Historical Jesus DID Exist – Bart Ehrman," YouTube, April 9, 2016, https://www.youtube.com/watch?v=43mDulN5-ww.

6. Ehrman, *Did Jesus Exist?*, 96.

7. Ehrman, *Did Jesus Exist?*, 4, 7.

almost everything about Jesus and the New Testament, wrote this: "Of course the doubt as to whether Jesus really existed is unfounded and not worth refutation. No sane person can doubt that Jesus stands as founder behind the historical movement whose first distinct stage is represented by the Palestinian community."[8]

You heard it from Bultmann himself: mythicists are insane.

But even though mythicism was murdered long ago by "a brutal gang of facts," social media and the internet have given it new life. In the scholarly community, however, nothing has changed since Van Voorst's comment in 2000: "The theory of Jesus' nonexistence is now effectively dead as a scholarly question."[9]

To be clear, it is not the affirmation of experts that confirms the Holocaust occurred or that Neil Armstrong and Buzz Aldrin walked on the moon or that Jesus existed. It is the robust historical evidence and facts. Within one hundred years of his death, primary sources for the existence of Jesus include Paul's early letters; Matthew, Mark, Luke-Acts, and John; Jewish historian Josephus; Roman historians Tacitus and Suetonius; and Roman governor Pliny the Younger (Josephus, *Ant.* 20.200; Tacitus, *Annals* 15.44; Suetonius, *Claudius* 25; Pliny the Younger, *Letter* 10.96).[10] After more than two hundred years of historical and biblical criticism, the careful evaluation of such evidence for Jesus and early Christianity on the part of experts from all different

---

8. Bultmann, *Jesus and the Word*, 13.

9. Van Voorst, *Jesus Outside the New Testament*, 14.

10. The primary sources definitively demonstrating the historicity of Jesus of Nazareth are conveniently laid out in Ehrman's *Did Jesus Exist?* and Van Voorst's *Jesus Outside the New Testament*.

backgrounds and worldviews has led to this overwhelming 99 percent consensus, despite a handful of mythicist hecklers.[11]

In short, Jesus of Nazareth most *certainly* did exist.

THE BEDROCK SOURCES

Jesus' existence is just one of many facts about Jesus and early Christianity that passes this 99 percent threshold of agreement among scholars. There are a lot more, many of which are not even included in this book. I am focused here on the bedrock facts that emerge from the earliest bedrock sources for Jesus and early Christianity: Paul's early letters. Over the past two hundred years of critical scholarship, these letters have been considered early and trustworthy sources in what they tell us about Paul and his movements, the historical Jesus, and some of his earliest followers like Peter. Seven of Paul's early letters are considered undisputed by virtually all scholars today: Galatians, 1 and 2 Corinthians, Romans, Philippians, 1 Thessalonians, and

---

11. Literally a handful. Richard Carrier's *On the Historicity of Jesus* (2014) is the first peer-reviewed academic book defending the mythicist position (the second is Raphael Lataster's *Questioning the Historicity of Jesus*, 2019). On his blog, Carrier lists eight scholars with credentials in either ancient history or biblical studies who he says, "are on record doubting the historicity of Jesus." If we look closer at Carrier's mythicist candidates, they do indeed have scholarly credentials, but the only current full-time professors on his list are Arthur Droge, Kurt Noll, and Hector Avalos. Avalos has used the word "agnostic" to describe his view on the historicity of Jesus. See Hector Avalos, "Who Was the Historical Jesus?," *Ames Tribune*, March 2, 2013, http://www.amestrib.com/sections/opinion/columns/hector-avalos-who-was-the-historical-jesus.html. The rest on the list are either retired professors (Brodie, Thompson) or are not full-time professors at all (Carrier, Price, Lataster). Carrier goes on to list five more teaching scholars who he says, "nevertheless endorse historicity but acknowledge we [mythicists] have a respectable point." Richard seems to be really reaching with this second list. In short, there may be a handful of current teaching professors (even according to Carrier only three) who "are on record doubting the historicity of Jesus," but this in no way affects the 99 percent threshold, and not *one* of these teaching professors identifies as a mythicist.

Philemon.[12] Even a mythicist such as Richard Carrier does not deny the undisputed letters were written by Paul and dates them to the 50s AD.[13]

Yet if we survey the past two hundred years of critical scholarship, we must narrow that undisputed list down to four *Hauptbriefe,* or "main letters": Galatians, 1 and 2 Corinthians, and Romans. In the entire history of biblical scholarship, the only teaching scholars on record to deny the Pauline authorship of the *Hauptbriefe* were from the Dutch school of W. C. van Manen in the nineteenth century, which has rightly been labeled "a critical aberration in the history of New Testament study."[14]

Along with Paul's four main letters, traditions and hymns concerning the historical Jesus within these early letters, preeminently the creedal tradition or formula found within 1 Corinthians 15:3–7, give us the bedrock facts concerning Jesus' death, resurrection, appearances, and key events during the first two decades of the Christian movement.

These four undisputed letters of Paul, and the bedrock traditions such as 1 Corinthians 15:3–7 quoted within them, will be the primary sources for the facts laid out in this book.

These bedrock facts and sources are indeed unalterable.

BEDROCK FACTS

In this book we will go on a journey through history to establish the unalterable bedrock facts concerning Jesus and early Christianity that virtually all scholars agree on. To emphasize again what was said above, this degree of agreement is true

---

12. Ehrman, *New Testament,* 308; see also Neill and Wright, *Interpretation of the New Testament, 1861–1986,* 362.

13. Carrier, *On the Historicity of Jesus,* 260–61.

14. Bruce, *Epistle to the Galatians,* 1. See also van Manen, "Wave of Hypercriticism."

not just today, but ever since the science of historical criticism began in the late eighteenth and early nineteenth century.[15] These unalterable facts have passed through the fires of biblical criticism since the Enlightenment. If you do not believe me, search the relevant scholars in history from Germany, France, England, or America. All agree on these bedrock facts.

If that seems incredible, it is! One might even call it miraculous.

Why is it important to know these bedrock facts? One of my goals for this book is to help followers of Jesus find the deepest, most foundational, solid-rock layer, historically speaking, on which they can rely for their faith. I want to demonstrate to you what New Testament scholar and agnostic Paula Fredriksen calls "historical bedrock, facts known past doubting."[16]

Pastor and author Tim Keller tells a story about when he realized that the historical facts surrounding the resurrection of Jesus of Nazareth were truly the bedrock of his faith. After reading N. T. Wright's *The Resurrection of the Son of God*, his understanding of the historical facts undergirding the resurrection sunk down into the depths of his heart.

Here is a brief account of his experience:

Did I believe the resurrection of Jesus Christ? I mean, of course, I'm a minister. Did I believe in the bodily resurrection of Jesus? Sure I did. Would you say I really believed

---

15. Historical criticism is the discipline that studies the prehistory of the text, its date, author, recipients, culture, background, and the final assembling of the text by the author or editor. One view is that historical criticism began with Johann Salomo Semler (1725–1791). Another foundational work, especially for our purposes, is David Strauss's *Life of Jesus*, which was published in 1835. Between Semler and Strauss is a good estimate for the beginning of the science of historical and biblical criticism.

16. Fredriksen, *Jesus of Nazareth*, 264.

it? Sure I really believed it. Does that give you peace? Sure it gives you peace. Then I got thyroid cancer and when I was recovering from thyroid cancer … I got a book by a bishop of Durham, N. T. Wright … called *The Resurrection of the Son of God.* … At the end of four weeks I put it down … and I said, "Oh my gosh, it really did happen." … I then felt the certainty go down three more floors, floors in my heart that I didn't even know were there. I thought I was at the basement but there were four or five more floors of things. It just sunk down all the way to the bottom. And maybe there is still more to go.[17]

It just sunk down all the way to the bottom.

With the resurrection of Jesus of Nazareth as the bedrock of your heart and faith, if it sinks down all the way to the bottom, even if new discoveries somehow demonstrated that most of the Bible was full of false information and contradictions, the bedrock facts concerning Jesus' death and resurrection would not be touched. They are unalterable. Even atheist and agnostic scholars who argue the Bible is full of errors and contradictions still affirm these bedrock facts as you will see. In other words, they are true independent of the inspiration and/or inerrancy of the Bible. While these are important Christian doctrines, whether you believe (and I do) in the inerrancy and/or inspiration of the Bible is independent of Jesus' death and resurrection and the facts surrounding this event. They are true regardless.

It is crucial that professing followers of Jesus all over the world know and understand the unalterable historical facts

---

17. Tim Keller, "Why Do You Have So Much Peace? Tim Keller at Veritas [11 of 11]," Veritas Forum at Columbia University, YouTube, November 29, 2011, https://www.youtube.com/watch?v=B4pA-KOUdQE&list=PL6A1AE952ADCB31FB&index=11.

undergirding their faith.[18] As the apostle Paul proclaimed to the philosophers of Athens: "He has … furnished proof to all men by raising Him from the dead" (Acts 17:31). This book lays out these unalterable proofs that all believers should know, not only in order to strengthen and solidify their own faith, but also so they will go on the offensive, not the defensive, with a skeptical and unbelieving world.

Another vital reason this book needed to be written is to let nonbelievers and skeptics who are interested in Christianity, or even seeking to critique it, know what these foundational, bedrock facts of Christianity are. There is an incredible amount of misinformation out there concerning Jesus and early Christianity. In this book, you will be able to find the common ground on which both believers and nonbelievers agree.

Another way to refer to this common-ground agreement is mere *historical* Christianity.

MERE *HISTORICAL* CHRISTIANITY

C. S. Lewis writes,

> The heart of Christianity is a myth which is also a
> fact. The old myth of the Dying God, without ceasing
> to be myth, comes down from heaven of legend and

---

18. The facts and arguments of this book stand on the shoulders of giants, specifically scholars Darrell L. Bock (*Who is Jesus?*), Gary Habermas (*The Historical Jesus*), Michael Licona (*The Resurrection of Jesus*), William Lane Craig (*Assessing the New Testament Evidence for the Resurrection of Jesus*; *The Son Rises*), and N. T. Wright (*The Resurrection of the Son of God*). To my knowledge, though, there is not a book that limits its scope to *only* the bedrock facts that are affirmed by 99 percent of scholars. Bedrock facts that pass this threshold are found primarily in the sources of Paul's early undisputed letters. This book is therefore unique as it is more limited in scope than these predecessors and seeks to demonstrate the bedrock, common-ground facts agreed on by virtually all scholars today and over the past two hundred years—what scholars have affirmed everywhere and always, in other words, mere *historical* Christianity.

imagination to the earth of history. It happens—at a
particular date, in a particular place, followed by defin-
able historical consequences. We pass from a Balder or
an Osiris, dying nobody knows when or where, to a historical Person crucified under Pontius Pilate.[19]

This book is in the spirit of Lewis's *Mere Christianity*, in
which Lewis sought to lay out the doctrines that are agreed on
by all branches of Christendom, whether Catholic, Orthodox,
or Protestant. These bedrock doctrines Lewis discusses—the
Trinity, Christ's incarnation, atonement, and others—are appro-
priately known as the essentials of Christianity, or as Lewis says,
"plain Christianity that no Christian disagrees with."[20]

In the chapters that follow, I want to lay out the plain *historical* facts that no ancient historian, classicist, or biblical scholar
disagrees with. These "plain facts" concern the essential of
the essentials: the death, resurrection, and post-resurrection
appearances of Jesus of Nazareth, *and* the rise of his indestructible movement, the Nazarenes.[21] These facts concern "a historical Person crucified ... under Pontius Pilate," as Lewis says.[22]

This is the Bedrock of Christianity.

As stated above, Christianity's bedrock is not the inerrancy or
even inspiration of the Bible. It is not any tradition, denomina-
tion, or saint. It is instead the historical man Jesus' agonizing

---

19. Lewis, "Myth Became Fact," 59.

20. Marsden, *C. S. Lewis's Mere Christianity*, 93.

21. Calling them "Christians" here would be anachronistic. The Jewish movement that arose after Jesus' death and resurrection was probably called the "sect"
of the "Nazarenes" (Acts 24:5) or "the Way" (see Acts 24:14–15, 22). They were
not called "Christians" until the church was founded at Antioch (Acts 11:26).

22. Lewis, "Myth Became Fact," 59.

death on a Roman cross and the extraordinary events and appearances that his earliest followers experienced soon after. This is the common ground where we must all, believers and nonbelievers, begin our discussions when dealing with arguably the greatest questions of human history: Who was Jesus? Did the historical Jesus rise from the dead? What was the cause of this world-changing movement known as Christianity? And how do *you* fit in to this story of Jesus?

For, as Stephen Neill and N.T. Wright have written, something extraordinary must have happened in history for Christianity to have endured these last two thousand years:

> Here is a great spiritual movement, which has withstood the changes and chances of nineteen centuries. How are we to account for it? The Roman Empire would be inexplicable without Julius Caesar and Augustus; what was the corresponding factor in the other movement in the first century A.D., which led to the birth and growth of the Christian Church?[23]

I will propose an answer to these questions, but only after we have traveled through history and understood the bedrock facts and sources concerning Jesus and his indestructible movement. As New Testament scholar George Caird wrote, "Christianity is based on indisputable facts. ... I do not say that Christianity is the indisputable interpretation of these facts."[24]

Before we discover the first of these indisputable facts, let us begin with one of the most important and foundational meetings of early Christianity. It was a meeting between the apostolic titans Peter and Paul. This meeting will also set the stage

---

23. Neill and Wright, *Interpretation of the New Testament*, 139.
24. Caird and Jenkins, *Jesus and God*, 26.

for the chapters that follow, laying out the bedrock facts. It is an exemplar for studying history and will help us learn to engage our historical imagination.

As Shakespeare suggests, "And let us, ciphers to this great account, on your imaginary forces work."[25]

---

25. Shakespeare, *Henry V*, act 1, prologue, line 15.

Prologue: When Titans Meet

It was three years later that I went to Jerusalem to obtain information from Peter, and stayed with him for two weeks.

Galatians 1:18 GNB

We may presume they did not spend all the time talking about the weather.

C. H. Dodd, *The Apostolic Preaching and Its Developments*

We have many examples of historic meetings of saints throughout history. George Müller, Hudson Taylor, and D. L. Moody, all three of them missionary titans of the nineteenth century, regularly visited and preached at Charles Spurgeon's Metropolitan Tabernacle, were Spurgeon's houseguests, and probably conversed about Jesus and the Scriptures into the late hours of the night. Oh to be a fly on the wall for those prayers and discussions!

In the last century, I think the most epic meeting of saints was between the myth-making giants C. S. Lewis and J. R. R. Tolkien. Lewis records their first meeting in his diary on May 11, 1926:

Tolkien managed to get the discussion round to the proposed English Prelim. I had a talk with him afterwards.

> He is a smooth, pale, fluent little chap—can't read
> Spenser because of the forms—thinks the language is
> the real thing in the school—thinks all literature is writ-
> ten for the amusement of men between thirty and forty.
> ... No harm in him: only needs a smack or so.[26]

Tolkien as a younger man must have had one of those punch-
able faces.

After this meeting, two of the most influential authors and
Christian apologists of the twentieth century met weekly at a
pub in Oxford discussing Narnia, Middle-Earth, Norse myths,
and how Christianity is the true myth.

In the history of Christianity, there was at least one meeting that is even more important than the meeting of Lewis and
Tolkien. It happened when the great apostles Peter and Paul
spent a fortnight together in Jerusalem. This is not legend but
real history! After Jesus, Peter and Paul are almost certainly the
two most influential figures in the history of Christianity. And
there they were, walking the streets of Jerusalem together, con-
versing, praying, and sharing their hearts.

An epic meeting indeed!

What were the first words shared between Peter and Paul
when they met? What did they talk about as they spent day and
night together during those two weeks? What sites did they see?
Who else joined them in their journeys? We do not know. History
is silent. But what we do know, what is a bedrock fact, is that
they did meet and spent these two weeks together. Scholars are
unanimous that this meeting took place in Jerusalem, even if we
don't know the content of their conversation or even the exact

---

26. Lewis, *All My Road before Me*, 392–93.

year of the meeting. It was most likely within five years of Jesus' crucifixion, sometime between AD 33 and 38.[27]

There is also unanimous agreement that Paul is telling the truth when he says he was Peter's houseguest for "fifteen days" (Gal 1:18). This is one of a handful of chronological markers Paul gives in his letters, especially in Galatians. In the same verse he mentions "three years later" (Gal 1:18), and the next chapter begins: "Then after an interval of fourteen years" (Gal 2:1). In addition, Paul uses the strongest language to say he is telling the truth: "Now in what I am writing to you, I assure you before God that I am not lying" (Gal 1:20). Paul makes it clear to the Galatians that these events really happened. Two thousand years later, critical scholars of all stripes, nonbelievers and believers alike, agree.

Two weeks is a long time to spend with someone, especially without the distractions of movies, television, or social media. They must have really bonded as fellow followers of Jesus and peered deep within each other's hearts. How could they not have become lifelong friends after this time? Early church father John Chrysostom sums it up well: "Now to remain with him was an act of honor, but to remain with him so many days was one of friendship and extreme love."[28] They were close enough friends, as we read later in Galatians (2:11–14), for Paul to feel comfortable enough to publicly rebuke Peter when he was not acting in line with the gospel.

27. See Dunn, *Epistle to the Galatians*, 72; Jewett, *Chronology of Paul's Life*, 32, 100; Lüdemann, *Paul, Apostle to the Gentiles*, 171–72.

28. John Chrysostom, "Homily on Galatians 1:18," in *Commentary on the Epistle to the Galatians*.

"TO OBTAIN INFORMATION FROM"

Let us visualize both bearded men offering each other the right hand of fellowship and embracing in that first meeting. If this meeting took place in AD 37, Peter would have been in his early forties and Paul in his late twenties.[29] They must have both referred to the other with that uniquely Christian greeting "Brother."

> Peter: Brother Paul. Greetings in the name of our Lord Jesus Christ!
>
> Paul: Greetings, Cephas.[30] I have eagerly desired to meet with you for years.
>
> Peter: And I as well, as soon as we heard the glorious news of our Lord appearing to you on the road.

Where did they go from there? Did Peter take Paul fishing? Did they pray at the temple? Did they travel around Jerusalem and visit the places where Jesus was arrested, put on trial, and crucified? If so, this would have been the first Christian pilgrimage to the holy sites of Jerusalem, and the tour guide was Saint Peter himself!

Or maybe Peter took Paul to the courtyard where he denied Jesus three times. Maybe he told him the dark story in much the same way we find it in the Gospel of Mark. In our historical imagination, we can hear Peter saying to Paul with tears in his eyes: "I denied him three times right here! I cursed myself!

---

29. Jewett, *Chronology of Paul's Life*, 100.

30. Both *Cephas* (Aramaic) and *Petros* (Greek) mean "rock." Paul almost exclusively refers to him as Cephas in his letters (Gal 1:18; 2:9, 11, 14; 1 Cor 1:12; 3:22; 9:5; 15:5), using "Peter" in only Gal 2:7, 8. According to the Gospels, "Cephas" would be the actual name Jesus gave him, replacing "Simon" (John 1:42; see also Matt 16:18). Since Peter is the more familiar name, I will use Peter throughout this book, except when I quote Paul.

I cursed Christ's name before men!" And Paul responding: "Cephas, you know how I persecuted the church of God. I have put many of his followers in prison and even to death! I forced many to blaspheme! I tortured them until they cursed Christ's name!"

It is a bedrock fact that these titans met, but exactly what they discussed and where they went is left to the historical imagination.

While we don't know exactly what they said to each other, there is one significant clue as to the content of their talks. Paul says, "I went to Jerusalem *to obtain information from* Peter" (Gal 1:18 GNB). This phrase "to obtain information from" is one word in the original Greek (*historeō*). It is where we get the English word "history." It is found nowhere else in the New Testament. What historical information would Paul want to learn from Peter?

As C. H. Dodd mentions above, they surely did not spend all their time talking about the athletic games or the weather! It is unimaginable that the primary content of their conversations did not involve the historical man Jesus.[31] In his commentary on Galatians, J. Louis Martyn says, "It is, of course, inconceivable that during the visit Cephas was silent about Jesus the Christ, about God's having raised him from the dead (cf. 1 Cor 15:5), and about the work among his fellow Jews to which God had called him."[32]

---

31. Von Campenhausen writes, "Even the most skeptical person, who rightly enough should deny to those concerned here a 'purely historical' interest, could hardly hold that they never spoke to one another about those crucial events, which the leading personalities had themselves experienced and used as the main topic of their preaching" ("Events of Easter and the Empty Tomb," 44).

32. Martyn, *Galatians*, 172.

It is important to point out that Paul did not *learn* the gospel from Peter. As Paul forcefully argues in Galatians 1:11–12, he learned the gospel directly through a "revelation of Jesus Christ," which occurred during his conversion about three years earlier.[33]

On the other hand, Paul did learn many historical facts and traditions about Jesus from Peter and others who knew the historical Jesus. This awareness of Jesus' life, exemplary character, and teachings is reflected all throughout his letters (see 1 Cor 7:10; 9:5, 14; 11:1, 2, 23–26; 15:3–7; 2 Cor 8:9; 10:1; Gal 1:19; 4:4; Rom 14:14; 15:3, 8; Phil 2:5; see also 2 Thess 2:15; 1 Tim 6:13).[34] From Galatians alone, we know that on the same visit when he spent fifteen days with Peter, Paul spent some time with James, Jesus' brother (Gal 1:19). During his second visit to Jerusalem (AD 46–47), Paul met John, the son of Zebedee and possibly others of the Twelve (Gal 2:9–10; 1 Cor 15:5).[35] There the proposed authors of twenty-one of the twenty-seven books of the New Testament

---

33. I will use the word "conversion" in this book to refer to the radical transformation Paul experienced because it is the one most commonly used. On the other hand, it may not be the best word to convey what happened to this young Pharisee. Paul did not see himself converting to an entirely different religion, but rather, by accepting Jesus as the Messiah, he remained a faithful Jew, but now was inside the Jewish movement that was truly the fulfillment of Judaism, "believing everything that is in accordance with the Law and that is written in the Prophets" (Acts 24:15). Ehrman writes: "Paul did not see himself as switching religions. He came to realize that Christ was the fulfillment of Judaism, of everything that God had planned and revealed within the sacred Jewish Scriptures. God had not abandoned the Jews or vacated the Jewish religion; Christ himself had not opposed the Jewish faith or proposed to start something new. Christ stood in absolute continuity with all that went before" (*Triumph of Christianity*, 56–57). See also Betz, *Galatians*, 69–70.

34. Ehrman conveniently lays out most of the key facts concerning the historical Jesus in Paul's early letters in his *New Testament*, 387. For a full discussion see Wenham, *Paul*.

35. "John must be the son of Zebedee, brother of the martyred James. As well as being one of the inner circle of Jesus' disciples (Peter, James and John), he is recalled by Luke as a regular companion of Peter in the early days of the new movement" (Dunn, *Epistle to the Galatians*, 109).

were together deciding the future of the church of Jesus Christ![36] Those same hands that once embraced the historical Jesus were now embracing Paul.

ANCIENT CREEDAL TRADITION

It is very likely that this was the meeting where Paul received the creedal tradition(s)[37] he cites in 1 Corinthians 15:3–7, among other traditions and hymns concerning the historical Jesus. "Creedal tradition" is a phrase that means this section is, first, pre-Pauline tradition, and second, was composed in the form of a creed (whether oral or written). Scholars are unanimous that this creedal tradition originated at the latest within a decade of Jesus' death and at the earliest "months" after Jesus' death.[38]

This is why we begin with this bedrock meeting between Peter and Paul. New Testament scholar F. F. Bruce says, "One piece of information which he most probably received during his visit was that Jesus, having been raised from the dead on the third day, 'appeared to Cephas' (1 Cor. 15:5). ... It may also have been from Cephas that Paul learned how, after his appearance to Cephas, Jesus appeared 'then to the twelve, then ... to

---

36. Paul: thirteen letters; Peter: 1–2 Peter; James: James; John: Gospel of John, 1–3 John, Revelation. Other than Paul's undisputed seven letters, the authorship of the rest of the NT books is debated among scholars. See Carson and Moo, *Introduction to the New Testament*; Ehrman, *Forged*. Regardless of what they discussed, the fact that the chief apostles behind most of the NT (according to Christian tradition) met in the mid-40s AD to make significant decisions regarding the future of the church is remarkable.

37. As we will see in chapter 3, there may be multiple traditions within this one creedal tradition Paul quotes in 1 Cor 15:3–7. There is scholarly agreement that 1 Cor 15:3b–5a represents the most primitive creedal formula that Paul received. The other appearances—to the five hundred, James, and to all the apostles—Paul may have received at other times. Either way, Paul received *all* of these creedal traditions within a decade after Jesus' death.

38. This bedrock source, 1 Cor 15:3–7, will be discussed in detail in chapter 3.

more than five hundred brethren at one time.' "[39] As evidenced throughout his letters, Paul learned many historical facts and traditions about Jesus from Peter, James, and others who knew the historical Jesus. Yet the creedal tradition in 1 Corinthians 15:3–7 is the most valuable of them all; indeed, as A. M. Hunter puts it, "it is our pearl of great price."[40] Ehrman writes that if this tradition goes back to "before the time when Paul himself joined the movement around the year 33 CE, some three years after Jesus had died ... it would be very ancient indeed! This passage almost certainly contains a pre-Pauline confession, or creed, of some kind."[41]

If Paul received this creedal tradition sometime in the mid-30s AD, then it must have been composed sometime *before* he received it, and of course after Jesus was crucified in AD 30 or 33.[42] This is what leads to the agreement among scholars that this creedal tradition should be dated no later than a decade after Jesus' crucifixion. Some scholars even date its composition to within *months* of Jesus' death, going back to the very "pillars" themselves: Peter, James (Jesus' brother), John, and possibly others of the Twelve. Dale Allison writes, "Indeed, Paul knew Peter and James and presumably others who claimed to have seen the risen Jesus. First Corinthians 15:3–8 is not folklore."[43]

---

39. Bruce, *Epistle to the Galatians*, 98; see also Ehrman, *How Jesus Became God*, 138–39.

40. Hunter, *Paul and His Predecessors*, 15.

41. Ehrman, *How Jesus Became God*, 138–39.

42. It is unclear whether Jesus was crucified in AD 30 or 33. As we will see in chapter 4, it is a bedrock fact that Jesus was crucified, but the exact year is debated. For chronological purposes I will assume 33 for Jesus' crucifixion, but none of the bedrock facts of this book are affected by whether it was in 30 or 33. For an excellent discussion of both sides of the debate see Brown, *Death of the Messiah*, 1350–78; Hoehner, *Chronological Aspects in the Life of Christ*.

43. Allison, *Resurrecting Jesus*, 234.

The creedal tradition found in 1 Corinthians 15:3–8 is the bedrock source for all the bedrock facts we will be discussing in this book concerning Jesus' death, resurrection, and appearances.

Now let us behold the bedrock, most ancient source of Christianity, which is unanimously dated on average within five years of Jesus' death:

> *That Christ died for our sins according to the Scriptures,*
> *and that he was buried,*
> *and that he was raised on the third day according to the Scriptures,*
> *and that he appeared to Cephas,*
> *then to the twelve.*
> *After that he appeared to more than five hundred brethren at one time ...*
> *then he appeared to James,*
> *then to all the apostles;*
> *and last of all, as to one untimely born, he appeared to me also.*[44]

Even though we don't know everything about this meeting between Peter and Paul that we would like, the fruit of this meeting, represented in Paul's *receiving* some or all of the traditions behind 1 Corinthians 15:3–7, forms the unalterable bedrock source of Christianity.

WHAT IS TO COME

In chapters 1 and 2 I will discuss what we know about the bedrock eyewitness, the "historical Paul," and key chronological aspects of his movements. In chapter 3, I will look in more detail

---

44. All scholars agree that Paul added the last sentence, which includes "He appeared to me" (1 Cor 15:8), to the ancient creed.

at the dating and content of the bedrock source, the creedal tradition(s) found in 1 Corinthians 15:3-7. For most of the rest of the book (chapters 4-6), I will focus on this creedal tradition line by line and reveal all the bedrock facts about Jesus that emerge from it. In chapter 7, I will look at one more bedrock fact of early Christianity, namely, that it became an indestructible movement that has gone on to be the most dominant and influential religion in the world.

In the conclusion, I will seek to answer those questions I asked in the introduction: Who was Jesus? Did the historical Jesus rise from the dead? What was the cause of this world-changing movement known as Christianity? And how do *you* fit in to the story of Jesus?

Like Horatio in *Hamlet*, we will see whether our philosophies are large enough to include the unexpected and extraordinary.

Come with me on this journey through history—a journey that I think should be likened to time traveling.

1: Studying History Is Time Traveling

We are like paleontologists struggling to piece together a set of bones which a dinosaur had used all its life without even thinking about it. Simply seeing and assembling the data is a monstrous task.

N. T. Wright, *The New Testament and the People of God*

Bill and Ted's Excellent Adventure is a cult movie classic from the 1980s. Like great wine, this movie only grows better with age.[45] The story is simple. Bill and Ted are failing their high school history class and need an A on their next presentation to graduate. Thankfully, a time-traveling phone booth (If you're not old enough, Google "phone booth" to learn what that is) falls out of the sky, with comedian George Carlin inside. Bill and Ted are enabled to travel back in time through history to kidnap (and learn from) Socrates, Genghis Khan, Joan of Arc, Abraham Lincoln, Sigmund Freud, and Billy the Kid. I don't want to spoil

---

45. Philosopher William Lane Craig ranks *Bill and Ted's Excellent Adventure* as one of his favorite movies because it is most consistent with his theory of time. See "God and Time," Reasonable Faith, December 2, 2007, https://www.reasonablefaith.org/media/reasonable-faith-podcast/god-and-time.

the ending for you, but they end up having a most excellent adventure.

If you could time travel to any time or place in history, where and when would you go? Is there an event you would most like to experience or a person you would most want to meet? What if you could travel to significant turning points in history such as the very moment when Socrates was walking to his trial before the citizens of Athens, when Lincoln was on his way to Ford's Theatre, or when Julius Caesar crossed the Rubicon? Imagine being able to interview them concerning their aims, beliefs, hopes and dreams.

I hate to be the one to tell you this, but you will never be able to *literally* travel through time. It is a logical impossibility. For example, could one travel back in time before one's own birth and kill one's parents or grandparents? Think about that question too long and you will be permanently cross-eyed.

But here is the good news. We do have the tools to travel back in time thousands of years in the past and observe historical events such as the Jewish war with Rome in AD 66–70. We can meet historical figures such as Socrates, Abraham Lincoln, and Julius Caesar, or even John the Baptist, Jesus, and Paul. We can discuss justice or courage with Socrates as we walk with him down the streets of Athens. We can behold the magnificent beauty of the temple in Jerusalem with Josephus or behold the horror of Jesus' crucifixion outside the city walls. We don't have time-traveling phone booths—we don't even have phone booths anymore—but we do have the tried and tested tools of the historical method.[46] These tools enable us to time travel through history.

---

46. NT historian Ben Meyer calls this "critical realism," meaning that there is a past that can be known to some extent (realism) and it is known through

WHAT HISTORIANS WANT

In one sense, "history" is everything that happened in the past, every second of every day since the beginning of the universe. However, I mean something more specific when I talk about studying history or the historical method. In this second and more useful sense, history is the "knowable past," the people and events of history for which reliable sources have survived.

In some cases, such as with Alexander the Great or many of the Roman Caesars and Egyptian Pharaohs, we have physical evidence of their existence such as coins, art, busts, statues, and even their mummies! However, most figures from history we only know through surviving written sources. Sometimes these are written by eyewitnesses to the events or person(s) they are describing, but in most cases, they are written by individuals many generations later. Like a paleontologist trying to piece together his newly discovered group of bones, historians work with what the sands of time have delivered them to piece together a particular historical event or understand the life, aims, beliefs, and death of a historical figure. How well they can do that really depends on the nature of the surviving sources.

We engaged in this art of time travel in the prologue when we sought to learn as much as we could from the epic meeting between Peter and Paul in Jerusalem. The one written source from Galatians 1:18 could only take us so far. Yet, since Galatians was written by a reliable eyewitness, Paul, we were able to explore in detail this event that occurred in Jerusalem sometime between AD 33 and 38.

---

rigorous historical analysis. In other words, the interaction between the historian and the subject matter is fully allowed for. See chapter 4 of Meyer's *Aims of Jesus*.

In Bart Ehrman's many books on early Christianity, he discusses what makes for a reliable source: "What historians want, in short, are lots of witnesses, close to the time of the events, who are not biased toward their subject matter and who corroborate one another's points without showing signs of collaboration."[47]

This can be laid out as four distinct items that constitute a historian's wish list:

(1) Early dating: sources that are very close to the time of the person or event

(2) Eyewitnesses: multiple people who saw and/or recorded the event

(3) Corroboration: eyewitnesses and sources that corroborate with one another without collusion

(4) Unbiased: sources that are not biased toward their subject matter

As Ehrman concludes, "Would that we had such sources for all significant historical events!"

Now, if we followed this criterion woodenly, we would have to throw out most of ancient history we now take for granted. In almost all cases, we don't have a person writing about an event who is unbiased or disinterested, and most of our sources date many generations, even hundreds of years, after the person or event that is being described.

For example, Oxford historian A. N. Sherwin-White says that historians of ancient history are usually

---

47. Ehrman, *How Jesus Became God*, 146. See also Ehrman, *Did Jesus Exist?*, 39–42.

dealing with derivative sources of marked bias and prej-
udice composed at least one or two generations after the
events they describe, but much more often, as with the
Lives of Plutarch or the central decades of Livy, from two
to five *centuries* later. Though connecting links are provided backwards in time by series of lost intermediate
sources, we are seldom in the happy position of dealing
at only one remove with a contemporary source.[48]

Sherwin-White goes on to say that even with many generations
separating an event from the person writing about it, this does
not prevent the historian from being able to say quite a lot concerning "what really happened."[49] To have the kind of sources
and eyewitnesses Ehrman is describing is almost unprecedented,
at least from the ancient world.

To be fair to Ehrman, that is why he calls it a wish list!

I will argue in chapter 3 that, incredibly, the creedal tradition found in 1 Corinthians 15:3–7 does pass this high threshold
for sources.

But for now, I want to emphasize that most of the history
we take for granted does not come even close to meeting the
wish-list criteria for reliable sources. Yet that does not present
a problem to ancient historians (or for us) who desire to time
travel to experience this event or meet that historical figure. As
Sherwin-White pointed out above, even with multiple generations separating an event from the author describing it, we are
still able to learn a lot concerning what really happened.

To illustrate this further, let's look briefly at four examples
from history: an emperor, an ancient war, a philosopher, and
a Baptist.

48. Sherwin-White, *Roman Society and Roman Law*, 186.
49. Sherwin-White, *Roman Society and Roman Law*, 186–90.

THE KNOWABLE PAST

Tiberius Caesar is one of the Roman emperors for whom we have multiple somewhat reliable biographical accounts. He ruled the Roman Empire from AD 14–37 and was the most powerful man in the world at that time. We have archaeological evidence of his reign in the coins he issued, but to learn about the man himself, we must rely on biographical material. Only a handful of written sources about him have survived, some of which were written long after his death. Sherwin-White discusses the evidence for Tiberius:

> The story of [Tiberius'] reign is known from four sources, the *Annals* of Tacitus and the biography of Suetonius, written some eighty or ninety years later, the brief contemporary record of Velleius Paterculus, and the third-century history of Cassius Dio. These disagree amongst themselves in the wildest possible fashion, both in major matters of political action or motive and in specific details of minor events. ... But this does not prevent the belief that the material of Tacitus can be used to write a history of Tiberius.[50]

Despite the lateness and disagreement among the biographies of Tiberius, this Caesar is still part of the knowable past. We can time travel to meet him through Tacitus and Suetonius, even though they were eighty to ninety years later. To put that time frame in perspective, the latest biography of Jesus in the New Testament is the Gospel of John, which dates to around sixty years after Jesus' death. Mark is the earliest, dating to somewhere between thirty and forty years after Jesus' death. Even better, we have Paul's early letters, which were written

---

50. Sherwin-White, *Roman Society and Roman Law*, 187–88.

within twenty to twenty-five years after Jesus' death. But with the traditions and hymns about Jesus quoted in Paul's early letters, we can reach back even further. In particular, 1 Corinthians 15:3–7, as we will see, is dated by 99 percent of scholars to within a decade after Jesus' death.

Tiberius was the most powerful man in the world of his day. Jesus was one of the poorest, belonging to the peasant class as a Jewish carpenter. He even died the most shameful death, a slave's death, on a cross during Tiberius' reign. Yet we have far more reliable written sources and closer to the time of Jesus' actual life and death than this Caesar of Rome.

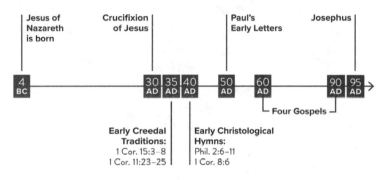

The second example is the events of the Jewish war with Rome, which began in AD 66 and ended in 70 when the Roman general Titus broke down the walls of Jerusalem and burned the temple to the ground. As a result of this event, we have archaeological evidence of the war to this very day. Yet how many contemporary eyewitness sources do we have for the most significant war in the first century? Only one. Jewish historian Josephus wrote down his eyewitness account in a book called *The Jewish War* only a few years after the event, around AD 75: "As for the History of the War, I wrote it as having been an actor myself in many of its transactions, an eyewitness in the greatest part of the rest, and as not unacquainted with anything whatsoever that was either said or done in it" (*Ag. Ap.* 1.55).

Using the tools of the historical method, historians do their best to distinguish clear exaggeration and the mix of legend and history from the places where Josephus is telling us "what really happened." All in all, Josephus gives us many bedrock facts about the Jewish war with Rome despite being on Emperor Vespasian's payroll, greatly exaggerating numbers,[51] and occasionally adding legendary events to the story. But through the historical method we can time travel and witness the massacre at Masada (*J.W.* 4.398–404; 7.252–406), observe that Titus' soldiers in jest played with different postures for crucified victims until they ran out of crosses (*J.W.* 5.449–551), and learn of many of the other horrors of the Jewish war with Rome.

For a third example, if we want to walk the streets of Athens with Socrates, listening to his philosophical wisdom, how do we do it? Like Jesus, Socrates didn't write anything. The only way we can meet the "historical Socrates" is through the undeniably biased writings about him from Plato's *Dialogues*, Xenophon's *Memorabilia* and *Symposium*, and Aristophanes' *Clouds*. These were all contemporary disciples of Socrates and wrote within decades after his death. We learn from all of them that the "historical Socrates" occupied himself primarily with ethics, seeking to help everyone around him toward excellence of character. He was the first to raise the problem of definitions and used a unique method of argument and debate known as the dialectic method.

---

51. An example of this is when he recounts the story of the Egyptian who rebelled under Felix. Josephus says that the Egyptian had thirty thousand followers (*J.W.* 2.261), and Acts 21:38 says it was four thousand. Most scholars believe the author of Acts uses a more reliable number.

According to Plato, Socrates was told by the oracle at Delphi that he was the wisest man on earth. Socrates was perplexed by this pronouncement. He thought of himself as someone who really knew nothing. Then he finally figured it out. He was the wisest because he was the only one who knew he was not wise, the only one who knew he did not know: "I am wiser than this man; for neither of us really knows anything fine and good, but this man thinks he knows something when he does not, whereas I, as I do not know anything, do not think I do either. I seem, then, in just this little thing to be wiser than this man at any rate, that what I do not know I do not think I know either" (Plato, *Apology* 21D–E).

Eventually, the leaders of Athens accused him of leading the youth astray, teaching "strange gods" (Xenophon, *Memorabilia* 1.1), and even "wizardry" (Plato, *Meno* 80B). The Athenian Senate condemned him to death by drinking hemlock. His last words, according to Plato ("Crito, we owe a cock to Aesculapius. Pay it and do not neglect it") are recorded in his famous dialogue *Apology*, which means "defense." He was seventy years old when he died in 399 BC (Plato, *Apology* 70D).

Scholars debate to this day whether Plato, Xenophon, and Aristophanes give us the historical Socrates or an idealized version of Socrates whom they used to teach their own philosophical theories and concepts. The majority view is that the historical Socrates is best represented in Plato's earliest dialogues (*Apology*, *Euthyphro*, *Crito*, etc.), and only in the later ones did Plato begin to put his ideas on Socrates' lips.[52] Classicists John Burnett and A. E. Taylor argue that Plato almost always gives us a faithful portrayal of the historical Socrates because he would not have done such an injustice to his master, especially while others

---

52. See Taylor, *Plato*; Vlastos, *Socrates*, 45–80.

were still alive to correct this view.[53] Even though these disciples of Socrates were clearly biased and interested in preserving their master's philosophical wisdom and legacy, we can learn a lot concerning the historical Socrates through their different, no doubt artistic, portrayals.

The fourth example, John the Baptist, like Socrates and Jesus, did not write anything—or at least nothing he wrote has survived. Our only first-century sources for John the Baptist come from the four Gospels, scattered references in primarily the sermons of Acts, and Josephus (Matt 3:1–17; 4:12; 9:14; 11:1–19; 14:1–13; 16:14; 17:13; 21:25–26, 32; Mark 1:1–14; 2:18; 6:14–32; 8:28; 11:30–32; Luke 1:5–25, 39–45, 57–80; 3:2–22; 5:33; 7:18–35; 9:7–9, 19; 11:1; 16:16; 20:4–6; John 1:6–8, 19–40; 3:23–36; 4:1; 5:33–36; 10:40–41; Acts 1:5, 22; 10:37; 11:16; 13:24–25; 18:25; 19:1–7; Josephus, *Ant.* 18.116–119). Bedrock facts concerning John the Baptist include his commencement of baptisms in the Jordan River between AD 26 and 28, his preaching a message of repentance, gathering multiple disciples (Matt 9:14; 11:2; Mark 2:18; Luke 7:18; 11:1; Acts 19:1–7), baptizing Jesus in the Jordan River,[54] and his arrest and imprisonment by Herod Antipas in the castle Machaerus.[55] While in prison, John sent his disciples to question Jesus whether he was the Messiah (Matt 11:1–9; Luke 7:18–35). Herod Antipas then had John put to death sometime between AD 28 and 32 (Mark 6:14–29; Josephus, *Ant.* 18.116–119).[56] Determining the historical reliabil-

---

53. Copleston, *History of Philosophy*, 100–101.

54. Ehrman writes, "There is little doubt about how Jesus began his ministry: he was baptized by John" (*New Testament*, 270).

55. For a description of the castle Machaerus see Josephus, *J.W.* 7.164–170.

56. Josephan scholar Louis Feldman writes, "In general, this famous passage, on the murder of John the Baptist has been accepted as authentic. ... According to Mark vi. 17–21, John was imprisoned because he questioned Herod's right to marry his sister-in-law. And there is nothing in Josephus of the story, told in Mark vi. 22–28, that Salome asked for John's head. But there is no necessary

ity of other passages about John the Baptist in the Gospels and Acts would give us even more historical information, but that is beyond the scope of this book. What is laid out above concerning the Baptist is historical bedrock, facts known past doubting.[57]

How do all these examples compare to the apostle Paul? Can we time travel to meet him, learn his beliefs, aims, and passions? Yes! Our sources for the "historical Paul," his undisputed four letters, are some of the most reliable historical sources in all the ancient world. Wright's analogy of the paleontologist in the epigraph of this chapter aptly describes our present circumstance. For over 99 percent of people who have lived on the earth, we have no "bones" to reconstruct who they were, what they believed, and how they lived. As the four examples above illustrate, for the remaining 1 percent we have few and precious bones to build with, though they are enough to draw a fairly accurate portrait.

Paul is a part of a very elite group from the ancient world for whom we have an abundance of trustworthy sources. To meet the historical Paul, we have just about all the bones we need (reliable and early sources) to know his beliefs, his aims, and even his heroes.

Get in the phone booth—we are going to do some time traveling to meet the Pharisaic persecutor transformed into the apostle of the crucified Nazarene.

---

contradiction between Josephus and the Gospels as to the reasons why John was put to death; the Christians chose to emphasize the moral charges that he brought against the ruler, whereas Josephus stresses the political fears that he aroused in Herod" (*Josephus: Jewish Antiquities*, 81–83).

57. For more on the "historical John the Baptist" see Kraeling, *John the Baptist*; Scobie, *John the Baptist*; Tatum, *John the Baptist and Jesus*.

PAUL THE PHARISEE

In order to time travel to the earliest days of Paul, his pre-Christian days of the 20s and early 30s AD, we must consult his autobiography in the first chapter of Galatians. If we met Paul[58] in Jerusalem in the late 20s AD, we would find a zealous young Pharisee, possibly even training under Rabbi Gamaliel, one of the most famous rabbis of his day (Acts 22:3). Incredibly, Paul's letters are the only writings we have from a Pharisee before the destruction of the temple in AD 70.[59] Even though Paul does not use the word "Pharisee" directly in Galatians, he presents himself as a young Pharisee "advancing in Judaism beyond many of my contemporaries among my countrymen, being more extremely zealous for my ancestral traditions" (Gal 1:14). According to New Testament scholar James Dunn, "The picture Paul here paints is of a dedication to excellence and to the most careful exposition of and living in accordance with the law, as interpreted within the sect of the Pharisees, which outstripped most even of his fellow Pharisees."[60]

The Pharisees were like the university and seminary professors of the first century AD. Paul is claiming in Galatians that he was running with the elite of the elite of Jewish sects of his day, graduating *summa cum laude*, and as to knowledge of Torah and zeal for God, he surpassed them all.

Paul's testimony in the books of Philippians and Acts further witnesses to this:

---

58. Since I am limiting my sources to Paul's early letters, I will not refer to him as "Saul" during this period as in the book of Acts (Acts 7:58; 8:1; etc.). "But Saul, who was also known as Paul…" (Acts 13:9) demonstrates that his name was not changed to Paul, but instead like many Jews in the Greco-Roman world (see Acts 1:23; 12:25; 13:1; Col 4:11), he possessed two names. Therefore, "Paul" was his gentile name before and after his conversion.

59. See Ehrman, *New Testament*, 313.

60. Dunn, *Epistle to the Galatians*, 60.

If anyone else has a mind to put confidence in the flesh,
I far more: circumcised the eighth day, of the nation of
Israel, of the tribe of Benjamin, a Hebrew of Hebrews;
as to the Law, a Pharisee; as to zeal, a persecutor of the
church; as to the righteousness which is in the Law, found
blameless. (Phil 3:4–6)

I am a Jew, born in Tarsus of Cilicia, but brought up in
this city, educated under Gamaliel, strictly according to
the law of our fathers, being zealous for God just as you
all are today. (Acts 22:3)

I lived as a Pharisee according to the strictest sect of our
religion. (Acts 26:5)

Notice the repetition of similar language, "as to the law, a
Pharisee," "extremely zealous for my ancestral traditions," educated "strictly according to the law of our fathers," and the sect of
the Pharisees is "the strictest sect of our religion." Even though
this testimony is not found in Paul's undisputed letters, it is
undisputed among scholars that Paul was a Pharisee. Even if
some scholars debate the historicity of Paul's speeches in Acts,
what Paul says about the Pharisees is historically accurate. The
Pharisees studied Torah and recited the Shema (Deut 6:4) daily
and were extremely zealous for their ancestral traditions, and
their zeal burned supremely for the God of Israel.

We know a lot about the Pharisees, not just from the only
pre-70 Pharisee author Paul, but also from the most significant
post-70 Pharisee author, Josephus. Josephus was born in Galilee
in AD 37, around the time Peter and Paul were having that epic
meeting we discussed in the prologue, and identifies himself as
a Pharisee in his *Life*: "So when I had accomplished my desires,
I returned back to the city, being now nineteen years old, and

began to conduct myself according to the rules of the sect of the Pharisees, which is of kin to the sect of the Stoics, as the Greeks call them" (*Life* 12).

We learn from Josephus that there were more than six thousand Pharisees in Jerusalem and throughout the diaspora in the first century AD (*Ant.* 18.14). The other two major sects of Judaism at this time, the Sadducees and the Essenes, had far fewer adherents than the Pharisees (*Ant.* 13.171–173). All three of these Jewish sects first show up in history during the Hasmonean Dynasty (143–63 BC). The Hasmonean Dynasty is still considered by many Jews today, along with the time of David and Solomon, to be a golden age of their history. This was a unique time in Jewish history, as it was the only time after the return from the Babylonian exile in 539 BC that the Jews had autonomy from their pagan neighbors. The Roman general Pompey put an end to this autonomous Hasmonean reign in 63 BC when Judea came under the authority of the Roman Empire.

The sect of the Pharisees first appeared under the reign of the Hasmonean ruler Alexander Jannaeus (103–76 BC), but may have emerged even earlier, during the reign of John Hyrcanus I (134–104 BC). According to Josephus, Alexander Jannaeus had eight hundred Pharisees crucified while he was feasting with his concubines for protesting his reign (*Ant.* 13.380). Even though the Pharisees did not have much political power, they did have a special sway over the Jewish people; as Josephus writes, they "had the support of the masses" (*Ant.* 13.298; see also 13.409). This agrees with how the leading Pharisees in Jerusalem are portrayed in all four Gospels. Some Pharisees, along with other religious leaders, are presented as conspiring to arrest Jesus and swaying the crowds to crucify him (Matt 27:62; Mark 3:6; Luke 6:7; John 18:3; see also Mark 15:1–10).[61]

Josephus also tells us about what the Pharisees believed. As Paul himself testifies in the quotes above, Josephus says the Pharisees "have the reputation of being unrivalled experts in their country's laws" (*Life* 191). Moreover, they "passed on to the people certain regulations handed down by former generations and not recorded in the laws of Moses" (*Ant.* 13.297), what Paul calls "ancestral traditions."

Josephus also testifies to the Pharisees' belief in bodily resurrection: "They believe that souls have power to survive death and that there are rewards and punishments under the earth for those who have led lives of virtue or vice: eternal imprisonment is the lot of evil souls, while the good souls receive an easy passage to a new life" (*Ant.* 18.14).[62] This agrees with the testimony of Acts 23:6–8:

> But perceiving that one group were Sadducees and the other Pharisees, Paul began crying out in the Council, "Brethren, I am a Pharisee, a son of Pharisees; I am on trial for the hope and resurrection of the dead!" As he said this, there occurred a dissension between the Pharisees and Sadducees, and the assembly was divided. For the Sadducees say that there is no resurrection, nor an angel, nor a spirit, but the Pharisees acknowledge them all.

---

61. The Gospels do not condemn *all* Pharisees at this time, but clearly *some* Pharisees with power and influence over the masses were directly involved in the death of Jesus.

62. This phrase "new life" is *anabiosis* in the Greek, and according to Feldman is "a clear reference to resurrection" (*Josephus: Jewish Antiquities*, 13). See 2 Macc 7:9, where the same word is used for bodily resurrection.

In sum, before Paul became a follower of this crucified man Jesus, he was a Pharisee surpassing all his contemporaries in zeal for Torah and God. It is a bedrock fact that the pre-Christian Paul was, by his own proud testimony, "circumcised on the eighth day," "a Hebrew of Hebrews," "an Israelite," "descended from Abraham," "of the tribe of Benjamin," "as to law, a Pharisee," and "as to zeal, a persecutor of the church" (see Rom 11:1; 1 Cor 15:9–11; 2 Cor 11:22; Phil 3:5–6; Gal 1:13–14, 22–24; see also Acts 7:58; 8:1, 3; 9:1–2, 13–14, 21; 22:4–5, 19–20; 23:6; 26:4–5, 9–11; Rom 9:3–4; 11:13–14; 1 Tim 1:12–13).

It is this word translated "zeal" (*zēlotēs*) that is most illuminating for us to understand Paul's passions, aims, and even heroes as a young Pharisee. The word "zeal" or "zealous" can be found three times on Paul's lips in the New Testament (the latter two of which are quoted above):

> I was advancing in Judaism beyond many of my contemporaries among my countrymen, being more extremely *zealous* for my ancestral traditions. (Gal 1:14)

> If anyone else has a mind to put confidence in the flesh, I far more ... as to the Law, a Pharisee; as to *zeal*, a persecutor of the church. (Phil 3:4–6)

> I am a Jew, born in Tarsus of Cilicia, but brought up in this city, educated under Gamaliel, strictly according to the law of our fathers, being *zealous* for God just as you all are today. (Acts 22:3)

It was this insatiable zeal for Torah, his ancestral traditions, and especially for God that led Paul the Pharisee to become Paul the persecutor, as he himself testifies, "I am the least of the apostles, and not fit to be called an apostle, because I persecuted the church of God" (1 Cor 15:9).

What does Paul mean that he was "extremely zealous," even "zealous for God"? In order to answer this question, we must go back to the stories of Phinehas, Elijah, Jehu, and Mattathias and Judas Maccabeus. All five of these men were highly praised in Jewish history for having great zeal for God, and it is reasonable to conclude that they were heroes to this young Pharisee Paul.

ZEAL FOR YHWH

Let us begin with Phinehas, the paradigmatic figure who had "zeal for YHWH."[63] When the Israelites were on the verge of entering the promised land, they committed idolatry with the god Baal of Peor, and part of this idolatry involved sexual immorality. During this time an Israelite man, Zimri, in full view of Moses, took a Midianite woman, Cozbi, into his tent (Num 25:1–6). Phinehas, who was the grandson of Aaron, Moses' brother, took a spear, went into the tent, and drove it straight through Zimri and Cozbi while they were having sexual relations (Num 25:7–8). As a result of Phinehas plunging his spear through their bodies, "the plague on the sons of Israel was checked" (Num 25:8). God himself even praises Phinehas, saying:

> Phinehas the son of Eleazar, the son of Aaron the priest, has turned away My wrath from the sons of Israel, for he was as zealous as I am for My honor among them, so that in My zeal I did not put an end to them. Therefore say, "Behold, I give him My covenant of peace; and it shall be for him and his descendants after him, a covenant of a perpetual priesthood, because he was zealous for his

---

63. "YHWH" is a transliteration of the Tetragrammaton, i.e., "the four letters" of God's personal name (usually pronounced "Yahweh"). This personal name of the God of Israel occurs over seven thousand times in the Hebrew OT. In most English translations of the Bible "YHWH" is rendered "the Lord."

God and made atonement for the sons of Israel." (Num 25:11–13)

This story may offend twenty-first century sensibilities. Many in our world today would probably argue that Phinehas was the one who was evil, not the couple in the tent. They might accuse Phinehas of being an intolerant bigot who shouldn't mind what people do in their own bedroom (or tent).

But the young Pharisee Paul, and all the Jewish commentators on this verse before him, would strongly disagree. Sins against God's honor, whether idolatry or sexual immorality, deserved the shocking punishment that Phinehas meted out. In fact, Phinehas went on to be praised for what he did in the Psalms:

Then Phinehas stood up and interposed,
And so the plague was stayed.
And it was reckoned to him for righteousness,
To all generations forever. (Ps 106:30–31)

Even later in Jewish history, in 180 BC, the grandson of the wise man Sirach recorded his grandfather saying this: "Phinehas son of Eleazar ranks third in glory for being zealous in the fear of the Lord, and standing firm, when the people turned away, in the noble courage of his soul; and he made atonement for Israel" (Sir 45:23). Moreover, the author of 1 Maccabees, around 100 BC, also revered Phinehas: "Phinehas our ancestor, because he was deeply zealous, received the covenant of everlasting priesthood" (1 Macc 2:54).

Even that other most famous first-century Pharisee, Josephus, has a long, glowing review of Phinehas' glorious deeds and zeal for God (*Ant.* 4.152–155). It is safe to say Phinehas was a shining example of zeal for Jews down through the centuries, especially for a young Pharisee such as Paul.

Another example of a zealous warrior hero of old would have been the prophet Elijah. The full account is recorded in the book of 1 Kings:

> Then he came there to a cave and lodged there; and behold, the word of the LORD came to him, and He said to him, "What are you doing here, Elijah?" He said, "I have been very zealous for YHWH, the God of hosts; for the sons of Israel have forsaken Your covenant, torn down Your altars and killed Your prophets with the sword. And I alone am left; and they seek my life, to take it away." (1 Kgs 19:9–10)

Elijah had been very "zealous" for YHWH, as he had just destroyed 850 of the prophets of Baal and Asherah on Mount Carmel. The text even says Elijah himself "brought them down to the brook Kishon, and slew them there" (1 Kgs 18:40). As with Phinehas, both Sirach[64] and 1 Maccabees[65] praise Elijah for his burning zeal for God. Paul even quotes the account where Elijah mentions his "zeal" in Romans 11:2–4.

A third example of a hero for Paul is the Israelite king Jehu, who was anointed by the prophet Elisha, Elijah's successor. Jehu was commissioned by the Lord to destroy the entire house of Ahab. Jehu, who should forever be known as "Jehu the Terminator," did this too well, killing so many people even beyond Ahab's line that he was rebuked by the prophet Hosea

---

64. "Then Elijah arose, a prophet like fire, and his word burned like a torch. He brought a famine upon them, and by his zeal he made them few in number" (Sir 48:1–2).

65. "Elijah, because of great zeal for the law, was taken up into heaven" (1 Macc 2:58).

(Hos 1:4). Jehu began doing the Lord's will by assassinating the kings Jehoram and Ahaziah. He then commanded that the Baal-worshiping witch Jezebel, Ahab's wife, be thrown down onto the street, with her blood splattering the walls. Later, he persuaded the leaders of Samaria, Israel's capital city, to behead the seventy sons of Ahab and piled all their heads into two heaps at the entrance to the gate.

Jehu's bloodlust seemed to have no limits once he began to slaughter anyone who even knew Ahab in Jezreel and Samaria. Jehu even deceived the priests of Baal and gathered many worshipers into a temple of Baal with the pretense that he and his friend Jehonadab were going to offer sacrifices. Instead, he ordered eighty men outside to kill every one inside, burn down the temple, and urinate all over the ashes of their corpses and Baal's ruins.[66]

The story of Jehu is an excellent Bible story to read to your kids at bedtime.

Jehu refers to all that he is doing as his "zeal" for YHWH: "Come with me and see my zeal for YHWH" (2 Kgs 10:16, my translation). And God does at least approve of Jehu's initial zeal in wiping out the house of Ahab: "YHWH said to Jehu, 'Because you have done well in executing what is right in My eyes, and have done to the house of Ahab according to all that was in My heart, your sons of the fourth generation shall sit on the throne of Israel' " (2 Kgs 10:30, my translation)

It seems from the testimony of the Hebrew Scriptures alone that to have zeal for YHWH is to be willing to defend his honor, even violently, against sinning Israelites and especially against heretics seeking to lead Israel astray. Ehrman writes concerning Paul's claim in 2 Corinthians 11:24 that he had received

---

66. For the entire account of Jehu the Terminator see 2 Kgs 9–10.

thirty-nine lashes that "it would mean he was caught out in a Jewish context of worship. Possibly we can infer that he himself meted out this punishment on others before he had converted. If so, this would make sense of his claim that when he 'persecuted the church,' he did so 'violently' (Galatians 1:13)."[67]

Finally, Paul also drew great inspiration from the Maccabean Revolt (167–164 BC), which is documented in 1-2 Maccabees.[68] In both of these accounts, Mattathias and his sons Judas, Simon, and Jonathan provide the model for a Jewish revolution against a wicked pagan ruler. When the ruler Antiochus Epiphanes came into Jerusalem beginning in 175 BC, he heavily persecuted the Jews, burned their Scriptures, disrupted Jewish festivals, and set up an altar of Zeus in the holy of holies of the temple. Antiochus even sacrificed a pig on Zeus's altar and spread pigs' blood all over the holy sanctuary (see 1 Macc 1:41–64; 2 Macc 6:1–17). The haunting title "abomination of desolation" forever after became its name (see Dan 11:31; 12:11; Mark 13:14; Matt 24:15; see also 1 Macc 6:7).

Some of the Jews, led by Mattathias and his sons, rebelled against Antiochus. They withdrew to the caves and the mountains and performed guerrilla warfare against Antiochus and his soldiers for the next three years. The rebellion began when Mattathias, seeing a Jew offering sacrifices before an altar to a pagan god, ran and killed him right on the altar:

---

67. Ehrman, *Triumph of Christianity*, 50.

68. Dunn writes of the word "zeal" in 1 Maccabees, "Here it may be significant that the word is used in 1 Maccabees to describe the faithful Maccabees' pursuit of 'the sons of arrogance' (including the apostate Jews) and the 'lawless' (1 Macc. 2:47; 3:5). It was certainly burned into Paul's memory of his past—'I persecuted the church of God' (1 Cor. 15:9; Gal. 1:13, 23; Phil. 3:6), and his resort to the word consistently in this sense in Galatians, and more frequently than anywhere else, shows how deeply the memory affected him (4:29; 5:11; 6:12)" (*Epistle to the Galatians*, 57–58).

When Mattathias saw it, he burned with zeal and his heart was stirred. He gave vent to righteous anger; he ran and killed him on the altar. At the same time he killed the king's officer who was forcing them to sacrifice, and he tore down the altar. Thus he burned with zeal for the law, just as Phinehas did against Zimri son of Salu. Then Mattathias cried out in the town with a loud voice, saying: "Let everyone who is zealous for the law and supports the covenant come out with me!" (1 Macc 2:24–27; see also Josephus, *Ant.* 12.270–271)

Notice that Mattathias "burned with zeal" and called everyone who is "zealous for the law" to join him. The author even invokes the story of Phinehas's zeal. Mattathias died soon after they fled, leaving his son Judas Maccabeus, "the Hammer," to lead the rebels from then on. Antiochus's horror came to an end on November 21, 164 BC, when Judas the Hammer demonstrated great heroism and led his fellow rebels to Jerusalem and retook the city and its temple. This event is still celebrated by Jews to this day as Hanukkah.[69]

There is little doubt that the young Pharisee Paul would have been greatly inspired by the Maccabean Revolt and seen Mattathias and Judas as great heroes of old, much like the Greeks looked back to Hector and Achilles, or the Romans looked back

---

69. Jesus attended the celebration of the Maccabean victory, known in the first century as the Feast of the Dedication, according to John 10:22–23. In 2011, Mel Gibson had in the works a film called *Judah Maccabee*, a *Braveheart* for Jewish history, telling this story of great heroism by the Maccabean Revolt. Gibson even had the script written and ready to go. Unfortunately, the project has been derailed and may never happen. See Sharon Waxman and Brent Lang, "Warner Bros. Shelves Mel Gibson Maccabee Movie," The Wrap, April 12, 2012, https://www.thewrap.com/warner-brothers-pulls-plug-mel-gibson-maccabee-movie-exclusive-36952/.

to Aeneas and Hercules. In that way he was just like many other Jews of his day, who were also "zealous." [70]

What led Paul the Pharisee to persecute this new and rising sect of Nazarenes? By his own testimony, it was his "zeal for God." Paul had the same burning zeal that Phinehas, Elijah, Jehu, Mattathias, and Judas had when they put sinners and heretics to death. Like his zealous predecessors, Paul knew Deuteronomy well:

> If a prophet or a dreamer of dreams arises among you and gives you a sign or a wonder, and the sign or the wonder comes true, concerning which he spoke to you, saying, "Let us go after other gods (whom you have not known) and let us serve them," you shall not listen to the words of that prophet or that dreamer of dreams; for the LORD your God is testing you to find out if you love the LORD your God with all your heart and with all your soul. ... But that prophet or that dreamer of dreams shall be put to death, because he has counseled rebellion against the LORD your God who brought you from the land of Egypt and redeemed you from the house of slavery, to seduce you from the way in which the LORD your God commanded you to walk. So you shall purge the evil from among you. (Deut 13:1–3, 5)

---

70. See Judith 9:4, as well as the first-century Jewish philosopher Philo's statement that "there are thousands, who are zealots for the laws, strictest guardians of the ancestral customs, merciless to those who do anything to subvert them" (*On the Special Laws* 2.253). In the book of Acts, see James's words recorded in Acts 21:20 ("You see, brother, how many thousands are there are among the Jews of those who have believed, and they are all zealous for the Law") and Paul's words to Jews in Jerusalem: "educated under Gamaliel, strictly according to the law of our fathers, being zealous for God just as you all are today" (Acts 22:3).

Deuteronomy 21:23 even says: "For he who is hanged is accursed of God." Paul was absolutely convinced that this so-called prophet, Jesus of Nazareth, had hung on a tree and was cursed by God. This crucified criminal could not be God's Messiah. All the Jews of Jerusalem and the surrounding areas following him had been led astray by this "dreamer." This sect of Nazarenes would continue to lead others from Israel astray if they were not stopped. As Deuteronomy makes clear, this blasphemer Jesus deserved to be put to death, and so did his followers unless they recanted from their blasphemy.[71]

The zealous attitude of Paul and many of his contemporaries is summed up well by New Testament scholar J. Louis Martyn: "In the collision between the crucified Jesus and the Law, then, there was in the mind of this zealous Pharisee no doubt at all as to where God stood. God stood on the side of the Law. Hence, Jesus, the Law-cursed criminal, could not be God's Messiah, and the church that venerated him as such could not be the church of God."[72]

The book of Acts agrees with this, recording Paul's pre-conversion aims this way:

So then, I thought to myself that I had to do many things hostile to the name of Jesus of Nazareth. And this is just what I did in Jerusalem; not only did I lock up many of the saints in prisons, having received authority from the chief priests, but also when they were being put to death I cast my vote against them. And as I punished them often

---

71. It is important to point out at this point that most Jews of the first century AD did not resort to violence. In fact, Rabbi Gamaliel, Paul's teacher, counseled the very opposite of what Paul ended up doing to the rising Christian movement (see Acts 5). The texts in Deuteronomy about destroying heretics were within the context of a Jewish theocracy, which in the first century AD the Jews were not.

72. Martyn, *Galatians*, 163.

in all the synagogues, I tried to force them to blaspheme; and being furiously enraged at them, I kept pursuing them even to foreign cities. (Acts 26:9–11)

This summary of Paul's aims fits well with the evidence provided from his letters. After his conversion, he continually looked back at this aim to "persecute the church of God" (Gal 1:13; 1 Cor 15:9) and even try to "destroy it" (Gal 1:13) as his chief sin.[73] In short, that Paul the zealous Pharisee was persecuting followers of Jesus and trying to destroy this new Jewish movement in the early 30s AD is a bedrock fact.

Then the unexpected, unthinkable, most extraordinary thing happened to this zealous Pharisaic persecutor. As convinced as Paul was that the crucified Jesus was cursed by God, suddenly, "in one of the most dramatic turnabouts in history,"[74] as Ehrman puts it, Paul became even more convinced this Jesus was God's Messiah, the Lord of the world, whom God raised from the dead.

Paul the Pharisaic persecutor was from this time forth known as Paul the apostle.

PAUL THE APOSTLE

Paul emphatically declares to the Corinthians: "Am I not free? Am I not an apostle? Have I not seen Jesus our Lord?" (1 Cor 9:1). While numerous theories about what happened to Paul have been offered over the last two hundred years, what is a bedrock fact is that Paul was convinced this transformation was for one reason and one reason alone: "He [Jesus] appeared to

---

73. The same Greek word for "destroy" here is also used in Acts 9:21. See also Gal 1:2.

74. Ehrman, *New Testament*, 307.

me" (1 Cor 15:8). Paul unequivocally believed the crucified man Jesus appeared to him alive, raised from the dead. Paul refers to this conversion experience all throughout his letters: as "when God ... was pleased to reveal His Son in me" (Gal 1:15–16); Jesus "appeared to me" (1 Cor 15:8; 9:1); "laid hold of" me (Phil 3:12); and that this was the moment when he was "called" to be an apostle (Rom 1:1; Gal 1:1; 1 Cor 1:1; 2 Cor 1:1). This Jesus, the false prophet and dreamer who Paul the persecutor had thought was leading Israel astray, Paul now proclaimed to be the Son of God, Savior, and the Lord of the world. Paul wrote, fewer than twenty years after his transformation, that this man Jesus "loved me and gave Himself up for me" (Gal 2:20). Quite extraordinary.

After his conversion, Paul must have spent lots of time in prayer and contemplation, poring over the Scriptures to understand how this crucified man Jesus could be God's Messiah and Lord of the world. The time frame for this, as we will discuss in the next chapter, possibly began with his time spent in Arabia (Gal 1:17) and especially during his "silent years" in Tarsus (AD 37–45). Soon after this, Paul wrote Galatians (AD 48)[75] and 1 Thessalonians (AD 50/51), where we find most of the fundamental doctrines of Paul's mature Christian theology already worked out. According to New Testament scholar Martin Hengel, all of Paul's theological understanding of Christ had already been achieved sometime within fifteen years of his conversion.

> This thoroughly bold, dynamic way of thinking took place in the astonishingly short space of hardly more than fifteen years. As Paul began his great missionary journeys toward the end of the 40s, it was already complete. In his letters no further Christological development

---

75. Whether Paul wrote Galatians in AD 48 or in the mid-50s is irrelevant to the arguments of this book. Critical scholars argue vigorously for either dating.

can be seen. The decisive basic development seems to have been completed ten years earlier.[76]

We see hints of this "working it out" especially in the third chapter of Galatians, where Paul the apostle reinterprets the accursed tree passage in Deuteronomy (21:23): "Christ redeemed us from the curse of the Law, having become a curse for us—for it is written, 'CURSED IS EVERYONE WHO HANGS ON A TREE'" (Gal 3:13). Paul the apostle still agrees with Paul the Pharisee that this crucified man Jesus was accursed of God. But after his conversion, Paul now understands Jesus was cursed by God "for us"; he hung on the cross bearing our sin and curse (Gal 3:13; 2 Cor 5:21), and he did it because he loved us (Gal 2:20; Rom 5:6-8). According to New Testament scholar Joachim Jeremias,

> The only explanation of this shocking phrase "God made Christ a cursed one" is that it originated in the time before the episode on the Damascus road. Jesus of Nazareth, a man ostensibly accursed by God—that was why Saul persecuted him in the guise of his followers, why he blasphemed him (1 Tim 1:13) and tried to compel blasphemy from his disciples (Acts 26:11), namely the cry *Anathema Jesus*—"Jesus be cursed" (1 Cor 12:3). But then, on the Damascus road, the accursed one appeared before Paul in divine glory. After this experience, Paul still went on saying, "God made Christ a cursed one," but now he added two words: "for us" or "for me" (Gal 2:20).[77]

Paul must have reinterpreted thousands of Scriptures in a similar way, now possessing new eyes that had "seen Jesus our

---

76. Hengel, *Studies in Early Christology*, 388.

77. Jeremias, *Jesus and the Message of the New Testament*, 77.

Lord" (1 Cor 9:1). It is indisputable and a bedrock fact that Paul believed the crucified man Jesus appeared to him alive, raised from the dead.

THE UNIQUENESS OF PAUL'S CONVERSION

I will be discussing this appearance of Jesus to Paul more in chapter 6. For now, it is important to point out why Paul's conversion was unlike so many other famous conversions of church history. In almost all cases of people converting to Christianity, by their own testimony, they were struggling with some kind of sin or guilt and sought Christ for forgiveness. This is the testimony of the two most famous (and influential) conversions after Paul: St. Augustine of Hippo in 386 and Martin Luther in 1516. They are both famous for the guilt they experienced before God, Augustine's guilt with sexual sin and Luther with guilt and terror of the wrath and judgment of God.

Paul's conversion was nothing like that. Paul was not a sinner struggling with sexual immorality, feeling the guilt in his soul, fearing the wrath and judgment of God. This important point of Paul's conversion is brilliantly argued by New Testament scholar Krister Stendahl in a famous article called "The Apostle Paul and the Introspective Conscience of the West."[78] Paul the Pharisaic persecutor did not believe God was against him but that God was on his side in this battle against the Nazarene heretics. He was not a sinner struggling with guilt; he was arresting and punishing the sinners! As to righteousness that came from the law, Paul confesses he believed he was "blameless" (Phil 3:6).

This is very different from Augustine and Luther. Paul was not seeking Christ. He was fighting against him and laying hold

---

78. Stendahl, "Apostle Paul and the Introspective Conscience."

of his followers for arrest. It was in his highest moment of burning zeal that Paul believed Jesus "laid hold of" him (Phil 3:12). The chief sin Paul referred back to from then on was not some inner struggle of guilt or even an outward struggle with idolatry or sexual immorality. Paul's great sin was that he persecuted the church of God. It was something Paul did not realize was sin until he was convinced Christ appeared to him. What Paul thought was righteousness before God was in reality the most severe evil and blasphemy against God.

So then, how do we account for Paul's conversion from persecuting Jesus to following Jesus? It was not because of a sinful conscience, and he was definitely not seeking the Nazarene who he considered accursed. Paul's answer is clear: the crucified man Jesus appeared to him, raised from the dead.

On the other hand, if Jesus stayed dead, then what did Paul see? What can historically account for this transformation that changed the course of human history? I will seek to answer these questions in the concluding chapter.

———

In sum, we don't have a phone booth that allows us to literally travel back in time, but the tools of the historical method enable us to time travel to learn about the knowable past, whether studying significant historical figures such as Tiberius Caesar and Socrates or historical events such as the Jewish war. Not all sources are equally reliable, but encountering the "historical Paul" is easier than most because the bedrock facts of his life and aims are found in bedrock sources. Paul the Pharisee, burning with zeal for Torah and God, sought to persecute, arrest, and even destroy the followers of this new Jewish movement, the Nazarenes. He believed Jesus was a "dreamer," leading Israel astray. Jesus' crucifixion was further proof that he was a false prophet and even accursed of God. Yet something unexpected and extraordinary happened to this Pharisaic persecutor. Paul had a radical transformation from Paul the Pharisee to Paul the world history–changing apostle. Paul unequivocally believed that the cause of his transformation was that the crucified man Jesus appeared to him alive, raised from the dead.

In the next chapter, we will see further why Paul is our bedrock eyewitness of this earliest stage of the Christian movement. He knew the earliest followers of Jesus and even received priceless creedal traditions and hymns from them long before his first letter was written.

2: Bedrock Eyewitness
The Apostle Paul

Of all the men of the first century, incomparably the most influential was the Apostle Paul. No other man exercised anything like so much power as he did in molding the future of the Empire. Among the Imperial ministers of the period there appeared none that had any claim to the name of statesman except Seneca; and Seneca fell as far short of Paul in practical influence and intellectual insight as he did in moral character.

Sir William Ramsay, Pauline and Other Studies in Early Christian History

Paul is the single most important author of the New Testament when it comes to studying the historical Jesus and the earliest days of the Christian movement. As we have already seen, he was a zealous Pharisee who believed Jesus was an accursed false prophet. Therefore, he persecuted followers of Jesus and tried to destroy this movement. Suddenly, he had an earth-shattering, world-changing, transformational conversion when he became convinced that the crucified man Jesus appeared to him, raised from the dead. After this appearance of Jesus, Paul the Pharisaic persecutor became forever known as Paul the apostle.

Paul's conversion, though, was just the beginning.

In addition to the bedrock facts of Paul's conversion and pre-conversion aims and beliefs, we know many of Paul's movements after his conversion during the earliest stages of the Christian movement. After his conversion, Paul spent time in Arabia and Damascus. Then, within five years of Jesus' crucifixion, he visited Jerusalem. During this visit, he met with Jesus' foremost follower, Peter, and Jesus' brother James. It was at this meeting, around AD 37 (or sometime after his conversion in Damascus, AD 34–37) that Paul received many traditions and hymns about Jesus' life, teachings, death, burial, resurrection, and appearances (see 1 Cor 7:10; 8:6; 9:14; 11:2, 23–26; 15:3–7; 16:22; 2 Cor 8:9; 10:1; Gal 1:4–5; Rom 1:3–4; 4:25; 6:3–4; 8:34; 14:14; 15:3, 8; 1 Thess 1:10; 4:14; Phil 2:6–11; see also 1 Tim 3:16). These travels of Paul during the 30s and 40s AD, referenced throughout his undisputed letters, are bedrock facts. We know more about the historical Paul and his movements in the first thirty years of the Christian movement than we know about any other figure of first-century Christianity, with the exception of Jesus himself.

ARCHIMEDEAN POINTS OF HISTORY

Below you will find a timeline of the life of Paul and his movements during the first two decades of Christianity. I have based the timeline on a few points where events in Paul's life mentioned in Scripture line up with events mentioned in other ancient sources. I call these "Archimedean points of history" after the ancient Greek mathematician Archimedes, who famously said, "Give me a place to stand and with a lever I will move the whole world."[79] I conclude the timeline with Paul standing before the proconsul Gallio in Corinth, recorded in

---

79. Diodorus Siculus, *Library of Diodorus Siculus*.

Acts 18:12-17, because this is one of those Archimedean points of history. At the end of the nineteenth century, an inscription from the Roman emperor Claudius was discovered at the temple of Apollo in Delphi, Greece (it was published in 1905). In the inscription, Claudius mentions Gallio as proconsul. This enables historians to accurately date Gallio as proconsul of Achaia from July 51 to July 52.[80] This is a bedrock fact in Paul's chronology.

We only need to work backward from here. According to Acts, Paul had been in Corinth for around eighteen months by the time he stood before Gallio (Acts 18:11). We then know Paul arrived in Corinth in either 49 or 50. In fact, another Archimedean point helps us further here. When Paul arrived in Corinth, Acts 18:2 says, "Paul found a Jew named Aquila, a native of Pontus, having recently come from Italy with his wife Priscilla, because Claudius had commanded all the Jews to leave Rome." Emperor Claudius expelled the Jews from Rome in AD 49, according to the Roman historian Suetonius: "Because the Jews at Rome caused continuous disturbances at the instigation of Chrestus, he expelled them from the city" (Suetonius, *Claudius* 25).

Paul then must have arrived in Corinth in AD 49.

We can then put the beginning of Paul's second missionary journey (Acts 15:36–18:22) toward the beginning of 49, and the apostolic council in Jerusalem (Acts 15:1-35) in the latter half of 48. Paul may have written his letter to the Galatians early in 48 after his first missionary journey (47-48). Moreover, Paul's second visit to Jerusalem, in 46 or early 47 (Acts 11:27-30; Gal 2:1-10) to aid in the famine, corresponds to when Josephus says

---

80. For the inscription and history of its discovery see Deissmann, *St. Paul*, 261–86. Paul could have stood before Gallio in 51 or 52; that is why we have a year or two on either side of the chronology of many events in Paul's life.

this famine occurred: "It was in the administration of Tiberius Alexander that the great famine occurred in Judaea, during which Queen Helena bought grain from Egypt for large sums and distributed it to the needy" (*Ant.* 20.101).[81]

In addition, Tiberius Alexander, the philosopher Philo of Alexandria's nephew, served as governor of Judea from AD 46 to 48 (*Ant.* 20.100-104). This all seems to fit quite well and enables us to create a timeline of dates related to the life of Paul and the early Christian movement (italics are used for events where there is not historical certainty):

6–4 BC	John the Baptist is born. Jesus is born.
4 BC	King Herod dies.
AD 9–12	*Saul of Tarsus/the apostle Paul is born.*[82]
August 19, 14	Augustus Caesar dies. Tiberius Caesar (AD 14-37) becomes emperor of Rome.
18	The high priesthood of Joseph (AD 18-36), called Caiaphas, begins.
26	Pontius Pilate (AD 26-36) becomes governor and the fifth procurator of Judaea.
26-28	John the Baptist begins his ministry, preaching and baptizing in the Jordan River.

---

81. See Wright, *Paul: A Biography*, 95.

82. "The best guess has [Paul] a little younger than Jesus of Nazareth; a birth date in the first decade of what we now call the first century is as good as we can get" (Wright, *Paul: A Biography*, 34).

27–30	Jesus is baptized in the Jordan by John the Baptist.
	Jesus' public ministry begins in Galilee and lasts three to four years.

| 28–32 | John the Baptist is arrested, imprisoned in the castle Machaerus, and soon after put to death by the orders of Herod Antipas. |

| 30/33 | Jesus is crucified under the procurator Pontius Pilate in the reign of Tiberius Caesar. Soon after, his followers Peter, the Twelve, and others claim he has appeared to them alive, raised from the dead. |

31/34	The Pharisee Paul begins persecuting followers of Jesus and attempts to destroy the movement (Gal 1:13, 22–24; 1 Cor 15:9–10; Phil 3:6).
	Paul becomes convinced that the crucified man Jesus appeared to him alive, raised from the dead, near Damascus (Gal 1:15–16; 1 Cor 9:1–2; 15:8).
	Paul immediately goes into Arabia (for an unspecified period of time) (Gal 1:17).

| 34–37 | Paul returns to Damascus and remains there for three years (Gal 1:18; 2 Cor 11:32–33). |
| | *Paul receives creedal traditions (1 Cor 11:2, 23–26; 15:3–7) and hymns (Gal 1:4–5; 1 Cor 8:6; 2 Cor 8:9; Rom 1:3–4; 4:25; 6:3–4; 8:34; 1 Thess 1:10; 4:14; Phil 2:6–11) about Jesus during this time.* |

| 36 | A rebel Samaritan's revolt and Pilate's massacre of his followers leads to his removal as governor of Judea. |

36	Joseph Caiaphas is removed as high priest in Jerusalem.
37	Josephus is born.
March 16, 37	Tiberius dies; Caligula (AD 37–41) becomes emperor of Rome.
37	Paul for the first time goes to Jerusalem, spends fifteen days with Peter (Gal 1:18), and sees James, the Lord's brother (Gal 1:19). *Paul receives creedal traditions (1 Cor 11:2, 23–26; 15:3–7) and hymns (Gal 1:4–5; 1 Cor 8:6; 2 Cor 8:9; Rom 1:3–4; 4:25; 6:3–4; 8:34; 1 Thess 1:10; 4:14; Phil 2:6–11) about Jesus during this time.*
37–45	Paul spends time in the regions of Syria (Caesarea) and Cilicia (Tarsus) (Gal 1:21), known as the "silent years."
42	*The apostle James, the son of Zebedee, is martyred by Herod Agrippa I (Acts 12:2).*
44–46	Barnabas recruits Paul to work with him in Antioch (Acts 11:25–26).
46–47	Paul goes to Jerusalem a second time (Gal 2:1–10; *Acts 11:27–30*) and with Barnabas meets with the "pillars" Peter, James, John, and possibly others of the Twelve. He then returns to Antioch (Acts 12:25).
47–48	Paul goes on his first missionary journey (lasting possibly around eighteen months) and returns to Antioch (Acts 13:4–14:26).

48   *Paul writes Galatians from Antioch.*
            Apostolic council is held in Jerusalem (Acts
            15). Paul and Barnabas return to Antioch (Acts
            15:30–33).

49–52   After a dispute between Paul and Barnabas,
            they part ways, and Paul begins his second
            missionary journey with Silas (Acts
            15:36–18:22).
            Paul and Silas travel to southern Galatia
            through Asia Minor, on to Macedonia
            to Philippi (Acts 16:9–40; 1 Thess 2:2),
            Thessalonica (Acts 17:1–9; 1 Thess 2:2; Phil
            4:15–16), Berea (Acts 17:10–15), then to Athens
            (Acts 17:16–31; 1 Thess 3:1) and to Corinth (Acts
            18:1–18).
            When Paul plants the church in Corinth, he
            delivers to them creedal traditions (1 Cor
            11:2, 23–26; 15:3–7) and a hymn (1 Cor 8:6) he
            received before this either in Damascus or
            Jerusalem.

51/52   Paul stands before Gallio's judgment seat in
            Corinth (Acts 18:12–17).
            Gallio, the Stoic philosopher Seneca's brother,
            serves as proconsul of Achaia from July 51 to
            July 52 (Tacitus, *Annals* 15.73; 16.17).

In order to time travel and follow in Paul's footsteps in the years before 46/47, we must again consult our most detailed chronology of Paul's movements from his own pen, his autobiography in the first two chapters of Galatians. In the rest of this chapter, I will show you how we can know the bedrock facts concerning the timeline of Paul's earlier life.

PAUL'S BEDROCK AUTOBIOGRAPHY

In the first two chapters of Galatians, Paul is defending his apostleship against attacks from false teachers infiltrating the churches he recently planted in Galatia. He wants to make crystal clear that he did *not* learn the gospel from those who were apostles before him, but instead it was given directly to him through a revelation of Jesus Christ (Gal 1:12). He is an apostle directly commissioned by the risen Jesus himself. This leads him to narrate his movements and significant people he met with, such as Peter and James, for example, during the first two decades after his conversion. As he defends his apostleship, he gives us the closest thing to an autobiography we possess from him. As a detailed, autobiographical sketch, it has no equal in the New Testament.

Beginning in Galatians 1:13, Paul takes us chronologically from his school days as a zealous, overachieving Pharisee (probably beginning sometime in the late 20s AD) to his showdown with Peter in Antioch, sometime around AD 46–47 (Gal 2:11–14). Jesus' appearance to Paul, which he describes as "when God, who had set me apart even from my mother's womb and called me through His grace, was pleased to reveal His Son in me" (Gal 1:15–16), occurred sometime between AD 31 and 34.

New Testament scholar and noted skeptic James Tabor expresses the inestimable historical value of this bedrock autobiography of Paul:

> Jesus was crucified in the year AD 30. Paul's Letters date to the 50s AD. For this twenty-year gap we have no surviving records. These are the silent years of the history

of earliest Christianity. What we can know we have to read backward from the records that survive. Fortunately, in Paul's letter to the Galatians, written about AD 50, he reached back at least fourteen years in recounting his own autobiography. This gives us an original first-person source, the most valuable tool any historian can work with, reaching back into the decade of the 30s AD.[83]

This autobiography is "the most valuable tool any historian can work with," and it is a bedrock fact. In his book *How Jesus Became God*, Bart Ehrman summarizes,

> It is reasonably clear that Paul became a follower of Jesus two or three years after Jesus' death, based on the chronological details he provides in some of his letters, especially Gal. 1–2, where he writes such things as "three years later" and "after fourteen years." When one crunches the numbers, it appears relatively certain that if Jesus died around the year 30, Paul became his follower around the year 32 or 33.[84]

What else can we learn from Paul's bedrock autobiography?

ARABIA AND DAMASCUS

Paul tells his Galatian churches that after his conversion he "went away to Arabia, and returned once more to Damascus" (Gal 1:17). This agrees with Acts that Paul's conversion happened somewhere near or within Damascus (Acts 9; 22; 26; cf. 2 Cor

---

83. Tabor, *Jesus Dynasty*, 251. See also Robinson's view in *Redating the New Testament*, 36: "Indeed we may say that the statements of Gal. 1–2 are the most trustworthy historical statements in the entire New Testament."

84. Ehrman, *How Jesus Became God*, 376–77. See also Ehrman, *New Testament*, 357–58.

11:31–32). Arabia probably refers to the ancient Nabataean kingdom founded in the second century BC, with its capital as Petra.[85]
It was very close to Damascus, included a lot of the area that is
today's Hashemite kingdom of Jordan, and, as Paul indicates
later in Galatians, included the Sinai Peninsula.

How long Paul spent in Arabia and what he actually did there
is left to the historical imagination. We do have some clues, however. For instance, Josephus tells us that "Moses went up into the
mountain called Sinai, which lies between Egypt and Arabia" (*Ag.
Ap.* 2.25). And Paul mentions "Arabia" one more time in Galatians,
saying, "Hagar is Mount Sinai in Arabia" (Gal 4:25). Is Paul giving
us a clue to where he went during this time—to Mount Sinai?
Did this earth-shattering news that the crucified man Jesus is
alive lead Paul to the same mountain to which his heroes Moses
and Elijah had fled during great crises in their lives? It seems
likely, but not certain.

One thing that is certain with a man like Paul is that he
prayed. He prayed long and hard. As a learned Pharisee, Paul
must have kept running his Scripture-filled mind through the
Torah, the Prophets, and the Psalms, seeking to understand them
in light of a crucified Messiah. Preeminent in his thoughts, one
can imagine, was this question: How it was that a man cursed
by God on a tree could be the Messiah, even Lord of the world?

It is a bedrock fact that Paul went for some amount of time
to Arabia during his three years at Damascus, but how long and
what exactly he did there is left to the historical imagination.

---

85. You can still visit Petra, which in 2007 was named as one of the "New
7 Wonders of the World" (https://world.new7wonders.com/wonders/). On a
personal note, I am living in Amman, Jordan, as I write this. I have visited Petra
three times and plan to go again and again. It is truly a wonder.

KING ARETAS OF THE NABATAEANS

Even if Paul did spend time in prayer and contemplation over the Scriptures in Arabia, evidence from another autobiographical chapter in Paul's letters indicates strongly that he was also preaching to all in Arabia and Damascus that Jesus is the Christ, "the Son of God."[86]

In 2 Corinthians 11, at the end of Paul's "fool's speech," where he recounts all his adventurous journeys, sufferings, and weaknesses to the Corinthians, he describes his first and possibly greatest humiliation soon after his conversion: "In Damascus the ethnarch under Aretas the king was guarding the city of the Damascenes in order to seize me, and I was let down in a basket through a window in the wall, and so escaped his hands" (2 Cor 11:32–33).[87]

In this passage, Paul describes probably the first attempt on his life, what John Calvin called his "first apprenticeship,"[88] after becoming a follower of Jesus. Its humiliating circumstances were no doubt seared into his memory, and according to many scholars, this may be another Archimedean point in

---

86. After Paul's conversion on the Damascus road as recorded in Acts 9, we are told "immediately he began to proclaim Jesus in the synagogues, saying, 'He is the Son of God' " (Acts 9:20). The title "the Son of God" occurs nowhere else in Acts, and here it is on the lips of Paul. Jesus is also called "Son" in Acts 13:33, where again it is on the lips of Paul quoting Ps 2:7. Paul refers to Jesus as "the Son of God" or "Son" fifteen times in his undisputed seven letters.

87. See also the parallel account in Acts 9:23–25: "When many days had elapsed, the Jews plotted together to do away with him, but their plot became known to Saul. They were also watching the gates day and night so that they might put him to death; but his disciples took him by night and let him down through an opening in the wall, lowering him in a large basket." In Acts it says "the Jews" plotted to kill Paul, but in Paul's own account he says it was Aretas who sought to capture him. The Jews in Damascus could very well have urged King Aretas to capture Paul, but we can't know for certain.

88. Calvin, *Commentaries on the Epistles of Paul the Apostle to the Corinthians*, 2:363.

Paul's chronology.[89] We possess coins of the Roman emperors Augustus, Tiberius, and Nero from Damascus, but not of Caligula (AD 37–41) or of Claudius (AD 41–54). There is a gap between the years 34 and 62. Although it is an argument from silence, a reasonable case may be made that during this time Damascus fell under the control of King Aretas of the Nabataeans (9 BC–AD 39) from AD 37–39.

During this period we also know from Josephus of some significant drama between Herod Antipas and Aretas (*Ant.* 18.109–142). King Aretas' daughter had been married to Antipas, but he divorced her in order to marry Herodias (the same wife who prompted her daughter Salome to ask for John the Baptist's head on a platter, according to Mark 6:14–19). This led to war between Aretas and Antipas, with Aretas as the victor. Antipas later convinced Tiberius to command the Roman governor Vitellius to capture Aretas and bring him to Rome dead or alive. While Vitellius was on his way to fulfill these orders, he received word that Tiberius had died (on March 16, AD 37) and called the whole thing off.

If this is accurate, then Paul was lowered from a basket to escape King Aretas sometime after Tiberius' death in March of 37 and before the death of Aretas in 39. New Testament scholar Robert Jewett's chronology is even more precise. He argues that after escaping Aretas, Paul paid his first visit to Jerusalem in October of 37. Again, even if these exact dates are debated among scholars, what is a bedrock fact according to Paul's autobiography is that Paul did escape from Aretas by being lowered from a wall in a basket. Paul is telling the truth.

---

89. Jewett: "This is a datum whose historical solidity is capable of anchoring a chronology" (*Chronology of Paul's Life*, 30–33). Campbell writes: "This dramatic episode creates the prospect of an absolute chronological marker for his life" ("Anchor for Pauline Chronology"). See also Bowersock, *Roman Arabia*, 65–69.

After this, according to Acts 9:26–29, he paid his first visit to Jerusalem.

JERUSALEM AND BEYOND

I already spent the prologue discussing Paul's first visit to Jerusalem. In Galatians 1:18–19, we are told Paul spent fifteen days with Peter and also some time with James, the Lord's brother. As I argued above, this is pivotal concerning the bedrock facts laid out in this book. It was likely during this visit that Paul received the bedrock source, the creedal tradition(s) found in 1 Corinthians 15:3–7.[90] I will discuss this bedrock source in detail in the next chapter, but for now let us finish Paul's autobiography as he recounts it in Galatians.

After Paul left Jerusalem, he tells us he "went into the regions of Syria and Cilicia" (Gal 1:21), probably right at the end of AD 37.[91] Paul also adds that "the churches of Judea" were glorifying God because of his conversion (Gal 1:22–24). Paul quotes the message he was hearing as "He who once persecuted us is now preaching the faith which he once tried to destroy" (Gal 1:23; see also Acts 9:21). These "churches of Judea" Paul speaks of are some of the most ancient congregations in the history of Christianity, "the oldest in Christendom," as Hans Dieter Betz notes.[92] As also mentioned in 1 Thessalonians 2:14 and Acts 9:31, they were formed probably sometime *before* Paul's conversion in AD 31 or 34. Here they are marveling at Paul's conversion story, and almost two

---

90. As I showed on the timeline above, it could have been even earlier that Paul received this information, during his three-year stay in Damascus. The bedrock fact is not *where* Paul received these creedal traditions and hymns, but *that* he received them within the first decade of the Christian movement.

91. The account in Acts 9:30 is in agreement with this chronology: "they brought him down to Caesarea and sent him away to Tarsus."

92. Betz, *Galatians*, 80.

thousand years later believers and nonbelievers alike are still marveling at Paul's transformation!

Paul's time in Syria and Cilicia, which Acts identifies more specifically as Tarsus, is known as Paul's "silent years." Bringing in the chronology in Acts, Paul would have spent almost a decade in his hometown of Tarsus before Barnabas brought him back to Antioch in AD 45 or 46. Like Paul's time in Arabia, we are left to our historical imagination as to what Paul did during these long years. As with Arabia, it must have been a time of prayer and contemplation, and, if we know Paul (and we do!), he spent time preaching Christ and him crucified and risen again. In fact, it is likely during this time Paul had the "visions ... of the Lord" in which he was "caught up to the third heaven," as he records in 2 Corinthians 12:1–6.

In his biography of Paul, New Testament scholar N. T. Wright imagines further:

> He reread Genesis. He reread Exodus. He reread the whole Torah and the prophets, especially Isaiah, and he went on praying the Psalms. With hindsight, he saw Jesus all over the place—not arbitrarily, not in fanciful allegory, but as the infinite point where the parallel lines of Israel's long narrative would eventually meet. These parallel lines are central to his mature thinking and foundational for what would later become Christian theology.[93]

Paul wrote all the letters we possess in the New Testament after this silent period. As I quoted Martin Hengel as saying in the previous chapter, more happened in Christology and theological advancement in this decade in Cilicia (and a little before in Arabia) than in all the later centuries of Christian theological

---

93. Wright, *Paul: A Biography*, 71.

development. It was during this time that Paul came to a mature understanding of the "gospel of God, which He promised before-hand through His prophets in the holy Scriptures, concerning His Son" (Rom 1:1–3).

These first two decades of the Christian movement would be almost completely lost to us if it were not for Paul's early letters. Whether in Jerusalem or Damascus or Arabia or Antioch, Paul was there meeting with Peter, James, John, and no doubt others who knew the historical Jesus. Through Paul we can reach back into the 30s and 40s AD of the Christian movement. To repeat Tabor from above, Paul "gives us an original first-person source, the most valuable tool any historian can work with." In addition, Ehrman makes this profound statement: "And so in the letter to the Galatians Paul states as clearly as possible that he knew Jesus' brother. Can we get any closer to an eyewitness report than this? … Paul knows one of these brothers personally. It is hard to get much closer to the historical Jesus than that."[94]

It is hard to get much closer to the historical Jesus than that.

———

Now that we have time traveled through history observing Paul's background and transformation, and why Paul is the bedrock eyewitness of the earliest stage of the Christian movement, in the next chapter we will begin to discuss this bedrock source that Paul *received* within a decade of Jesus' death: 1 Corinthians 15:3–7. It is from this source/creedal tradition(s) that we learn all of the bedrock facts discussed in the remainder of this book, with the exception of the rise of the Nazarenes in chapter 7.

In this "pearl of great price" we have the bedrock source for the unalterable bedrock of Christianity.

---

94. Ehrman, *Did Jesus Exist?*, 145, 148.

3: Bedrock Source:
1 Corinthians 15:3–7

This tradition, we can be entirely confident, was formulated as tradition within months of Jesus' death.

James Dunn, *Jesus Remembered*

What counts is that the heart of the formula is something Paul knows the Corinthians will have heard from everyone else as well as himself, and that he can appeal to it as unalterable Christian bedrock.

N. T. Wright, *The Resurrection of the Son of God*

Come back with me into our phone booth and let's time travel to Palestine in the spring of 1947. We are on the northwestern shore of the Dead Sea, following a young Bedouin shepherd named Muhammad. Like shepherds throughout history, Muhammad has lost one of his goats, and being a good shepherd, he chases after it. The goat jumps up some rocks of the mountainous regions nearby and wanders into a cave. Muhammad begins to throw some rocks to get the goat to come down and then hears something unfamiliar. One of his rocks has shattered a clay pot inside the cave the goat has wandered into. As Muhammad climbs up the rock and enters the cave, he discovers other clay pots, one of which contains seven ancient Hebrew scrolls. This was the beginning of arguably the greatest of archaeological treasures discovered in the twentieth century: the Dead Sea Scrolls.

Don't miss the real hero of the story: the goat!

After nineteen hundred years of these scrolls sitting in this cave undisturbed, this goat wanders in. This cave was the first of a total of eleven caves excavated over the next eight years (1948–1956). A grand total of 930 scrolls, all over two thousand years old, now for the first time became available to the world, not to mention the ancient pots, coins, seeds, and other artifacts discovered in these caves.[95]

Of these 930 scrolls, 230 of them are from books of the Old Testament. Most of them are in Hebrew, but some are in Aramaic and Greek. All twenty-four (according to the Jewish numbering) or thirty-nine (according to the Protestant numbering) books of the Old Testament canon are represented, with the exception of Esther. It is virtually unanimous among scholars today that these surviving scrolls are a portion of a library belonging to the Jewish sect of the Essenes, who were active from roughly 150 BC to AD 70. Therefore, most of these scrolls, especially the biblical ones, date to around 150 BC, and some even earlier—a scroll with portions of Ecclesiastes housed in the Jordan Museum dates to 250 BC! The most valuable of all the 930 scrolls discovered is the Great Isaiah Scroll, which Muhammad and his goat found in Cave 1. This complete scroll of the book of Isaiah indisputably dates between 150 and 100 BC.[96] Before this discovery, the earliest Hebrew scroll of Isaiah

---

95. For the entire Indiana Jones–like story of the discovery of the Dead Sea Scrolls, see Vermes, *Story of the Scrolls*. To read the scrolls themselves, see Vermes, *Dead Sea Scrolls in English*, for the nonbiblical scrolls, and Abegg, Flint, and Ulrich, *Dead Sea Scrolls Bible*, for the biblical scrolls.

96. The Great Isaiah Scroll has been digitized and is online here for all to behold its wonder: dss.collections.imj.org.il/isaiah.

we possessed dated to the ninth century AD. This means that with the discovery of the Dead Sea Scrolls, we are taken back over one thousand years in the history of the Hebrew texts of the Old Testament! When you compare the Dead Sea scroll of Isaiah and the Masoretic Text scroll of Isaiah, separated by over one thousand years, they are almost identical, with only minor textual variants. It is difficult to fully explain the inestimable value of these treasures discovered at Qumran.

Now let's engage our historical imagination again ("on your imaginary forces work") and imagine that tomorrow archaeologists find an ancient scroll buried in Jerusalem. This scroll was able to be accurately dated to within a decade or so of Jesus' death, and all the evidence suggests it originally came from Jesus' earliest followers: Peter, James, John, and others of the Twelve. Even more importantly, the writing on the scroll is in a creedal formula, laying out the core beliefs of this very young and rising Jewish movement.

What a priceless, irreplaceable treasure that would be!

Incredibly, within Paul's Letter to the Corinthians, this is *almost* exactly what we possess. We do not have an actual scroll, but what we do have is a creedal tradition or traditions dating to within a decade of Jesus' death, with its ultimate source going back to Jesus' earliest followers.

This is a bedrock fact among believing and nonbelieving scholars.

Even if all that survived from the Christian movement in the first century AD were this creedal tradition (1 Cor 15:3–7), we would still have the unalterable bedrock source for the most essential claim of Christianity: Jesus died for our sins, he rose again on the third day, and he appeared to individuals and groups of people alive again as proof of his resurrection.

In this chapter, I will discuss 1 Corinthians 15:3–7 in detail, answering the following questions in turn: How do we know it is a creedal tradition that Paul is quoting? How early can we date it? Who originally composed it, and where? Is it only one creedal tradition, or does it contain multiple, distinct traditions?

PRE-PAULINE TRADITIONS

The discovery of pre-Pauline creedal traditions and hymns within Paul's early letters is one of the greatest fruits of historical-critical scholarship.[97] The early church fathers, medieval theologians, and Reformers all knew, quoted, and commented on 1 Corinthians 15, yet it was not until the turn of the twentieth century that anyone realized that 1 Corinthians 15:3–7 was not originally composed by Paul, but instead contains a creedal tradition that Paul had *received* almost two decades earlier.[98]

The two main reasons for this are found within the text itself. The first sign that this is a creedal tradition is the way Paul introduces it with the words "delivered" and "received": "For I delivered to you as of first importance what I also received" (1 Cor 15:3). When Paul planted the church in Corinth between AD 49 and 51, he delivered certain traditions to the Corinthians that further illuminated the gospel of Jesus Christ (see 1 Cor 11:2). These must have included some teachings and stories of the historical Jesus (1 Cor 7:10; 9:14; 11:1; 2 Cor 10:1), the account of the Lord's Supper (1 Cor 11:23–26), possibly hymns (1 Cor 8:6;

---

97. According to NT scholar Gerd Lüdemann, "the discovery of pre-Pauline confessional formulations is one of the great achievements of recent New Testament Scholarship" (*Resurrection of Christ*, 37).

98. It seems the first to argue that this is a pre-Pauline formula was Alfred Seeberg in *Der Katechismus der Urchristenheit*, 48–50. Kloppenborg writes: "That 1 Corinthians 15:3b–7 contains a pre-Pauline confessional/kerygmatic statement has been almost universally acknowledged" ("Analysis of the Pre-Pauline Formula," 351).

2 Cor 8:9), and this creedal tradition concerning the death, burial, resurrection, and appearances of Jesus. Since Paul is also saying he "received" these traditions, we can definitively date them at least *before* the founding of the church of Corinth between AD 49 and 51.

We will discuss below where and when Paul received these creedal traditions, but let us spend a little more time on this language of "receiving" and "delivering."

According to New Testament scholar Richard Hays,

> The language of "receiving" and "handing on" indicates clearly that Paul is referring here to early Christian tradition. ... This passage shows clearly that Paul's original preaching and teaching included the narration of the events of Jesus' passion (cf. 1 Cor. 15:3–5; Gal. 3:1b). Even though there were no written Gospels in Paul's time, the telling of the story of Jesus' death and resurrection stood at the center of Christian proclamation from the beginning. Paul is not giving the Corinthians new information here; rather, he is recalling to mind the story that he told them about the foundational redemptive event, a story that they themselves repeat—or *should* repeat—every time they gather at table.[99]

"Received" and "delivered" are technical terms we find in other Jewish writings of the first century AD and afterward. These terms refer to the oral transmission of religious traditions.[100] I quoted Josephus in chapter 1 saying the Pharisees deliv-

---

99. Hays, *First Corinthians*, 197–98.

100. "There should never have been any doubt that 'to receive' (παραλαμβάνειν) and 'to deliver' (παραδίδοναι) represent the rabbinical technical terms *qibbēl min* and *māsar le* (P. Ab. 1.1ff. etc.)" (Jeremias, *Eucharistic Words of Jesus*, 101). See also Gerhardsson, *Reliability of the Gospel Tradition*, 19–25.

ered to the Jewish people many traditions that they themselves had received from their ancestors (*Ant.* 13.297). These traditions were believed to go back ultimately to Moses and had been handed down by a succession of leaders up to and beyond the days of Paul and Josephus. According to the Mishnah, a Jewish source dating to around AD 200, "Moses received Torah at Sinai and handed it on to Joshua, Joshua to elders, and elders to prophets. And prophets handed it on to the men of the great assembly" (Mishnah Pirqe Abot 1.1).

The earliest Christians also delivered traditions that came down from the earliest apostles, with the Lord Jesus being the ultimate source (1 Cor 7:10; 9:14; 11:2, 23–25; 15:3–7; 2 Cor 10:1; Gal 1:9; Rom 14:14; 1 Thess 1:6; 2:13; 4:1; Phil 4:9; see also 2 Thess 3:6; Heb 2:3). We know from Paul that he served as a mediator, relaying these traditions to the churches he planted, such as this one in Corinth. In fact, in the other most significant tradition that Paul relayed to the Corinthians, we have not only the earliest account of the Lord's Supper, but most likely the earliest recorded words of Jesus in all of history![101]

> For I received from the Lord that which I also delivered
> to you, that the Lord Jesus in the night in which He was
> betrayed took bread; and when He had given thanks, He
> broke it and said, "This is My body, which is for you; do
> this in remembrance of Me." In the same way He took

---

101. Jeremias: "The Pauline account of the Lord's Supper, the oldest written form of a pronouncement of Jesus himself, was probably written in the spring of 54. When Paul said that he has transmitted orally the words of the account to the Corinthians (1 Cor. 11.23, 'what I also delivered to you'), this brings us back to the autumn of 49, i.e. the beginning of the missionary work in Corinth. The further statement of the Apostle that the report was transmitted to him (11.23, 'for I received from the Lord') points back still farther. When did Paul himself receive the Eucharistic tradition? At his conversion? That is quite probable!" (*Eucharistic Words of Jesus*, 188).

the cup also after supper, saying, "This cup is the new covenant in My blood; do this, as often as you drink it, in remembrance of Me." (1 Cor 11:23–25)

Notice the same language of "received" and "delivered" as found later in 1 Corinthians 15:3. Paul is aware of Jesus' Last Supper tradition, which later made its way into the Gospels of Mark, Matthew, and Luke (Mark 14:22–26; Matt 26:26–30; Luke 22:14–20).[102] Paul only relayed this tradition to the Corinthian church because of the "unworthy" manner in which many Corinthians were partaking in the Lord's Table. It is truly incredible that the only reason we know Paul and his churches celebrated the Lord's Supper is the controversies at the table in Corinth. Paul probably had knowledge of many other Jesus traditions that simply did not come up in his surviving letters because there was not a particular controversy he needed to address.

In short, like the tradition of the Lord's Supper, this creedal tradition found within 1 Corinthians 15:3–7 was something Paul "delivered" to the Corinthians at the founding of their church, meaning he must have "received" it sometime earlier—before about AD 49.

The second most prominent reason we know this is a pre-Pauline formula is linguistic. Paul uses a number of words here that he uses nowhere else in his letters. Phrases such as "died for our sins," "according to the Scriptures," "He was buried," "He was raised," "on the third day," "He appeared," and "the twelve" are either only used here or, if used elsewhere, there has

---

102. Interestingly, in light of Luke's relationship to Paul according to early church tradition, Luke's account of the Last Supper is closest to the tradition within 1 Cor 11:23–26.

been influence from tradition.[103] Why would he not use phrases like these elsewhere, especially when he uses words and phrases similar to these throughout his letters? We must conclude that to have at least seven unique phrases and/or words within just a few verses is improbable if it were originally composed by Paul himself.

These considerations above have persuaded 99 percent of scholars today and for the past one hundred years that we have in 1 Corinthians 15:3–7 a pre-Pauline creedal tradition. This means it dates before Paul's earliest letters, but how early?

DATING THE CREEDAL TRADITION

As we saw two chapters ago, New Testament scholar and historian Bart Ehrman talks about a "wish list" for historians trying to get to the truth of (or, to use my words, "time travel to") a historical person or event. This wish list includes having sources

---

103. For a full discussion see Jeremias, *Eucharistic Words of Jesus*, 101–2. "Died for our sins": Paul uses *hamartia* ("sin") sixty-four times, three in the Pastorals and five in OT quotations. Of the remaining fifty-six times, fifty instances of *hamartia* are singular and without the genitive case. In the six cases where *hamartia* is plural (as in 1 Cor 15:3), influence from "tradition" can be seen (1 Cor 15:3, 17; Gal 1:4; Rom 7:5; Eph 2:1; Col 1:14). "According to the Scriptures" occurs only here Paul's letters. Paul usually introduces an OT passage with *kathōs gegraptai*, "just as it is written" (Rom 9:33; 10:15; 11:8; etc.). "He was buried" only occurs here in Paul's letters. The phrase "He was raised" with the perfect passive indicative is only found in Paul repeated in this same chapter (1 Cor 15:4, 12–14, 16, 20) and in 2 Timothy (2:8). Paul is always proclaiming Christ's resurrection in his letters, but besides these examples, he never uses this same phrase. Paul seems to be repeating the word from the creedal tradition to make his point about the continuity between Jesus' resurrection (1 Cor 15:4, 12–14, 16, 20) and all believers' future resurrection (1 Cor 15:12–14, 16, 20). "On the third day" occurs here only in Paul's letters. "He appeared" appears only five times in all of Paul's letters, four times here in this creedal formula (1 Cor 15:5, 6, 7, 8) and once elsewhere, in 1 Tim 3:16 (another creedal formula). "The twelve" occurs only here in Paul's letters. Paul elsewhere uses the phrase "the apostles" to refer to those who followed Christ before him (Gal 1:17, 19; Rom 16:7; 1 Cor 9:5; 12:28, 29; 15:9; 2 Cor 11:5; 12:11; see also Eph 2:20; 3:5; 4:11).

that date very close to the time of the person or event; having multiple, reliable eyewitnesses; having these eyewitnesses and sources corroborate with one another; and having them not to be biased toward their subject matter.

I argued in that chapter that if we followed these "wish list" criteria rigidly, we would have to throw out most of ancient history we now take for granted. In almost all cases, we do not have a person writing about an event who is unbiased or disinterested, and most of our sources date many generations, even hundreds of years, after the person or event that is being described.

For instance, consider another example that is appropriate to compare to Jesus, another founder of a world religion: Gautama Buddha. Gautama Buddha is believed to have lived from 563 to 483 BC.[104] What is our earliest source for the "historical Buddha"? The first mention in history of the Buddha is found in inscriptions from the Edict of Ashoka, which are dated to the reign of Emperor Ashoka of the Mauryan Empire (269–232 BC). That is a gap of more than two hundred years between when the Buddha died and our earliest source referencing him.[105] The first biography of the Buddha laying out his life and teachings is not written down until the first century AD.[106] That is a gap of almost five hundred years,[107] the very opposite of a historian's wish list for reliable sources!

Now compare this to our earliest source for the historical Jesus: 1 Corinthians 15:3–7.[108] This creedal tradition seems to

---

104. The time frame the Buddha lived is not certain. Other scholars of Buddhism date his life from 480 to 400 BC.

105. Even if the Buddha died in 400 BC, that is still a gap of over 130 years.

106. See Olivelle, *Life of the Buddha*, xix.

107. Even if we compare Jesus' four biographies, Mark, Matthew, Luke and John, they all date within thirty-five to sixty years of Jesus' death.

108. Other early teachings of Jesus repeated in 1 Corinthians date to the same time frame and are found in 7:10; 9:14; 11:23–25.

pass the highest of bars of rigorous historical analysis.[109] Not only does it contain the reliable testimony of eyewitnesses who knew the historical Jesus, but, as you will soon see, this creedal tradition dates from as early as months after Jesus' death to, at the very latest, a decade after his death. This is not even one generation removed from the person and events they describe, let alone two hundred years removed!

Again, this is not the conclusion of only Christian scholars. Here is just a sample of what nonconservative, "critical" historians say about the dating of this creed:

- "It is among the earliest confessions of Christian faith that we have, going back to the time of Paul's conversion and calling to become the apostle to the Gentiles, about three years after Jesus' crucifixion, and perhaps even earlier."[110]

- "The analysis of the formula tradition about the resurrection of Jesus allows the following conclusion: a tradition in 1 Cor 15.3b–5, which goes back very close to the events themselves, attests appearances to both individuals and groups. The credibility of this tradition is enhanced, because it is in part confirmed by the narrative tradition, which is independent, and because in the case of Paul we have the personal testimony of an eye-witness who knew many of the other witnesses."[111]

---

109. Von Campenhausen: "This account meets all the demands of historical reliability that could possibly be made of such a text as things stood" ("Events of Easter and the Empty Tomb," 44).

110. Scott, *Resurrection of Jesus*, 78.

111. Theissen and Merz, *Historical Jesus*, 490.

- "The formation of the appearance traditions mentioned in 1 Cor. 15.3–8 falls into the time between 30 and 33 CE, because the appearance to Paul is the last of the appearances and cannot be dated after 33 CE."[112]

- "This tradition, we can be entirely confident, was formulated as tradition within months of Jesus' death."[113]

What is bedrock concerning this creedal tradition is that it cannot be later than a decade after Jesus' death.[114] Depending on whether Jesus' crucifixion is dated to AD 30 or 33, most put the composition of this creedal formula sometime in the early 30s AD.[115]

---

112. Lüdemann, *Resurrection of Jesus*, 38.

113. Dunn, *Jesus Remembered*, 855.

114. The only detractors against the authenticity and early dating of the creed I am aware of are Marxsen, *Jesus and Easter*, 54, 95; O'Neill, *Recovery of Paul's Letter*, 27; and Price, "Apocryphal Apparitions." It may be relevant to point out that Price is one of the handful of scholars who self-identify as mythicists. See Allison's note in *Resurrecting Jesus*, 234n134. The other well-known mythicist, Richard Carrier, does believe this passage has "become multiply corrupted, deliberately and accidentally," but he concedes: "However, to avoid needlessly controversial premises here, I will simply assume the passage as we have it is what Paul wrote" (*On the Historicity of Jesus*, 516).

115. Between AD 30 and 35 (Seeberg, *Der Katechismus der Urchristenheit*, 189–93); "between its creation and the event it conveys, hardly more than a decade could have elapsed, and probably only half of one" (von Campenhausen, "Events of Easter and the Empty Tomb," 44); "five to six years after the crucifixion of Jesus" (Schweizer, "Resurrection: Fact or Illusion?," 145); "dating from only a few years after Jesus' death" (Burridge and Gould, *Jesus Now and Then*, 46); "most probably in the first half of the 30s" (Wedderburn, *Beyond Resurrection*, 113); "in the early 30s CE" (Hengel, *Studies in Early Christology*, 384); "cannot be later than some seven years after the death of Jesus Christ" (Dodd, *Apostolic Preaching and Its Developments*, 16); "within a decade of the death of Jesus" (Bockmuehl, *Cambridge Companion to Jesus*, 102); "a couple of years or so after Jesus' death" (Ehrman, *Did Jesus Exist?*, 130–32); "The formula itself, if Paul had received it soon after his conversion, must have reached back to the first five years after Jesus' death" (Pannenberg, *Jesus: God and Man*, 90); "It was probably formulated within the first two or three years after Easter itself, since it was already in

As Ehrman notes well: "The best sources, of course, are those nearest the time of Jesus himself."[116]

The creedal tradition in 1 Corinthians 15:3–7 is *very* near the time of Jesus.

I believe that New Testament scholar James Dunn has the best estimate, namely, that only "months" after Jesus' death this creedal formula was already being memorized and taught to new converts, possibly during the planting of churches by many of the apostles.[117]

I have contended above that Paul received this and other traditions and hymns when he met with Peter (and spent time with James) in AD 37 (Gal 1:18–19).[118] Many scholars agree with this contention, but some put the reception of these creedal formulas even earlier: either right after Paul's conversion in Damascus or sometime during his three-year stay in Damascus. They could be right, but it makes more sense that he received such information as "He appeared to Cephas … He appeared to James" (1 Cor 15:5, 7) at the time he first met with Peter and James (Gal 1:18–19). Whether it was right after Paul's conversion or three or five years after Paul's conversion, it is a bedrock fact that this creedal tradition was formulated sometime in the 30s AD.

---

formulaic form when Paul 'received' it" (Wright, *Resurrection of the Son of God*, 319); "must have been formulated within the first five years after Jesus' death" (Craig, *Son Rises*, 48).

116. Ehrman, *Jesus: Apocalyptic Prophet*, 22.

117. "There is no reason to doubt that this information was communicated to Paul as part of his introductory catechesis" (Dunn, *Jesus Remembered*, 855). According to Ernst Käsemann, it is "a tradition of catechical instruction on the subject of the Resurrection events" (*Essays on New Testament Themes*, 49).

118. Ehrman: "This visit is one of the most likely places where Paul learned all the received traditions that he refers to and even the received traditions that we otherwise suspect are in his writings that he does not name as such" (*Did Jesus Exist?*, 130–32).

Now that we know when the creedal tradition of 1 Corinthians 15:3–7 originated, let us look at where it came from and who originally composed it.

ORIGIN OF THE CREEDAL TRADITION

Over the last century, scholars have debated where this creedal tradition came from. The two major options are that it originated in Damascus, or even Antioch, with Greek-speaking Christians, or in Jerusalem with Aramaic-speaking Christians.

German New Testament scholar Joachim Jeremias has been the leading advocate for its originating in Jerusalem and possibly even being translated into Greek from a Semitic (Aramaic) source.[119] Others follow another German New Testament scholar, Hans Conzelmann, who vigorously argued against Jeremias's position, instead contending this creedal tradition originated with a Greek-speaking Jewish community in Damascus or even Antioch.[120]

Overall, this particular scholarly debate is not that important to our discussion. Whether this creedal tradition was originally composed in Jerusalem, Damascus, or Antioch, the ultimate source of the content of 1 Corinthians 15:3–7 comes from Jerusalem.[121] It was in Jerusalem that Paul met with Peter and James (and most likely other members of the Twelve), who are specifically mentioned in the creedal tradition.

Paul himself declares at the end of his discussion of Jesus' death, burial, resurrection, and appearances, "Whether then it was I or they, so we preach and so you believed" (1 Cor 15:11).

---

119. See Jeremias, *Eucharistic Words of Jesus*, 101–5.

120. Conzelmann, "On the Analysis," 18–20. See also Héring, *1 Corinthians*, 158; Bousset, *Kyrios Christos*, 76; Dibelius, *From Tradition to Gospel*, 18n2; Kramer, *Christ, Lord, Son of God*, 36–37.

121. See Lüdemann, *Resurrection of Christ*, 36.

The "they" here are the Jerusalem apostles, Peter, James, John, and others of the Twelve Paul has just referenced (1 Cor 15:5–7). Paul is making it crystal clear that he and all the Jerusalem apostles are preaching the same gospel, namely, the content of the creedal tradition in 1 Corinthians 15:3–7. This is a bedrock fact.

Hengel agrees: "This later forms the basis of Paul's gospel and, by his own report (1 Cor 15:11), was the original 'Jerusalem confession' that formed the bedrock for the proclamation of Cephas, the Twelve, James, and all the Apostles."[122]

In sum, whether this particular creedal tradition Paul received was originally composed by Greek-speaking Christians in Damascus or Antioch or in Aramaic by the apostles in Jerusalem, the testimonies concerning Jesus' death, burial, resurrection, and appearances ultimately came from some of the earliest followers of Jesus.

EXTENT OF THE CREEDAL TRADITION

What, then, did Paul actually receive in the 30s AD? Was it a written or an oral formula? If it was written, was it originally composed in Aramaic or in Greek? Did he receive the entire tradition in 1 Corinthians 15:3–7 or different parts of it at different times?

It is impossible to know for certain the answer to these questions. They are interesting to speculate about, but not important for the purposes of this book. Most scholars would agree that the creedal tradition originally contained 1 Corinthians 15:3–5 and then Paul added to it more traditions he received, such as Jesus' appearances to more than five hundred eyewitnesses (1 Cor 15:6), to James (1 Cor 15:7a), to all the apostles (1 Cor 15:7b),

---

122. Hengel, *Studies in Christology*, 11. Ehrman adds: "There are no grounds for assuming that Paul, whose views of Jesus were taken over from the Palestinian Jewish Christians who preceded him, held a radically different view of Jesus from his predecessors" (*Did Jesus Exist?*, 256).

and to himself (1 Cor 15:8). This makes the most sense of the data, as there is a clear break from the formulaic wording after verse 5.[123]

However, remember the bedrock facts concerning this bedrock source: Paul received this information sometime in the 30s AD, either soon after his conversion in Damascus or when he met with Peter in Jerusalem, and all testimonies found within cannot be dated later than a decade after Jesus' crucifixion. Technically, then, we can say that the most ancient creedal tradition speaks of Christ's death, burial, resurrection, and appearances to Peter and to the Twelve. The other traditions concerning Jesus appearing to more than five hundred at one time, to James, and to all the apostles, while possibly added to the original creedal formula, still must be dated no later than a decade after Jesus' death. This is why, even if 1 Corinthians 15:3-7 can be broken up into different traditions/sources, they all make up the unalterable bedrock source of Christianity.

OLDEST ON RECORD

I hope you have seen by now what a priceless, irreplaceable treasure we have in 1 Corinthians 15:3-7. To be sure, we have other ancient, possibly creedal statements concerning Jesus' death and resurrection in Paul's early letters (Gal 1:4-5; Rom 1:3-4; 4:25; 6:3-4; 8:34; 1 Thess 1:10; 4:14), yet none can compare to the antiquity and extent of 1 Corinthians 15:3-7. It preserves the most

---

123. Fitzmyer: "To the fragment of the kerygma quoted in vv. 3b-5a, Paul has added part of a list of early witnesses of the risen Christ in vv. 5b-7. The appearance to James and the apostles is a parallel to Cephas and the Twelve, and it undoubtedly comes from an equally early pre-Pauline tradition, but was not necessarily part of the primitive kerygma itself" (*First Corinthians*, 541). On the creedal tradition ceasing after verse 5, see von Campenhausen, "Events of Easter and the Empty Tomb," 44; Jeremias, *Eucharistic Words of Jesus*, 101ff; Hays, *First Corinthians*, 257; Kramer, *Christ, Lord, Son of God*, 19.

ancient statement of Christianity and "the oldest record of the Christian belief in the resurrection of Jesus of Nazareth," as Joseph Fitzmyer notes.[124] It is unparalleled in the New Testament. In fact, it is unparalleled in all of ancient literature![125]

Let me highlight again what I said above: even if this creedal tradition were the only thing to survive from the early Christian movement, we would still have the unalterable bedrock source for the most essential claim of Christianity: Jesus' death, burial, resurrection, and appearances. This is why I believe this bedrock source became the foundation for all later preaching (and writing) concerning the Christ event.

To show you what I mean, the chart on page 88–89 demonstrates the development from this ancient creedal tradition into the sermons in Acts and then later into the literary accounts of the Gospels.

———

We have now time traveled to the 30s AD to follow our bedrock eyewitness (Paul) during the earliest days of the Christian movement and to learn everything we can concerning our bedrock source: the creedal tradition he quotes in 1 Corinthians 15:3–7. In the next three chapters, we will walk through this creedal tradition line by line to clarify exactly what we can know from

---

124. Fitzmyer, *First Corinthians*, 543. Von Campenhausen: "The oldest and most reliable account we have of what the disciples experienced at Easter is that of Paul in the fifteenth chapter of his first Epistle to the Corinthians. This is universally admitted" ("Events of Easter and the Empty Tomb," 43). It is "the oldest source about the appearances of the Resurrected Lord" (Bornkamm, *Jesus of Nazareth*, 150) and the "oldest faith statement about the resurrection" (Lapide, *Resurrection of Jesus*, 98).

125. "So also with the catalogue of resurrection appearances (vv. 5-7), the like of which there is nothing else in the early literature" (Fee, *First Epistle to the Corinthians*, 719).

this bedrock source concerning Jesus' death, burial, resurrection, and appearances.

Chapter 4 will focus on Jesus' crucifixion and burial, chapter 5 the extraordinarily innovative *belief* in Jesus' resurrection, and chapter 6 on the appearances to Peter, the Twelve, the more than five hundred, James, to all the apostles, and last of all, to Paul himself. By the end of these chapters, you will see just how many bedrock facts emerge from this priceless bedrock source.

We begin by witnessing the horror of Roman crucifixion in the first century AD.

	1 Corinthians 15:3–5, 8 30s AD	Acts 10:39–40; 13:28–31 40s AD
Death	"Christ died for our sins according to the Scriptures" (1 Cor 15:3a)	"they asked Pilate that He be executed" (Acts 13:28) "They also put Him to death by hanging Him on a cross" (Acts 10:39)
Burial	"and that He was buried" (1 Cor 15:4)	"they took Him down from the cross and laid Him in a tomb" (Acts 13:29)
Resurrection	"and that He was raised on the third day according to the Scriptures" (1 Cor 15:4)	"God raised Him up on the third day" (Acts 10:40) "But God raised Him from the dead" (Acts 13:30)
Appearances	"and that He appeared to Cephas" (1 Cor 15:5) "then to the twelve" (1 Cor 15:5) "then He appeared to James" (1 Cor 15:7) "and last of all, as to one untimely born, He appeared to me also" (1 Cor 15:8)	"and for many days He appeared to those who came up with Him from Galilee to Jerusalem, the very ones who are now His witnesses to the people" (Acts 13:31) "and granted that He become visible" (Acts 10:40) "The Lord Jesus, who appeared to you on the road" (Acts 9:17)

Mark 15–16; Luke 24:34 60s AD	John 19–20; Luke 24:36 AD 80–90
"It was the third hour when they crucified Him" (Mark 15:25) "And Jesus uttered a loud cry, and breathed His last" (Mark 15:37)	"Therefore when Jesus had received the sour wine, He said, 'It is finished!' And He bowed His head and gave up His spirit" (John 19:30)
"Joseph bought a linen cloth, took Him down, wrapped Him in the linen cloth and laid Him in a tomb which had been hewn out in the rock" (Mark 15:46)	"So they took the body of Jesus and bound it in linen wrappings with the spices. ... Now where He was crucified there was a new tomb in which no one had yet been laid. ... Since the tomb was nearby, they laid Jesus there" (John 19:40–42)
"Do not be amazed; you are looking for Jesus the Nazarene, who has been crucified. He has risen; He is not here; behold, here is the place where they laid Him" (Mark 16:6)	"For as yet they did not understand the Scripture, that He must rise again from the dead" (John 20:9)
"The Lord has really risen and has appeared to Simon" (Luke 24:34) "But go, tell His disciples and Peter, 'He is going ahead of you to Galilee; there you will see Him, just as He told you'" (Mark 16:7)	"So when it was evening on that day, the first day of the week ... Jesus came and stood in their midst and said to them, 'Peace be with you'" (John 20:19) "While they were telling these things, He Himself stood in their midst and said to them, 'Peace be to you'" (Luke 24:36)

4: Crucifixion

"Christ Died for Our Sins and He Was Buried"

The fact of Jesus' death as the consequence of crucifixion is indisputable.

Gerd Lüdemann, *The Resurrection of Jesus*

That Jesus was crucified is as sure as anything historical can ever be.

John Dominic Crossan, *Jesus: A Revolutionary Biography*

One thing at least can be said with certainty about the Crucifixion of Christ; it was manifestly the most famous death in history. No other death has aroused one hundredth part of the interest, or been remembered with one hundredth part of the intensity and concern.

Malcolm Muggeridge, *Jesus Rediscovered*

C rucifixion was invented by the Persians, advanced by the Greeks, but perfected by the Romans.[126] Crucifixion as a capital punishment came to an end only by the orders of the Roman emperor Constantine the Great in the early fourth century AD after he converted to Christianity. It is arguably the most brutal, shameful, and inhuman death penalty to ever enter the mind

---

126. For a brilliant, concise history of crucifixion in the ancient world see Hengel's *Crucifixion*.

of humankind. Josephus referred to it as the "most wretched of deaths" (*J.W.* 7.203). Among all the historical records we possess concerning crucifixion, only one person is said to have survived. Josephus, who was working for Rome at the time, tells us that the Roman general Titus sent him to a certain village called Thecoa in order to know whether it was a place fit for a camp. On his way back, he saw many captives crucified, three of his personal friends among them. Josephus persuaded the soldiers to take them down and give them the best medical care they could. Only one survived (*Life* 420–421).

Roman statesman and orator Cicero was also appalled at the barbarity of crucifixion, calling it a "cruel and disgusting punishment" and the "worst extreme of the tortures inflicted upon slaves" (*Against Verres* 2.5.166, 169). In fact, in a famous trial of the first century BC, Cicero publicly rebuked a Roman official named Gaius Verres who had a Roman citizen, Publius Gavius of Compsa, flogged and then crucified. Death by crucifixion was mostly reserved for slaves; Roman citizens were almost never crucified. Publius Gavius was a well-known exception. In his condemnation of Verres, Cicero's oratory reaches a climax when he says: "It is a crime to bind a Roman citizen; to flog him is an abomination; to put him to death is like murdering your own father; to crucify him—what? There is no fitting word that can possibly describe so horrible a deed" (*Against Verres* 2.5.170).

Cicero could not find a word in his vast Latin vocabulary that could accurately describe this monstrosity. All he could say was, "What?"

JESUS AND YEHOHANAN

For a very long time, the primary historical evidence we had for crucifixion in the ancient world was in the writings of people such as Josephus, Cicero, Plutarch, and even the four Gospels.

Then in 1968, archaeologists unearthed the first physical evidence of death by crucifixion.

During the first century, many Jews in Jerusalem buried their dead in rock-cut tombs. After a year, the bones of the dead would be collected and put into small stone boxes called ossuaries. In 1968, one of these was discovered that bore the Hebrew name "Yehohanan, the son of Hagkol." Inside, archaeologists found an ankle bone through which was driven a curved nail. Yehohanan is to this day the only victim of crucifixion ever discovered.[127]

We don't know why Yehohanan was crucified, but it may have been for a political crime against the Roman Empire. This was the most common reason the Caesars would crucify someone, as it was a strong deterrent to others not to fight against Rome. Archaeologists learned from the bones of Yehohanan that his arms were tied (not nailed) to the wooden crossbeam, or *patibulum*, but he was fastened to the vertical stake with nails through his ankle bones. Yehohanan's famous ankle bone can now be viewed at the Jerusalem Museum:

---

127. See Vassilios Tzaferis, "Crucifixion—the Archaeological Evidence."

Here is how archaeologists believe Yehohanan was crucified:

Let us time travel to the moment Yehohanan was condemned to death by crucifixion and behold the horror. He picks up his heavy *patibulum* over his shoulders and behind his neck and is forcibly led away like an animal toward his place of execution.[128] As he walks, a placard with his crime(s) written on it is hanging from his neck (see Suetonius, *Domitian* 10). During this shameful walk to crucifixion, Roman soldiers are whipping him with leather ropes containing animal bones and glass shards.[129] When he makes it to the vertical stake in the ground that awaits his

128. "Every criminal condemned to death bears his cross on his back" (Plutarch, *Moralia* 554A/B).

129. "Tearing his naked body with whips" (Dionysius of Halicarnassus, *Roman Antiquities* 7.69.1–2).

arrival, Yehohanan is stripped completely naked, tied with ropes to the crossbeam, and lifted up to the top of the vertical stake, and nails are driven through each of his ankles into the wood (Dionysius of Halicarnassus, *Roman Antiquities* 7.69.1–2). Listen to Yehohanan's screams of agony as they drive the nails through his ankle bones. After hanging there in agony, possibly for days, most likely cursing the day of his birth, exposed to the crows and wild animals, starving and dying of thirst, he starts to gasp for breath. Due to exhaustion, he can no longer lift himself up to breathe. Yehohanan is dying by asphyxiation. He suffocates and is dead within minutes.

Crucifixion is where we get the word "excruciating," literally meaning "out of the cross."

Tens of thousands of people died this way in the ancient world—some under the Persians and the Greeks, but most of them under the Caesars of Rome. Yehohanan was one of them. Jesus of Nazareth was another. The other tens of thousands of people crucified in the ancient world have been erased from history, and if it were not for the curved nail that stuck in his ankle bone, we would never have known how Yehohanan died. Yet somehow this crucified man Jesus of Nazareth is to this day the most influential person in human history. As Malcolm Muggeridge says, his is "the most famous death in history."

Who was this crucified Nazarene?

"CHRIST DIED"

It is a bedrock fact that Jesus of Nazareth was crucified in AD 30 or 33 during Passover, under the governor Pontius Pilate during the reign of Tiberius Caesar. Renowned New Testament scholar E. P. Sanders puts Jesus' crucifixion on a list of "almost indisputable facts ... which can be known beyond doubt."[130] Jesus' crucifixion is a bedrock fact in part because, within 130 years of his death, it is attested by Paul (1 Cor 1:13, 23; 2:2; 15:3; 2 Cor 13:4; Gal 2:20; 3:1, 13; 6:14; Rom 6:6), all four Gospels (Mark 15:22–25; Matt 27:33–36; Luke 23:32–34; John 19:18, 23–24), Acts (2:23; 3:13–15; 5:30; 10:39; 13:29), Josephus (*Ant.* 16.63–34),[131] the Roman historian Tacitus (*Annals* 15.44),[132] and Lucian of Samosata (who calls Jesus "that crucified sophist" in *The Passing of Peregrinus* 11–13). According to Luke-Acts and John, Jesus was nailed to the cross by both his hands and his feet (Luke 24:39–40; Acts 2:23; John 20:20, 25, 27).

But the earliest evidence of Jesus' death, dating somewhere between months to ten years afterward, is the beginning of the creedal tradition in 1 Corinthians 15:3: "Christ died." Even though it does not mention crucifixion specifically, 99 percent of scholars agree this refers to Jesus' crucifixion under Pontius Pilate.

---

130. Sanders, *Historical Figure of Jesus*, 11. See also Dunn: "Two facts in the life of Jesus command almost universal assent. They bracket the three years for which Jesus is most remembered, his life's work, his mission. One is Jesus' baptism by John. The other is his death by crucifixion" (*Jesus Remembered*, 339).

131. Though there are Christian interpolations in this passage of Josephus, it is almost universally agreed among Josephan scholars that the core does belong to Josephus himself, especially the reference to Jesus' crucifixion. Feldman captures in a sentence the current scholarly consensus, "The most probable view seems to be that our text represents substantially what Josephus wrote, but that some alterations have been made by a Christian interpolator" (*Josephus: Jewish Antiquities*, 51). Ehrman writes, "It is far more likely that the core of the passage actually does go back to Josephus himself" (*Did Jesus Exist?*, 64). See also Meier, *Marginal Jew*, 68.

132. Ehrman: "Some mythicists argue that this reference in Tacitus was not actually written by him—they claim the same thing for Pliny and Suetonius, where the references are less important—but were inserted into his writings (interpolated) by Christians who copied them, producing the manuscripts of Tacitus we have today. (We have no originals, only later copies.) I don't know of any trained classicists or scholars of ancient Rome who think this, and it seems highly unlikely" (*Did Jesus Exist?*, 55).

The first part of the creed, "Christ died," is "as historical as anything can ever be," as John Dominic Crossan says.

But what about the next two phrases: "for our sins" and "according to the Scriptures"? What do they mean? Are these claims also bedrock facts? Did he just hang on that cross and die, like Yehohanan and tens of thousands of others from the ancient world? Or did he hang on that cross and die *for our sins*, yours and mine?

"FOR OUR SINS ACCORDING TO THE SCRIPTURES"

Whether this theological statement about Jesus' historical death is true largely hinges on the question of Jesus' resurrection. Did the historical Jesus rise from the dead? If he did, then one can reasonably conclude that he died "for our sins." As you will see below, the historical Jesus himself said to his followers the night before he was crucified at the Last Supper: "This cup is the new covenant in My blood" (1 Cor 11:25). The promise of the "new covenant" from the prophet Jeremiah would have resounded in these Jewish followers' minds: " 'Behold, days are coming,' declares the LORD, 'when I will make a new covenant with the house of Israel and with the house of Judah ... for I will forgive their iniquity, and their sin I will remember no more' " (Jer 31:31, 34).

The critical question of the historicity of the resurrection must await the final chapter. For now, let us at least briefly explore what the earliest followers of Jesus *meant* when they proclaimed, "Christ died for our sins according to the Scriptures."

Isaiah 53 is the only place in all the Hebrew Scriptures that contains a statement corresponding to "died for our sins." The suffering servant, a mysterious figure that appears throughout Isaiah 40–55, is said in 53:12 to bear the sins of many and even intercede for their sins. This means Isaiah 53 is almost certainly in the background to 1 Corinthians 15:3b: "Christ died for our sins."[133]

Commentators on 1 Corinthians almost universally agree that Isaiah 53 is in the background of this passage when it says "according to the Scriptures."[134] Specifically these texts from the prophet Isaiah:

- "But He was pierced through for our transgressions, He was crushed for our iniquities;[135] the chastening for our well-being fell upon Him, and by His scourging we are healed. All of us like sheep have gone astray, each of us has turned to his own way; but the LORD has caused the iniquity of us all to fall on Him" (Isa 53:5-6)

- "He Himself bore the sin[136] of many, and interceded for the transgressors"[137] (Isa 53:12)

Notice the key phrases "pierced through for our transgressions," "crushed for our iniquities," "bore the sin of many," and "interceded for the transgressors." Those last two phrases in the

---

133. *Christos apethanen hyper tōn hamartiōn hēmōn.*

134. Conzelmann writes, "Dependence on Isa 53 is accepted by most exegetes (e.g., Jeremias, Lohse)" (*1 Corinthians*, 255). Early church father John Chrysostom seems to be the first commentator to make the connection between 1 Cor 15:3 and Isa 53: "For, 'for the sins of my people,' says one, 'is He come to death': and, the Lord delivered Him up for our sins: and, 'He was wounded for our transgressions'" (*Homilies on the Epistles of Paul to the Corinthians* 38.3-4).

135. LXX Isa 53:5: *dia tas hamartias hēmōn.*

136. LXX Isa 53:12a (*hamartias*, "sins"), according to the Septuagint (Greek translation of the Hebrew Scriptures) and the Dead Sea Scrolls versions of Isaiah (1QIsa[a], 1QIsa[b], 4QIsa[d]).

137. LXX Isa 53:12b (*dia tas hamartias auton paredothē*): "their transgressions" according to the Septuagint (Greek translation of the Hebrew Scriptures) and the Dead Sea Scrolls versions of Isaiah (1QIsa[a], 1QIsa[b], 4QIsa[d]).

versions of Isaiah from the Greek Septuagint and found among the Dead Sea Scrolls have "sins" instead of "the sin" and "their transgressions" instead of "the transgressors." Therefore, the most ancient reading of this passage (and the one Paul would have been familiar with) declares: "He Himself bore *the sins* of many, and interceded for *their sins*" (Isa 53:12).

The earliest followers of Jesus believed that Jesus' death was in some way in substitution for them, specifically *for* their sins.[138] Paul makes these substitutionary claims even more explicit in other passages in his early letters:

- "For the love of Christ compels us, having concluded this, that one died *for all*, therefore all died" (2 Cor 5:14)

- "He made Him who knew no sin to be sin *on our behalf*, so that we might become the righteousness of God in Him." (2 Cor 5:21)

- "Christ redeemed us from the curse of the Law, having become a curse *for us*—for it is written, 'Cursed is everyone who hangs on a tree'" (Gal 3:13)

- "For while we were still helpless, at the right time Christ died *for the ungodly*. For one will hardly die for a righteous man; though perhaps for the good man someone would dare even to die. But God

---

138. According to the standard Greek lexicon of the NT and other ancient literature, the preposition *hyper* primarily means "on behalf of, for the sake of." Here, it should be taken in the substitutionary sense of "in place of, instead of." See Sir 29:15; 2 Macc 7:9; 8:21; Josephus, *Ant.* 13.6 ("to die for them"); *J.W.* 2.201 ("for the sake of so many I shall readily give my life") (Arndt, Danker, Bauer, and Gingrich, *Greek-English Lexicon*, 1030-31).

demonstrates His own love toward us, in that while we were yet sinners, Christ died *for us*" (Rom 5:6–8)

- "He who did not spare His own Son, but delivered Him over *for us all*, how will He not also with Him freely give us all things?" (Rom 8:32)

As was already quoted above, Paul even personalizes Christ's death as "for me": "I have been crucified with Christ; and it is no longer I who live, but Christ lives in me; and the life which I now live in the flesh I live by faith in the Son of God, who loved me and gave Himself up *for me*" (Gal 2:20; see also Rom 14:15; 1 Cor 8:11).

If the earliest apostles from Jerusalem—Peter, James, John, the Twelve and the others—are preaching the same thing as Paul (see 1 Cor 15:11), then they are all teaching the substitutionary death of Jesus *for our sins*.

"THIS IS MY BODY, WHICH IS FOR YOU"

Even if Isaiah 53 may be the scriptural background to the phrase "for our sins," and the early church taught that Jesus' death was substitutionary in nature, could the historical Jesus himself have suggested this? It seems very likely. As referenced above, the other most significant tradition that Paul *received* is the Last Supper tradition he quotes in 1 Corinthians 11:23–26. Within these verses we have the earliest recorded sayings of the historical Jesus.[139]

---

139. Dodd writes, "Jesus was saying that in order that the 'covenant' might become effective, or in other words that the new people of God might come into existence, he was voluntarily taking a course which would lead to his death. ... 'During supper,' we read, 'he took bread, and having said the blessing he broke it and gave it to them, with the words, 'Take this; this is my body.' No words of his are more firmly attested" (*Founder of Christianity*, 109). See also Hengel, *Studies in Early Christology*, 6, 44.

And what does Jesus say?

"This is My body, which is for you; do this in remembrance of Me." (1 Cor 11:24)

"This cup is the new covenant in My blood; do this, as often as you drink it, in remembrance of Me." (1 Cor 11:25)

It seems very unlikely that the early church would have put these words in Jesus' mouth if he did not actually say them. Jesus, an observant first-century Jew, here shockingly reinterprets the more-than-one-thousand-years-old (at that point) Jewish Passover meal so that when his followers eat it they will think not of the plagues and the exodus from Egypt, but now of the bread and the wine as his body and his blood. Who has the authority to reinterpret a more-than-one-thousand-years-old Jewish tradition, even the greatest event commemorated in Jewish history?

Moreover, Jesus uses the phrase "for you." Jesus' imminent death, the breaking of his body and the shedding of his blood, was "for you" (plural), that is, his followers.[140] This Last Supper meal was to be commemorated by his disciples to remember what he did *for them* in his death. Jeremias argues that Jesus was speaking here of his death in terms of the Servant Songs from Isaiah 40–55, primarily 52–53.[141] Like the claim that Jesus died "for our sins," Jesus' words at the Last Supper have Isaiah in the background. If these are the actual words of the historical Jesus,

---

140. Fitzmyer writes, "This is the intention of the word reinterpreting the Passover bread of old; it also implies a soteriological aspect of Jesus' handing over his body in death for others" (*First Corinthians*, 440). See also Thiselton, *First Epistle to the Corinthians*, 882–85.

141. Jeremias, *New Testament Theology*, 287–88.

then we have the ultimate source for the substitutionary nature of Jesus' death for sins: Jesus himself.[142]

To recap what we have seen so far this chapter, that Jesus was crucified ("Christ died") in either AD 30 or 33 under Pontius Pilate is as historical as anything can ever be. It is a bedrock fact of history. In addition, the scriptural and theological interpretation of his death ("for our sins according to the Scriptures") goes back to the earliest followers of Jesus, is even more explicitly proclaimed by Paul in his letters, and is corroborated by Jesus' own words at the Last Supper, recorded in 1 Corinthians 11:23-25.

Of course, as I mentioned earlier, the truth of these claims ultimately hinges on whether Jesus did in fact rise from the dead. But before we discuss the *belief* in Jesus' resurrection in the next chapter, let us briefly look at the next phrase in the creedal tradition: "and that He was buried" (1 Cor 15:4a).

"HE WAS BURIED"

What happened to Yehohanan after he gave his last breath hanging from that Roman cross? Josephus testifies that in some cases Jews were taken down from the cross and buried: "The Jews used to take so much care of the burial of men, that they took down those who were condemned and crucified, and buried them before the going down of the sun" (*J.W.* 4.317).

Jewish philosopher Philo of Alexandria (20 BC–AD 50) also testifies to this burial process for crucified Jews, especially on the eve of a holiday such as Passover: "On the eve of a holiday of this kind, people who have been crucified have been taken down and their bodies delivered to their relatives, because it was

---

142. Not only are they the earliest recorded words of Jesus, dating to within a decade of his death, but they have multiple attestation (Mark 14:22-26; Matt 26:26-30; Luke 22:14-20; 1 Cor 11:23-25).

thought well to give them burial and allow them ordinary rites" (*Flaccus* 83–84). Since we have discovered Yehohanan's bones in an ossuary in Jerusalem, it seems that what Josephus and Philo said above was true of at least his situation. His body was taken down from the cross, and he was buried in some way, perhaps by his family or friends. Later his bones were preserved in the ossuary that was discovered in the twentieth century.

In contrast, Martin Hengel says that most non-Jewish criminals and rebels who were crucified in the ancient world were probably either thrown in some ditch or left to be eaten by the dogs. "Crucifixion was aggravated further by the fact that quite often its victims were never buried. It was a stereotyped picture that the crucified victim served as food for wild beasts and birds of prey. In this way his humiliation was made complete."[143]

What, then, happened to Jesus' body? Was he left to be eaten by wild dogs? (This is exactly what John Dominic Crossan believes happened.)[144] Or was he given a proper burial in a tomb on the eve of Passover?

What exactly happened to Jesus' body after it was taken down from the cross, along with the discovery of the empty tomb three days later, are not considered bedrock facts. While many scholars agree with the creedal tradition that Jesus received some kind of burial, others entertain wild theories such as Crossan's idea that Jesus' corpse was consumed by dogs. For this reason, we cannot consider the burial or the empty tomb among the bedrock facts. On the other hand, let us still explore the background

---

143. Hengel, *Crucifixion*, 87.

144. See Crossan, *Jesus: A Revolutionary Biography*. Not many scholars, if any, have followed him in this contention. See, for example, Fitzmyer's critique: "To claim, as had been done in modern times, that Jesus' body was either left lying on the ground or thrown into a common grave for criminals is a preference for speculation that goes against the multiple attestation of NT witnesses about the burial (Synoptics, John, Paul)" (*Gospel according to Luke X–XXIV*, 1525).

of this ancient phrase "and he was buried" (1 Cor 15:4a) along with the later empty-tomb traditions. That Jesus was buried and that the women found his tomb empty three days later is not a bedrock fact *only* means it does not meet the high bar of 99 percent of scholars' affirmation, but that does not mean these events are not historical. There are good reasons to believe Jesus was buried just as the ancient creed testifies.

First, the Gospels testify unanimously that a ruling member of the Jewish council, or Sanhedrin (Mark 15:1, 43), Joseph of Arimathea, courageously asked Pilate for Jesus' body and buried him in his new tomb (Mark 15:42–47; Matt 27:57–61; Luke 23:50–55; John 19:38–42).

Second, the early sermons of Acts are another source that preserves possibly another burial tradition. Paul is recorded as saying in a synagogue sermon: "When they had carried out all that was written concerning Him, they took Him down from the cross and laid Him in a tomb. But God raised Him from the dead" (Acts 13:29–30).

The one possible difficulty between the Acts tradition and the Gospels is that it is unclear who the "they" were who took Jesus' body down from the cross and laid him in a tomb. However, when we look at it closely, it is not much of a difficulty after all. It is virtually unanimous among scholars (a bedrock fact) that whoever wrote the Gospel of Luke also wrote Acts.[145] So even if Acts 13 preserves a separate tradition concerning the burial of Jesus, it seems incredible that the author thought someone different from Joseph of Arimathea carried Jesus down from the cross (see Luke 23:53, which states that Joseph of Arimathea

---

145. It is debated among scholars whether Paul's companion, the doctor Luke, is the author of Luke and/or Acts, but that these two works were written by the same author (whoever he was) is indisputable.

"took [Jesus' body] down and wrapped it in a linen cloth, and laid Him in a tomb cut into the rock, where no one had ever lain"). Would a rich man such as Joseph not have servants to help him take Jesus' body down from the cross? Does anyone imagine Joseph climbing up there and carrying Jesus down by himself? It seems reasonable to conclude the "they" in Acts 13:29 were Joseph and his servants.

What about the testimony in our earliest creedal tradition, 1 Corinthians 15:3-7: "and that He was buried"?[146] Does this brief account support the stories in the Gospels concerning Joseph of Arimathea and the empty-tomb narratives? It is likely, but not historically certain.

First and foremost, the creedal tradition seems to be giving definitive evidence that Jesus did indeed die, in the same way that the list of appearances is giving definitive evidence that Jesus did indeed rise from the dead.[147] It may also imply a proper burial in some kind of tomb. Of the eleven occurrences of this word for "buried" in the New Testament, in most cases a proper burial in a tomb is assumed (see Matt 8:21-22; Luke 9:59-60; Luke 16:22; Acts 2:29). This is also true when this word is used in the Septuagint, the Greek translation of the Old Testament (Gen 35:8, 19; Num 20:1; Deut 10:6; Judg 10:2, 5; 12:7, 10, 12, 15; see also Josephus, *J.W.* 4.317; *Ant.* 4.78; 8.264). The reference to King David's tomb in Acts is a most interesting parallel to 1 Corinthians 15:4a because the exact phrase *kai etaphē* ("and

---

146. The creedal tradition's "and he was buried" only consists of two words in the Greek (*kai etaphē*). The four instances of "that" (*hoti*) in vv. 3-5 were most likely added to the creedal tradition by Paul. See Murphy-O'Connor, "Tradition and Redaction," 583-84.

147. Conzelmann: "The expansions ἐτάφη, ὤφθη, are added as verifications on the two statements on salvation. Thus the two fundamental statements (dead-raised) are each provided with a twofold proof: from Scripture and from a verifying fact" (*1 Corinthians*, 251-53).

he was buried") is used, and then "his tomb" is mentioned right after: "Brethren, I may confidently say to you regarding the patriarch David that he both died and was buried, and his tomb is with us to this day" (Acts 2:29). It is possible that Jesus' tomb was assumed in the words "and he was buried."

In addition, Paul echoes this creedal death, burial, and resurrection language when he discusses the Christian's baptism in Romans 6:3–4: "Or do you not know that all of us who have been baptized into Christ Jesus have been baptized into *His death*? Therefore *we have been buried* with Him through baptism into *death*, so that as Christ *was raised from the dead* through the glory of the Father, so we too might walk in newness of life." Paul sees the Christian reenacting the historical death, burial, and resurrection of Jesus when he or she is baptized into water. This implies a proper burial that the Christians in Rome no doubt gave to fellow believers who had died. In the same way as believers' graves would be empty after they physically rose from the dead at the general resurrection, so was Jesus' burial place empty after he "was raised from the dead."[148]

Last, the Greek word for "He was buried" (*etaphē*) is in the passive form, meaning he was buried by someone. Even though it does not say it explicitly, everyone agrees that that the first phrase "Christ died" implies *under Pontius Pilate*. Therefore, it may have been originally understood that "He was buried" implies *by Joseph of Arimathea*. But we cannot be sure.

All in all, while it does not meet the 99 percent threshold of a bedrock fact, it is reasonable to conclude with our earliest and multiply attested sources that say Jesus was given a proper burial in a tomb after his crucifixion.

---

148. Paul regularly compares believers' future bodily resurrection to Jesus' resurrection (1 Cor 6:14; 15:23; 2 Cor 4:14; Rom 8:11, 23; Phil 3:20–21).

THE EMPTY TOMB

Before we move on to examine the bedrock facts concerning the resurrection, there is one final question to ask about Jesus' death: Is it significant that our creedal tradition does not explicitly reference the empty tomb? As I will discuss in detail in the next chapter, the phrase "He was buried" being followed by "He was raised" assumes the burial place was empty. Resurrection meant Jesus' followers believed something happened to his corpse. As New Testament scholar Markus Bockmuehl writes: "Any known place of burial must have been empty: Paul's argument leaves no room for any form of Jesus' body to remain buried."[149] We can be pretty certain that Jesus' body was nowhere to be found when his followers began proclaiming he had risen from the dead. If the location of Jesus' corpse was known to the authorities or anyone else in Jerusalem, it seems incredible that this movement would have even lasted a day, or even "a single hour."[150]

That does not mean that the creedal tradition definitively confirms the empty-tomb narratives in the Gospels. On the other hand, there is nothing in this phrase that contradicts those accounts, and, as illustrated above, I believe it undergirds these accounts from the Gospels. N. T. Wright says on this point, "The fact that the empty tomb itself, so prominent in the gospel accounts, does not appear to be specifically mentioned in this passage, is not significant; the mention here of 'buried, then raised' no more needs to be amplified in that way than one would need to amplify the statement 'I walked down the street' with the qualification 'on my feet.' "[151]

---

149. Bockmuehl, *Cambridge Companion to Jesus*, 109. See also Hays, *1 Corinthians*, 256.

150. Pannenberg, *Jesus: God and Man*, 100.

151. Wright, *Resurrection of the Son of God*, 321.

The point of a creedal tradition is not that it includes everything about everything. Rather, a creed is intended to be easily memorized after learning the more detailed account concerning Jesus' burial and the empty-tomb traditions. When the early Christians cited this simple phrase, the stories of Joseph of Arimathea and the women finding the tomb empty may have immediately come to mind.

In fact, the phrase "on the third day" added to "and that He was raised" in 1 Corinthians 15:4b could be an early historical reference to the fact that the women found the tomb empty "on the third day," that is, on the first day of the week (Sunday). This was also the reason that Sunday was the day Christians gathered for worship according to sources as early as Paul's letter to the Corinthians (see 1 Cor 16:2; Acts 20:7; Rev 1:10; Didache 14.1; Ignatius, *To the Magnesians* 9.1).[152]

Even though Jesus' burial by Joseph of Arimathea and the empty-tomb traditions as recorded in the Gospels are not bedrock facts, many critical scholars do accept them as historical.[153]

---

152. Dunn writes, "Nor should we forget the striking but often neglected fact that from as early as we can trace, Sunday had become a day of special significance for Christians, 'the Lord's day,' precisely because it was the day on which they celebrated the resurrection of the Lord" (*Jesus Remembered*, 860). For a full discussion, see Rodorf, *Sunday*.

153. Vermes: "When every argument has been considered and weighed, the only conclusion acceptable to the historian must be that the opinions of the orthodox, the liberal sympathizer and the critical agnostic alike—and even perhaps of the disciples themselves—are simply interpretations of the one disconcerting fact: namely that the women who set out to pay their last respects to Jesus found to their consternation, not a body, but an empty tomb" (*Jesus the Jew*, 41). Fitzmyer writes: "Joseph of Arimathea is otherwise unknown; but in all four Gospels he is linked to the burial of Jesus, clearly a historical reminiscence being used. Who would invent him?" (*Gospel according to Luke X–XXIV*, 1526). Ehrman has affirmed in the past the historicity of Jesus' burial by Joseph of Arimathea and the empty-tomb traditions (see *Jesus: Apocalyptic Prophet*, 225; *Did Jesus Exist?*, 258), but he now says he doubts both (*How Jesus Became God*, 159–63). On the other hand, Ehrman affirms my main contention in this section, namely, that wherever Jesus was buried, his followers would have believed it was empty

Numerous robust arguments can be put forth for the historicity of the empty-tomb narratives, but since this concerns the four Gospels, not Paul, this is beyond the scope of this book.

One last point on the empty-tomb narratives. The stories surrounding the empty tomb were not proclaimed in Paul's letters or the sermons in Acts, nor do the Gospels say Jesus' followers believed in the resurrection as a result of finding Jesus' tomb empty.[154] According to the Gospels, the discovery of the empty tomb generally led to more puzzlement and confusion than belief. It was, instead, the appearances of the risen Jesus to the women, to Peter, to the Twelve, and to Paul that led to their conviction that God raised him from the dead. The appearances, then, are the definitive evidence for Jesus' resurrection according to this creedal tradition, Paul, the Gospels, and the sermons in Acts—*not* the empty tomb.

If we want to maintain our focus on the bedrock facts available to us from the earliest sources, we can say that Jesus certainly died by crucifixion, but we cannot then include the empty-tomb traditions. However, we can conclude that *some* type of burial place had to have been empty for the claim "He was raised" to make any sense to first-century Jews.

———

We are now ready to turn to this most crucial phrase in the creedal tradition: "And that He was raised on the third day, according to the Scriptures."

This is unparalleled, pure innovation.

---

because they claimed he was physically raised from the dead. "They wouldn't need an empty tomb to prove it. Of course, for them, the tomb was empty. It goes without saying and without seeing. Jesus is alive again, which means his body has been raised from the dead" (*How Jesus Became God*, 186).

154.   John 20:8 is a notable exception to this.

The composers of this creedal tradition were the first ever to make such a claim, namely, that a single individual, this crucified man Jesus, in the middle of history, has risen from the dead.

5: Resurrection
"He Was Raised on the Third Day"

What made Jesus different from all the others teaching a similar message was the claim that he had been raised from the dead. Belief in Jesus' resurrection changed absolutely everything. Such a thing was not said of any of the other apocalyptic preachers of Jesus' day, and the fact that it was said about Jesus made him unique.

Bart Ehrman, How Jesus Became God

The New Testament writers speak as if Christ's achievement in rising from the dead was the first event of its kind in the whole history of the universe. He is the "first fruits," the "pioneer of life." He has forced open a door that has been locked since the death of the first man. He has met, fought, and beaten the King of Death. Everything is different because He has done so. This is the beginning of the New Creation: a new chapter in cosmic history has opened.

C. S. Lewis, Miracles

J. R. R. Tolkien, creator of *The Hobbit* and *The Lord of the Rings*, once gave a fascinating lecture called "On Fairy Stories" that lays out his philosophy of fairy stories and fantasy in general. In it, he argues that the genre of faerie should not be only associated with children, but is primarily for adults. Within this lecture, Tolkien coins a wonderful word: *eucatastrophe*, literally meaning "a good catastrophe." Tolkien defines it as "the sudden happy turn in a story which pierces you with a joy that brings tears."[155] Every great fantasy story must have a eucatastrophe. According to Tolkien, *The Hobbit*'s eucatastrophe is toward the end, during the Battle of Five Armies, when Bilbo is beginning to think that all hope is lost:

> The clouds were torn by the wind, and a red sunset slashed the West. Seeing the sudden gleam in the gloom Bilbo looked round. He gave a great cry: he had seen a sight that made his heart leap, dark shapes small yet majestic against the distant glow.
>
> "The Eagles! The Eagles!" he shouted. "The Eagles are coming!"[156]

Tolkien concludes his lecture discussing what he believes is the greatest eucatastrophe of the real world: "The Birth of Christ is the eucatastrophe of Man's history. The Resurrection is the eucatastrophe of the story of the Incarnation. This story begins and ends in joy."[157] Describing the lecture in a letter, he writes, "I concluded by saying that the Resurrection was the greatest 'eucatastrophe' possible in the greatest Fairy Story— and produces that essential emotion: Christian joy which produces tears because it is qualitatively so like sorrow, because it comes from those places where Joy and Sorrow are at one, reconciled, as selfishness and altruism are lost in Love."[158]

When we think of the devastating blow the crucifixion was for the earliest followers of Jesus, how can we rightly describe

---

155.   Christopher Tolkien, *Letters of J. R. R. Tolkien*, Letter 89.

156.   J. R. R. Tolkien, *The Hobbit*, 214.

157.   J. R. R. Tolkien, "On Fairy Stories," 83–84.

158.   Christopher Tolkien, *Letters of J. R. R. Tolkien*, Letter 89.

their experience of suddenly being convinced that Jesus was alive, risen from the dead? Eucatastrophe! This was truly a sudden, happy turn that pierced the depths of their being, bringing tears of joy and wonder. We witness this unexpected joy and wonder in the responses to the risen Jesus in the resurrection stories found in the four Gospels.

Focused as we are on the bedrock facts that we can discern from the earliest sources (Paul's undisputed letters), we will not look in detail at the resurrection accounts in the Gospels. But we do want to visit the earliest followers of Jesus on the night of Jesus' crucifixion. It is the unanimous testimony of the Gospels, and one of the many bedrock facts from the Gospels, that on the night before the crucifixion, the night Jesus was arrested, Judas betrayed Jesus, Peter denied him, and the rest of his disciples fled (Mark 14:43–50; Matt 26:47–56; Luke 22:47–53; John 18:1–11). All, except perhaps his women followers, abandoned him. Ehrman writes, "What is abundantly clear is that at the end, no one stood up for or put his or her neck out for Jesus. He was tried and executed alone."[159]

Let us then time travel to this very night, Good Friday night, in Jerusalem, to the place(s) where the disciples are hiding. Whether they were all together or scattered in different places throughout Jerusalem, we do not know. What we do know is that all their hopes and dreams of Jesus as the Messiah had been crushed. The crucifixion of their leader was a death blow to their movement, as it was to a dozen or so other messianic movements around this time, as we will see below. A crucified messiah was

---

159. Ehrman, *Jesus: Apocalyptic Prophet*, 219. That the disciples fled Jesus after his arrest is a fact that is "almost beyond dispute," according to Sanders, *Historical Figure of Jesus*, 11.

a contradiction in terms in first-century Judaism(s).[160] What we don't know is their attitude toward Jesus at this moment. They had followed this extraordinary man for over three years, and now he was dead. Were they sad for him, weeping floods of tears for their dead master? Or were they angry, enraged at Jesus for leading them astray all these years?[161] We can't know for sure, but either one seems plausible historically.

What we can say with historical certainty, the bedrock fact that I want to focus on in this chapter, is that sometime very soon after this, possibly "on the third day" after the crucifixion (Sunday), these same overwhelmingly devastated followers were suddenly convinced that their crucified leader had risen from the dead. This is the next line in the creedal tradition: "He was raised on the third day according to the Scriptures"[162] (1 Cor 15:4b).

---

160. Judaism in the first centuries BC and AD was not monolithic. Jews of this time had many different beliefs concerning most theological and political topics. One thing they all agreed on was that a dead, let alone crucified, Messiah was no Messiah at all.

161. John Chrysostom was the first to hypothesize such an enraged mind-set for the apostles at this time. See his *Homily* on 1 Cor 1:22–25.

162. Wright says, "Paul does not mean that there are one or two biblical prophecies which, taken by themselves, point in this direction. He refers to the entire scriptural narrative, stretching forward as it does towards the climax of God's purpose for Israel, and characterized throughout by the powerful grace which brings hope out of disaster and life out of death" (*Paul: Fresh Perspectives*, 224). Interestingly, the creedal tradition used an aorist tense for both "Christ died" and "he was buried," but with "he was raised" the perfect tense is used. According to a grammar of NT Greek, "Ἐγήγερται sets forth with the utmost possible emphasis the abiding results of the event, which supply the main thought of the whole passage" (Moulton, *Grammar of New Testament Greek*, 137). Wright adds, "The Greek perfect tense indicates the ongoing result of a one-off event, in this case the permanent result that Jesus is now the risen Messiah and Lord" (*Resurrection of the Son of God*, 321). As was said in the previous chapter, I believe "on the third day" is most likely a chronological reference to the women finding the tomb empty on Sunday morning, as recorded in the Gospels (Luke 24:46; see also Acts 10:40). Yet there are Hebrew scriptures that the earliest Christians also saw being fulfilled by this historical fact. Most scholars agree that the primary scripture referred to here is Hos 6:2, "He will revive us after two days; He will raise us up on the third day, That we may live before Him."

That Jesus' earliest followers, soon after his death, became convinced that Jesus rose from the dead and appeared to them, is, like the crucifixion, as historical as anything can ever be. In this chapter I want to focus on this unparalleled, innovative claim of the earliest Nazarenes: this crucified man Jesus rose from the dead.

Where did they get this idea of their crucified leader rising from the dead? (We are, of course, for now assuming Jesus remained dead and did not appear to them.)

Many Jews at this time believed in a future, bodily resurrection. Many Jews expected a Davidic Messiah figure to arrive and rescue them from their pagan oppressors. Yet not *one* of them envisioned a two-stage resurrection in which the Messiah would die and be resurrected first, and then the general resurrection would take place at the end of this present age, let alone a Messiah that would be crucified by their pagan oppressors! According to N. T. Wright, "There are no traditions about a Messiah being raised to life: most Jews of this period hoped for resurrection, many Jews of this period hoped for a Messiah, but nobody put those two hopes together until the early Christians did so."[163]

The historian is pressed for an explanation for this unparalleled innovation among these first-century Jewish Nazarenes. If Jesus did not appear to them, then where did these ideas come from? From the mind of Peter? Mary Magdalene? James? Their claims concerning Jesus were unique not only in the history of Judaism, but in the history of ideas in general.

See Conzelmann, *1 Corinthians*, 255; Kloppenborg, "Analysis of the Pre-Pauline Formula," 363. Jeremias observes that the first to make this connection was the early church father Tertullian in *Against the Jews* 13; see also Cyril of Jerusalem, *Catechetical Lectures* 14.14.

163. Wright, *Resurrection of the Son of God*, 205.

We must first look at the ancient Jewish understanding of resurrection and expectation of the Messiah(s) to see how utterly innovative and revolutionary this claim about this crucified man Jesus really was.

RESURRECTION HOPE

The Greeks and the Romans knew enough about the idea of resurrection to deny it. The lack of belief in or even outright rejection of resurrection is found in many Greek and Roman writers, especially Homer and Plato. We see this clearly when Paul proclaims the resurrection of Jesus to the Epicurean and Stoic philosophers and they mock him, as recounted in Acts 17. Another famous example comes from the Greek playwright Aeschylus: "Oh, monsters utterly loathed and detested by the gods! Zeus could undo fetters, there is a remedy for that, and many means of release. But when the dust has drawn up the blood of a man, once he is dead, there is no resurrection (*anastasis*)" (*Eumenides* 647–648).

On the other hand, according to Josephus, many Jews at this time, like the Pharisees, believed in a future, bodily resurrection "at the revolution of the ages" when the souls of the righteous "return to find in chaste bodies a new habitation" (*J.W.* 3.374; see also *Ant.* 18.14–15). Other Jews, such as Philo of Alexandria, opted more for the Greek idea of the immortality of the soul; and some, such as the Sadducees, denied any afterlife at all (see Acts 23:6–8). Those who believed in resurrection primarily based it on a passage from the prophet Daniel. There were other texts about a national resurrection of Israel, such as Isaiah 26:19 and Ezekiel 37:1–14, but Daniel contains the most unambiguous teaching of bodily resurrection in the Hebrew Scriptures: "Many of those who sleep in the dust of the ground will awake, these to everlasting life, but the others to disgrace and everlasting contempt.

Those who have insight will shine brightly like the brightness of the expanse of heaven, and those who lead the many to righteousness, like the stars forever and ever" (Dan 12:2–3).

This is physical, bodily resurrection of the righteous and the wicked—all those corpses who have turned into dust. Resurrection from this point forward was understood to mean the physical revivification of bodies in a future, renewed creation.[164] There was no place in Jewish understanding for resurrection understood as the post-death existence of disembodied souls. Ehrman writes,

> If an apocalyptic Jew … were to come to believe that the resurrection of the dead had begun—for example, with the raising of God's specifically favored one, his messiah—what would that resurrection involve? It would naturally and automatically involve precisely a bodily resurrection. That's what resurrection meant to these people. It did not mean the ongoing life of the spirit without the body. It meant the reanimation and glorification of the body.[165]

---

164. See 1 Enoch 51.1; 62.14–16; 2 Baruch 49–51; Testament of Judah 25.4–5; Testament of Benjamin 10.6–10. For full discussion see Nickelsburg, *Resurrection, Immortality, and Eternal Life.*

165. Ehrman, *How Jesus Became God,* 186. Compare Brown: "It is not really accurate to claim that the New Testament references to the resurrection of Jesus are ambiguous as to whether they mean bodily resurrection—there is no other kind of resurrection" (*Virginal Conception and Bodily Resurrection,* 70). See also Allison: "To my knowledge, nowhere in the Bible or in old Jewish or Christian literature does the language of resurrection refer to a materially new body, physically unconnected to the old. A resurrected body is always the old body or a piece of it come back to life and/or transformed" ("Resurrection of Jesus and Rational Apologetics," 317).

We see this resurrection hope most clearly expressed in the records of the Maccabean martyrs killed during the second century BC:

> And when he was at his last breath, he said, "You accursed wretch, you dismiss us from this present life, but the King of the universe will raise us up to an everlasting renewal of life, because we have died for his laws." After him, the third was the victim of their sport. When it was demanded, he quickly put out his tongue and courageously stretched forth his hands, and said nobly, "I got these from Heaven, and because of his laws I disdain them, and from him I hope to get them back again." (2 Macc 7:9–14)

Even if his tongue is cut out and they saw his arms off, this bold martyr believes he will at the resurrection receive them back again. Outside of the early Christians, this is probably the best example of resurrection hope one can find. Notice that it involves only a future resurrection of bodies in the renewed creation. This is what resurrection meant to the Jews who believed in it as well as to those who denied it.

MESSIANIC HOPE

The fervor of messianic expectation reached a boiling point in the first century AD. Many Jews were eagerly expecting the arrival of the Messiah or even multiple messiahs.[166] Similar to beliefs about resurrection and the afterlife, messianic expectations were incredibly diverse among first-century Jews. The

---

166. Mowinckel, *He That Cometh*, 3. See Luke 3:15; Josephus, *J.W.* 6.312 ("at that time one from their own country could become ruler of the world"); Suetonius, *Vespasian* 4; Tacitus, *Histories* 5.13.

Essenes who wrote the Dead Sea Scrolls, for example, were expecting at least two messiahs, a priestly messiah like Aaron and a kingly messiah like David.[167] The second one, a kingly Schwarzenegger-like warrior (from *Commando* and *Predator*, not the older Schwarzenegger from *The Expendables*) messiah, seems to have been the most dominant view.[168] In the same way the warrior David of old had rescued them from their pagan enemies, this Messiah figure would violently remove the boot of the Roman Empire from Israel's neck and rule over God's kingdom from Jerusalem.

This may very well be the kind of expectation that many of Jesus' disciples had. James and John, for example, asked Jesus to sit at his right and at his left in a *physical* kingdom in Jerusalem (Mark 10:35–40). Judas may even have betrayed Jesus in order to force his hand against Rome, and Peter was increasingly vexed every time Jesus predicted his coming execution (see Mark 8:27–33). Even John the Baptist may have had such a messianic expectation, leading him to momentarily doubt whether Jesus was the Messiah and sending his disciples to ask him: "Are you the Expected One, or do we look for someone else?" (Luke 7:19–20).

Clearly, many of the things Jesus was doing and teaching during his public ministry defied the messianic expectations of the day.

Then he was crucified.

---

167. Community Rule (1QS) column IX, lines 7–11. Compare the Qumran community's collection of messianic prophecies in the Florilegium (4Q174) and the Testimonia (4Q175), which include some OT texts that are applied to Jesus in the NT.

168. As a prime example of the hope of a Davidic warrior-messiah, see Psalms of Solomon 17.23–30, which dates to around 100 BC. See also Targum of Isaiah 53, but this is dates to hundreds of years after Jesus. See Vermes, *Jesus the Jew*, 130–34; Neusner, Green, and Frerichs, *Judaisms and Their Messiahs*.

There could be no greater death blow to a Jewish messianic movement than crucifixion.

As N. T. Wright rightly notes,

> The Messiah was supposed to win the decisive victory over the pagans, to rebuild or cleanse the Temple, and in some way or other to bring true, god-given justice and peace to the whole world. What nobody expected the Messiah to do was die at the hands of the pagans instead of defeating them. ... The violent execution of a prophet ... still more of a would-be Messiah, did not say to any Jewish onlooker that he really was the Messiah after all, or that YHWH's kingdom had come through his work. It said, powerfully and irresistibly, that he wasn't and that it hadn't.[169]

We know this because we can compare Jesus and his movement to a dozen or so failed Jewish messianic type movements of his day. Jesus was seen as a would-be Messiah because he was crucified with his crime inscribed on a *titulus* and nailed to the cross above his head. It read, according to Mark 15:26, "THE KING OF THE JEWS." The historicity of the inscription of Jesus' crime is another bedrock fact from the Gospels, and it demonstrates that Jesus was seen by the Romans as just another failed messianic pretender.[170]

But how do we know that these other messianic movements died with their founders or, as Rabbi Gamaliel says describing

---

169. Wright, *Resurrection of the Son of God*, 557–58.

170. Fitzmyer writes, "The inscription on the cross is the only thing we know of which was written about Jesus during his lifetime. Anything else that might have been written about him has disappeared" (*Gospel according to Luke X–XXIV*, 1502). Wright adds: "There can be no doubt, historically speaking, that Jesus was executed as a messianic pretender" (*Jesus and the Victory of God*, 522).

a few of them, were "overthrown" (Acts 5:38)? Couldn't their followers just have continued on without their leader—maybe even saying that the spirit of their leader lived on or even that he was raised from the dead?

To help further our understanding of messianic hope at this time, let us take a look at these other messianic movements and compare them to Jesus' movement.

MESSIANIC PRETENDERS

As the figure below demonstrates, we know of at least a dozen other messianic type movements between 40 BC and AD 135 that all came to an abrupt end after their leader died or disappeared.

The leaders of these movements that bear the most resemblance to Jesus are:

- Judas the Galilean (AD 6), who is described in Acts 5:37 and Josephus, *Ant.* 18.4–10, 23–25

- the Samaritan (AD 36) who is described in Josephus, *Ant.* 18.85–87

- Theudas (AD 45), who is described in Acts 5:36 and Josephus, *Ant.* 20.97–99

- Jesus, son of Ananus (AD 60s), who is described in Josephus, *J.W.* 6.289–309

- Menahem, son of Judas the Galilean (AD 66), who is described in Josephus, *J.W.* 5.510

- Simon bar Giora (AD 70), who is described in Josephus, *J.W.* 7.25–36, 153–154

- Simon bar Kochba (AD 132–135), who is described in Cassius Dio, *Roman History* 69.12–14 and Justin Martyr, *First Apology* 31

MESSIANIC MOVEMENTS

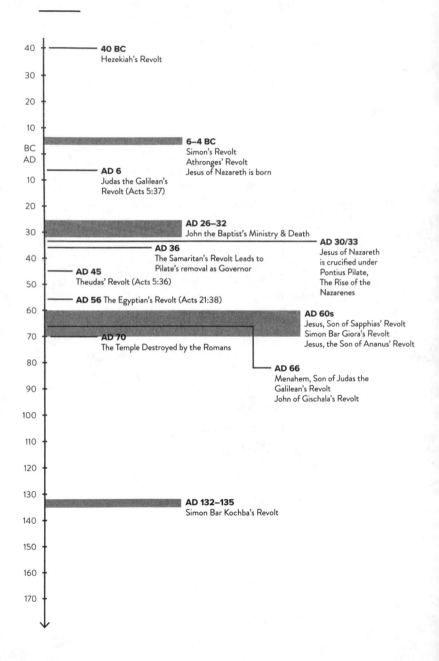

40 — **40 BC**
Hezekiah's Revolt

30

20

10

BC
AD — **6–4 BC**
Simon's Revolt
Athronges' Revolt
Jesus of Nazareth is born

10 — **AD 6**
Judas the Galilean's
Revolt (Acts 5:37)

20

30 — **AD 26–32**
John the Baptist's Ministry & Death

AD 30/33
Jesus of Nazareth
is crucified under
Pontius Pilate,
The Rise of the
Nazarenes

36 — **AD 36**
The Samaritan's Revolt Leads to
Pilate's removal as Governor

40

45 — **AD 45**
Theudas' Revolt (Acts 5:36)

50

56 — **AD 56** The Egyptian's Revolt (Acts 21:38)

60

AD 60s
Jesus, Son of Sapphias' Revolt
Simon Bar Giora's Revolt
Jesus, the Son of Ananus' Revolt

70 — **AD 70**
The Temple Destroyed by the Romans

80 — **AD 66**
Menahem, Son of Judas the
Galilean's Revolt
John of Gischala's Revolt

90

100

110

120

130 — **AD 132–135**
Simon Bar Kochba's Revolt

140

150

160

170

Some of these revolutionary figures claimed to be prophets (for example, Theudas). Others claimed to be kings, which in those cases was probably a messianic claim—Josephus tells us that anyone with a group of followers at this time might "make himself king" (*Ant.* 17.285). All of them made grand promises concerning the future, gathered disciples around themselves, and eventually had a bloody showdown with Rome. After a Roman general, of the sort played by Russell Crowe in *Gladiator*, came out and crushed them, these leaders were beheaded (such as Theudas), crucified (such as Judas the Galilean's sons, James and Simon), or otherwise executed, and the movement they led came to a disastrous end. The followers who survived either looked for another messiah figure to follow or settled down and got jobs.

In a strikingly similar example to Jesus, Simon bar Giora was executed by the general Titus in Rome in AD 70, forty years after Jesus' crucifixion under Pontius Pilate in Jerusalem. Simon had a large number of disciples he led like a king. Once captured, he was paraded through the crowds in Rome to celebrate Titus' magnificent triumph. Today in Rome, you can still see a snapshot of this victorious celebration inscribed on the Arch of Titus at the east end of the Forum. Simon bar Giora is among

those Jewish prisoners pictured being led to their inevitable deaths, along with the last known visual of the menorah from the temple in Jerusalem. Simon was scourged with whips along the way and then executed before cheering crowds (*J.W.* 7.154). The so-called Jewish Messiah was dead, and Rome rejoiced.

In Simon bar Giora's case, as in the case of all the messianic pretenders that had come before, the movement he led came to an end with his death. Wright asks us to engage our historical imagination a few days after Simon's execution: "Imagine two or three of Simon's supporters—if there were any of them left, hiding in caves or secret cellars—a few days later. Supposing one said to another, 'Actually, I think Simon really was the Messiah.' The kindest view the others might take would be that the speaker had gone mad."[171] Even if they claimed they had received visions of Simon or had a heartwarming spiritual experience, none of this would have made any of them think that Simon had risen from the dead, let alone was the Messiah or the Lord of the world.

Knowing that this is what usually happened, in Acts 5:34–40 Rabbi Gamaliel compares two of these leaders of messianic movements, Judas and Theudas, to Jesus of Nazareth. He argues that since their movements came to nothing after these leaders died, so too this young, rising movement of the Nazarenes will also soon fail.[172] But, he adds, if this movement of the Nazarenes is of God, then it will prove to be indestructible.

Gamaliel spoke better than he knew because the Jesus movement, the Nazarenes, not only continued despite his execution

---

171. Wright, *Resurrection of the Son of God*, 558–59.

172. We will look at Gamaliel's speech more closely in chapter 7 below.

by Rome, but for the next 280 years expanded and conquered the Roman Empire, not with armies, but with love and sacrifice.[173]

Why, then, did this movement continue after Jesus' execution when these dozen or so other movements came to nothing? Wright captures one possible answer well: "Jewish revolutionaries whose leader had been executed by the authorities, and who managed to escape arrest themselves, had two options: give up the revolution, or find another leader. Claiming that the original leader was alive again was simply not an option. Unless, of course, he was."[174]

PURE INNOVATION

Let me wrap up this chapter by summarizing the unparalleled, innovative claims of the Nazarenes. As we look at each of them we have to ask: What made them respond to the death of their Messiah differently from anyone else before or since? Could it be, as Wright suggests, the reason they in unparalleled fashion claimed their leader Jesus was alive again was that he actually was?

The first pure innovation we find from the early Christians is their positive interpretation of a crucified Messiah. We do not possess another example of a positive view of crucifixion and/or the person crucified from the ancient world.[175] As we heard from Cicero above, "to put [a Roman citizen] to death is like murdering your own father; to crucify him—what?" If there are

---

173. From the crucifixion of Jesus (AD 33) to the Emperor Constantine's conversion to Christianity and his famous Edict of Milan (AD 313) is exactly 280 years.

174. Wright, *Who Was Jesus?*, 63.

175. Hengel: "There remains the question whether there is any evidence in the ancient Roman world for a non-Christian, positive interpretation of death by crucifixion, say as the manner of death of a philosopher or a national martyr. After all, the death of such figures was a familiar feature in the ancient world. I have not been able to discover a real historical instance" (*Crucifixion*, 64).

no words to describe the crucifixion of a Roman citizen, how do we describe the crucifixion of God's Messiah? This is why Paul the Pharisee rejected Jesus—because his crucifixion proved he was under God's curse.

This was no doubt the same thing Jesus' disciples thought on Good Friday evening. Even if they still loved him and wept for him, Jesus' death meant he could not be God's Messiah. The testimony of one of Jesus' disciples on the Emmaus road captures this thinking well: "the things about Jesus the Nazarene, who was a prophet mighty in deed and word in the sight of God and all the people, and how the chief priests and our rulers delivered Him to the sentence of death, and crucified Him. But we were hoping that it was He who was going to redeem Israel" (Luke 24:19–21).

"We were hoping," but now all our hopes and dreams concerning this Jesus have been shattered due to his crucifixion. This mind-set fits with everything we know about how ancient peoples viewed crucifixion, and Jews especially, in light of the dozen or so failed messianic movements. And yet Paul says within two decades of Jesus' crucifixion: "I want to know nothing among you except Jesus Christ, and Him crucified" (1 Cor 2:2). The cross became, for followers of Jesus, "the power of God and the wisdom of God (1 Cor 1:24). Again, this is extraordinary, and the historian is pressed for an explanation.

The second unparalleled innovation was the claim that this crucified Messiah had risen from the dead (1 Cor 15:4b). Nowhere else do we find the claim of a two-stage resurrection in which the Messiah would rise from the dead and then everyone else at the still-future resurrection (1 Cor 15:23). As we saw at the beginning of this chapter, any Jewish belief in a resurrection was always in the future. There was no expectation for a single person to be resurrected in the middle of history. But in Christianity we find, as New Testament scholar Christopher Evans observes, "a precise, confident and articulate faith in which resurrection has moved from the circumference to the center."[176] It is not enough to attempt to explain the Christian belief that Jesus had risen from the dead by claiming that many Jews believed in resurrection. As Raymond Brown writes, "The contention that the Jewish mind had to express Jesus' victory over death by resurrection language is simply inaccurate, for we know of several other models current in Judaism which might have been employed. On the contrary, since there was no expectation of an isolated resurrection within history, the choice of the category of resurrection must be explained."[177]

How did resurrection become the central belief of the early Christians? Moreover, where did they get this idea of a two-stage resurrection, and why did they claim this happened to the crucified man Jesus? Why did they not say Jesus was translated to heaven, like Enoch (Gen 5:24) or Elijah (2 Kgs 2:11–12) or Job's children (Testament of Job 39.1–40.6) or the two witnesses (Rev 11:12)? There were many categories of exalted saints, Ezra (4 Ezra 14:48) and Baruch (2 Baruch 76.1–5) and martyred heroes of the past, that could have been applied to Jesus (see Jubilees 23.31).[178] The Maccabean martyrs were believed to have gained eternal life after death, but the general bodily resurrection was still future (2 Macc 7:36; 12:43–44). None of these figures, until Jesus, were ever claimed to be raised from the dead. Resurrection was consistently seen as a future event; it would happen to all the saints and martyrs, but in the renewed creation. It was the earliest Christians who, with pure innovation, brought these ideas of crucifixion, resurrection, and the Messiah together.

---

176. Evans, *Resurrection and the New Testament*, 40.

177. Brown, *Virginal Conception and Bodily Resurrection*, 76.

178. Allison: "There is no evidence that Jews believed resurrection began immediately after their deaths" (*Resurrecting Jesus*, 244n182).

As James Dunn summarizes, "Why draw the astonishing conclusion that the eschatological resurrection had already taken place in the case of a single individual quite separate from and prior to the general resurrection? There must have been something very compelling about the appearances for such an extravagant, not to say ridiculous and outrageous conclusion to be drawn."[179]

The third unparalleled innovation was that this crucified Messiah, whom God raised from the dead, was also divine and Lord of the world. This is the most shocking of them all, especially in the Jewish monotheistic context from which this idea arose. No one expected the Messiah to be crucified and resurrected, but neither did anyone expect the Messiah to be in some sense God (Phil 2:6; Rom 9:5)!

In the creedal tradition of 1 Corinthians 15:3–7, we do not have such a claim of Jesus' divinity, only his death, burial, resurrection, and appearances. However, in Paul's early letters and other hymns Paul quotes, Jesus is presented as preexisting (Phil 2:6; 1 Cor 8:6; 2 Cor 8:9), involved in the creation of the universe (1 Cor 8:6), being worshiped (Phil 2:9–11), prayed to (Rom 10:13; 1 Cor 1:2; 16:22; 2 Cor 12:8–9), sharing in YHWH's unique identity and sovereignty (Phil 2:10–11; 1 Cor 8:6; Rom 10:13), and even called "Lord" (1 Cor 12:3; Rom 10:9; Phil 2:11) and "God" (Rom 9:5).

Many scholars argue that Paul is quoting another early tradition (or hymn) that he *received* in 1 Corinthians 8:6: "For us there is but one God, the Father, from whom are all things and we exist for Him; and one Lord, Jesus Christ, by whom are all things, and we exist through Him."[180]

---

179. Dunn, *Jesus and the Spirit*, 132.

180. Ehrman writes, "This verse may well incorporate another pre-Pauline creed of some kind, as it divides itself neatly, as can be seen, into two parts, with two lines each. The first part is a confession of God the Father, and the second a

Paul (and if not Paul, then the original composer of this hymn) is redefining the Shema, which he would have quoted at least daily as a devoted Pharisee: "Hear, O Israel! YHWH is our God, YHWH is one!" (Deut 6:4). These Jewish Nazarenes are still monotheists, but they began proclaiming that this crucified man Jesus shares in the unique identity with YHWH, the one God of Israel. Dunn agrees this is unparalleled: "Paul here splits the Shema ... between God the Father and Christ the Lord in a way that has no earlier parallel."[181]

The chart on the following page demonstrates the radical mutation within Paul's strict monotheism.

New Testament scholar and leading expert on early Christian worship Larry Hurtado says: "In early Christian circles Jesus is recipient of the sorts of expressions of devotion that are otherwise reserved for God alone, and which simply have no analogy in Jewish tradition of the Second-Temple period. Put simply, this worship of the risen/exalted Jesus comprises a radical new innovation in Jewish monotheistic religion."[182]

How does the historian account for this "radical new innovation" within first-century Jewish monotheism? How is it possible that within two decades of Jesus' crucifixion, he was already being worshiped and presented as participating in the unique divine sovereignty of YHWH, the God of Israel? As Hengel pointedly says: "The Easter appearances alone do not suffice as an

confession of Jesus Christ. It is 'through' Christ that all things come into being and that believers themselves exist. This sounds very much like what non-Christian Jewish texts occasionally say about God's Wisdom. And God's Wisdom was itself understood to be God, as we have seen" (*How Jesus Became God*, 268).

181. Dunn, *Christology in the Making*, 180. "The binary formula is the first step on the way to the doctrine of the Trinity" (Hengel, *Studies in Early Christology*, 280).

182. Hurtado, *How on Earth Did Jesus Become God?*, 47–48.

TRACING JESUS TO YHWH

HEBREW	GREEK	ENGLISH
YHWH ⟶	**KURIOS** ⟶	**LORD**
God's personal name in the Old Testament.	The title used to translate YHWH into Greek and most commonly applied to Jesus.	The English title almost always applied to Jesus Christ in the New Testament.
ELOHIM ⟶	**THEOS** ⟶	**GOD**
The title for God in the Old Testament.	The title used to translate Elohim into Greek and most commonly applied to God the Father.	The English title almost always applied to God the Father in the New Testament.
THE SHEMA ⟶	**THE SHEMA REDEFINED** ⟶	**1 CORINTHIANS 8:6A**
shema yisrael YHWH elohenu YHWH ehad	all' hēmin heis theos, ho patēr, ex hou ta panta hai hēmeis eis auton, kai heis kurios, Iēosous Christos...	yet for us there is one God, the Father, from whom are all things and for whom we exist, and one Lord, Jesus Christ...

explanation for why the crucified one came to be recognized as the Messiah, Son of God, and Lord."[183]

The earliest confession of Jesus' divinity could not be due *only* to the belief in his resurrection. Even if his followers believed Jesus rose from the dead, why would monotheistic Jews worship and pray to him, and say that Jesus participated in the creation of the world and shares in the identity and sovereignty

---

183. Hengel, *Studies in Early Christology*, xii.

of YHWH himself? Along with their belief in the resurrection, the historical Jesus must have made claims concerning his divinity during his public ministry. To discuss the historical Jesus' claims to divinity, however, is beyond the scope of this book.

———

In sum, a coming Messiah, resurrection, and monotheism were all concepts known in the ancient Jewish and Greco-Roman world. Yet no one mutated them and put them together the way the early Christians did concerning Jesus. They uniquely, with unparalleled innovation, proclaimed that the crucified man Jesus was the Messiah, whom God raised from the dead, and was also Lord of the world.

These ideas arose within a monotheistic Jewish context and over a period of fewer than two decades after Jesus' crucifixion. This presses the historian for an explanation.

Why did the early Christians begin to view Jesus' crucifixion in a positive manner?

Why did they say Jesus rose from the dead as the first stage of a two-stage resurrection event?

Or, as Dunn succinctly asks: "So our question returns with added force: why was the first articulation of post-Easter faith in just these terms—'resurrection,' the beginning of the resurrection of the dead?"[184]

Why did these monotheistic Jews, such as Paul, claim that Jesus was divine, pray to him, and worship him, even claiming he shared in the unique identity and sovereignty of YHWH, the God of Israel?

Who did this threefold innovation originate with? Peter? Mary Magdalene? James? Some unknown follower? If Jesus

---

184. Dunn, *Jesus Remembered*, 870.

remained dead, the historian must ask how it was that these innovations were created *ex nihilo*.

On the other hand, if Jesus burst through all the contemporary expectations of messiahship and resurrection and really did rise from the dead, then this was the unparalleled event in history that led to such unparalleled claims. Jesus' resurrection would then be the most unexpected and radically new innovation that the world had ever seen.

In their innovative beliefs, then, the earliest followers of Jesus were attempting to explain an extraordinary and even haunting event. They could not fully grasp all of its implications, but what they could not deny was that Jesus being resurrected meant the beginning of a new creation, a new chapter in cosmic history.

The repeated phrase in the creedal tradition, "He appeared" (1 Cor 15:5–8), is the key to unlock the origins of these extraordinary innovations.

6: Appearances

To Peter, the Twelve, More than Five Hundred, James, and Paul

It may be taken as historically certain that Peter and the disciples had experiences after Jesus' death in which Jesus appeared to them as the risen Christ.

Gerd Lüdemann, *What Really Happened to Jesus*

I do not regard deliberate fraud as a worthwhile explanation. Many of the people in these lists were to spend the rest of their lives proclaiming that they had seen the risen Lord, and several of them would die for their cause. Moreover, a calculated deception should have produced greater unanimity. Instead, there seem to have been competitors: "I saw him first!" "No! I did."

E. P. Sanders, *The Historical Figure of Jesus*

This is the sort of truth that is hard to explain because it is a fact; but it is a fact to which we can call witnesses.

G. K. Chesterton, *The Everlasting Man*

I t is a bedrock fact that soon after Jesus' crucifixion, individuals and groups, men and women, followers and *at least one* enemy, became convinced that Jesus appeared to them alive, raised from the dead. According to Bart Ehrman, "There can be no doubt, historically, that some of Jesus' followers came to believe he was raised from the dead—no doubt whatsoever. This is how Christianity started."[185] We discussed in the last chapter the threefold innovative claims of the earliest Christians concerning Jesus. There I argued that the ultimate reason for this pure innovation must have been that the early Christians believed these resurrection appearances happened. We know that with certainty.

Yet whether Jesus really did rise from the dead and appear to these individuals and groups, or whether these experiences happened in some way in their minds (i.e., hallucinations), is still the debate between Christians and the rest of the world. What is a bedrock fact is that the early Christians *believed* and *proclaimed* that they saw Jesus risen from the dead.

RESURRECTIONS AND THE MIRACULOUS

Jesus' resurrection appearances and the number of people who claimed to witness them is unparalleled in history. Dunn concurs, "Appearances of Jesus which impacted on the witnesses as resurrection appearances did not conform to any known or current paradigm. Instead, they created their own."[186] Where do we find anything like this list of resurrection appearances in the ancient world or even up to the present day?

The only similar examples from the ancient world one could possibly point to are Romulus, Aristeas, Alcestis, the prophet Samuel, and Apollonius of Tyana.

---

185. Ehrman, *How Jesus Became God*, 174. See also Perrin: "The more we study the tradition with regard to the appearances, the firmer the rock begins to appear upon which they are based" (*Resurrection according to Matthew, Mark, and Luke*, 80).

186. Dunn, *Jesus Remembered*, 874–75.

But even though these figures are said to appear after their death in some way, not one of them is said to have been raised from the dead. Moreover, when historians consider the sources for these figures, it becomes immediately clear that most of these are legendary accounts. Romulus, for example, the legendary founder of Rome, is said to have lived in the eighth century BC. Our primary accounts for Romulus's life are from Plutarch, Ovid (*Metamorphoses* 14.800–851), and Livy writing in the first century AD. That is more than a seven-hundred-year separation between the written accounts and the events being described. In his fifty-fourth year of life, Romulus is said to have "disappeared" and was "caught up to heaven" (Plutarch, *Romulus* 27, 29). In the same source, others say he was murdered by the senators in the temple of Vulcan. Livy claims that he descended from the sky and appeared to at least one individual (*History of Rome* 1.16). Because this was recorded seven centuries after it happened, historians today consider the story of Romulus' afterlife excursions to be legend, not history.

The same can be said about Aristeas and Alcestis. We learn about Aristeas over three hundred years after he supposedly lived from the Greek historian Herodotus, who introduces his account by saying, "I will now relate a tale which I heard" (*Histories* 4.13). Since hearsay is never a good place to start for historical investigation, we can only conclude that both Aristeas' existence and the story of his resurrection are legendary. Alcestis' story is also clearly legendary and was never meant to be considered historical. According to the Greek playwright Euripides, Hercules rescued Alcestis from Hades and brought her back to her husband alive again. Again, this is not resurrection, and it is not history.

In the Hebrew Scriptures, the only time a figure appears to a person after death is the prophet Samuel to King Saul (1 Sam

28). Yet this is also not presented as Samuel being raised from the dead. He is a "divine being" (verse 13) who ascends out of the realm of the dead (called "Sheol" elsewhere in the Old Testament) to pronounce judgment on Saul and then returns to the underworld.

The only real possible parallel figure to Jesus' resurrection appearances in the ancient world would be Apollonius of Tyana. Apollonius was a Pythagorean philosopher who is indeed a historical figure who died sometime during the reign of the Roman emperor Nerva (AD 96–98). In the introduction to his translation of the earliest account of Apollonius' life, Christopher Jones writes, "There is no reason to doubt that the historical Apollonius was an itinerant Pythagorean philosopher, traveling mainly in the eastern part of the Roman Empire."[187] However, we know next to nothing about him, and Jones adds, "The 'historical' Apollonius is very difficult to recover."[188]

Consider the sources.

Our earliest account of Apollonius' life was written by a man named Flavius Philostratus sometime between AD 220 and 230. That is over a 120-year gap between when Apollonius died and when the first account about him was written. Remember, the Gospels date to within thirty-five to sixty years of Jesus' death, Paul's early letters within twenty to thirty years, and our creedal tradition (1 Cor 15:3–7) within a decade. Philostratus does claim to be using a source from an eyewitness named Damis, though many believe that Damis is an invention of Philostratus.[189] In fact, many scholars are convinced that the entire account of Apollonius' life, written as it was around 150 years after the latest

---

187. Jones, introduction to *Apollonius of Tyana*, 11.

188. Jones, introduction to *Apollonius of Tyana*, 7.

189. See Jones, introduction to *Apollonius of Tyana*, 6.

canonical Gospel (John), is more likely a polemic against the Christians, with Apollonius parodying miracles of Jesus from the Gospels.[190]

Moreover, Apollonius does not rise from the dead, and he does not appear to individuals and groups. At the end of Philostratus' account, Apollonius dies and then appears as a "spirit" (*daimoniois*) in the dream of *one* of his disciples (*Apollonius of Tyana* 8.31.3). This is hardly a parallel to Jesus' resurrection appearances.[191]

A last example from the ancient world that has been compared to Jesus concerns a miracle performed by Emperor Vespasian (AD 68–79). According to three sources, Tacitus (*Annals* 4.81) and Suetonius (*Vespasian* 7), written roughly forty years after the event, and Cassius Dio (*Roman History* 65.8), written over a hundred years afterward, Vespasian healed two

190. See Jones, introduction to *Apollonius of Tyana*, 12. Fitzmyer writes: "One thing is certain: this story about a resuscitation by Apollonius does not stem from a writer prior to the NT Gospels themselves. Where this story about Apollonius' resuscitation can be traced to a source earlier than those of the NT evangelists is not clear. Can one exclude the possibility that the tradition about Jesus' resuscitations has influenced that used by Philostratus?" (*Gospel according to Luke I–IX*, 657). See also Bovon: "The story of Philostratus is more recent than the Gospels and so could be a pagan resumption of this theme as a polemic directed against the holy books of Christians" (*Commentary on the Gospel of Luke 1:1–9:50*, 269n24).

191. It is surprising to find some even comparing the resurrection appearances of Jesus to Joseph Smith's claim that the angel Moroni appeared to him. For instance, Ehrman writes, "Maybe there is an angel Moroni and maybe he did reveal secret truths to Joseph Smith, but there is no way for historians to establish any of that. ... Historical evidence has to be open to examination by everyone of every religious belief" (*How Jesus Became God*, 147). His latter statement is completely correct, so let us then examine the evidence of the Moroni appearance. We have one witness, Joseph Smith, not many individuals and groups, not an enemy of Moroni, who claimed to see him. Moreover, this one witness, by many non-Mormon testimonies of his contemporaries and to this present day, was a fraud and a con man. See Abanes, *One Nation under the Gods*. In contrast, even non-Christians, such as Ehrman, for example, would testify to the credibility and moral character of our bedrock eyewitness Paul.

beggars, one lame and the other blind. Can this really be compared to the multiply attested, early, eyewitness accounts of Jesus' resurrection appearances? Incredibly, philosopher and skeptic David Hume calls this "one of the best attested miracles in all profane history"![192] Did Hume ever investigate the historical evidence for the resurrection of Jesus? The emperor Vespasian, according to Suetonius, said a joke as he was dying: "Dear me! I must be turning into a god" (*Vespasian* 23). History, I think, has vindicated this, and his miracles, as nothing more than a joke.

We should be open to miraculous accounts from the ancient world and to this present day. Like Hamlet said to Horatio, our philosophies should be large enough to include the unexpected, strange, and extraordinary. But the most important question that must be asked of any miraculous claim is "What is the evidence?" Anyone who impartially investigated the evidence for each of these miraculous claims from the ancient world must admit the evidence for Jesus' resurrection is in a class of its own.[193]

In contrast to the historically flimsy accounts of the miraculous I have recounted above, we have a bedrock source that asserts that multiple eyewitnesses—individuals and groups, *even an enemy*—saw the risen Jesus. And this source, the creedal tradition of 1 Corinthians 15:3–7, dates to no later than a decade after Jesus' crucifixion, and probably earlier.

---

192. Hume, *Of Miracles*, 117.

193. Muhammad's claim in the early seventh century AD that the angel Gabriel appeared to him multiple times is also parallel here. Here we have a single witness (Muhammad) to this supernatural claim, not multiple individuals and groups, and there were no enemies who witnessed the appearances of Gabriel. This is nothing like the resurrection appearances of Jesus.

"HE APPEARED"

In this ancient list of appearances in 1 Corinthians 15:5-8, Jesus is said to have "appeared" (*ōphthē*)[194] to three individuals:

> Peter
> James
> Paul

And to three groups:

> the Twelve
> more than five hundred (!)
> all the apostles

The most glaring omission in this list, for anyone with knowledge of the Gospel stories, is the women, specifically Mary Magdalene. In all four Gospel accounts, Mary Magdalene is first to see the risen Jesus (Mark 16:1-8; Matt 28:1-8; Luke 24:1-8; John 20:11-18).[195] We really don't know why Mary Magdalene and the other women are not included. The best guess is that the testimony of women did not count for much in the ancient world, as we see from the testimony of Josephus: "Put not trust in a single witness, but let there be three or at least two, whose

---

194. This word *ōphthē* is also used to refer to Jesus' postresurrection appearances in Luke 24:34; Acts 9:17; 26:16. See also Acts 13:31: "And for many days He appeared [*ōphthē*] to those who came up with Him from Galilee to Jerusalem, the very ones who are now His witnesses to the people." Dunn writes, "The very early formulation, 'he appeared (*ōphthē*),' indicates by its passive form the assumption/impression that there was something to be seen" (*Jesus Remembered*, 872).

195. Ehrman: "It is also significant that Mary Magdalene enjoys such prominence in all the Gospel resurrection narratives, even though she is virtually absent everywhere else in the Gospels. She is mentioned in only one passage in the entire New Testament in connection with Jesus during his public ministry (Luke 8:1-3), and yet she is always the first to announce that Jesus has been raised. Why is this? One plausible explanation is that she too had a vision of Jesus after he died" (*How Jesus Became God*, 192).

evidence shall be accredited by their past lives. From women let no evidence be accepted, because of the levity and temerity of their sex" (*Ant.* 4.219).[196]

Moreover, the eyewitness testimony of the women is not appealed to in the sermons of Acts, even though the same author wrote Luke 24:1–8. The male eyewitnesses to the risen Jesus receive the primary emphasis (Acts 1:3; 10:40–41; 13:30–31). It is reasonable to assume, then, that Mary and the other women were not included in this earliest list of witnesses because its primary purpose, like the sermons in Acts, was evangelistic and apologetic.[197] This list of witnesses to Jesus' resurrection was primarily meant to give proof that Jesus did indeed rise from the dead, in the same way that "he was buried" was meant to give proof that Jesus died. A list of female eyewitnesses to the risen Jesus, not being regarded as solid testimony in the ancient world, were then not included. This seems like the best answer to this puzzle, but we can't be certain.

In addition to this list of witnesses being presented as proof of Jesus' resurrection, it was most likely meant to be chronological, though not exhaustive.[198] Among Jesus' male followers,

---

196. This was also true in Greco-Roman culture. For instance, see Celsus's attack: "But who really saw this? A hysterical woman, as you admit" (Hoffman, *Celsus on the True Doctrine*).

197. Even Bultmann sees this list of witnesses to Jesus' resurrection as Paul seeking to demonstrate it as historical fact: "Paul is betrayed by his apologetic into contradicting himself" (*Theology of the New Testament*, 1:83). See also Pannenberg: "The intention of this enumeration is clearly to give proof by means of witnesses for the facticity of Jesus' resurrection" (*Jesus: God and Man*, 89).

198. The repetition of the Greek word *eita* ("then") indicates the chronology: *kēfa eita ... epeita ... epeita ... eita eschaton de pantōn ... kamoi.* Von Campenhausen writes, "There should never have been any doubt that Paul's account was intended to be chronological" ("Events of Easter and the Empty Tomb," 45). Resurrection appearances mentioned in the NT but missing from the creedal tradition are Jesus' appearance to the two on the Emmaus road (Luke 24) and to

Jesus first appeared to Peter (Cephas), then soon after that to the Twelve, sometime later (even weeks later?) to more than five hundred men and women at once, after this to James, then to all the apostles, and one to two years later he appeared to Paul.[199] There are no resurrection appearances after Paul, not only from early Christianity, but from all of church history. Many people over the past two thousand years, including Paul (see 2 Cor 12:1-6), have claimed to have visions and/or dreams of Jesus, but not *one* of them has claimed this was a resurrection appearance in the same order as the kind we see in 1 Corinthians 15:5-8. These resurrection appearances were truly unique: they occurred over a limited period of time (one to two years), beginning with Mary Magdalene and Peter, and Paul was "last of all" (1 Cor 15:8).

WHAT DID THEY SEE?

In 2000, when interviewed by news anchor Peter Jennings for his documentary *The Search for Jesus,* agnostic New Testament scholar Paula Fredriksen said of the early Christians, "I know in their own terms what they saw was the raised Jesus. That's what they say and then all the historic evidence we have afterwards attests to their conviction that that's what they saw. I'm not saying that they really did see the raised Jesus. I wasn't there.

---

the seven disciples at the Sea of Tiberias (John 21). Paul may have not had knowledge of these appearances, but for whatever reason they were not included.

199. We also are not certain where all these resurrection appearances took place. It seems clear that Peter's appearance occurred in Jerusalem and the appearance to the Twelve that same Sunday evening in Jerusalem (Luke 24; John 20). As we will see, the appearance to more than five hundred at once most likely occurred in Galilee, which is also likely where the appearance to James occurred. "To all the apostles" is the most mysterious, but I will argue later that the story of Jesus' ascension in Jerusalem accounts for this appearance (Acts 1:9-11). Last, I already discussed the appearance to Paul happened somewhere near or in Damascus (Gal 1:15-17).

I don't know what they saw. But I do know that as a historian that they must have seen something."[200]

They must have seen something.

Besides Jesus rising from the dead, the two most prevalent answers today to the question "What did they see?" are either that they had hallucinations or "I don't know."[201] I will discuss the earliest apostolic proclamation, namely, that the historical Jesus did rise from the dead, along with what I call the "cautious agnostic approach," in the final chapter. For now, let us look briefly at the hallucination theory.

Most who argue that Jesus' earliest followers had hallucinations usually compare their experiences to the bereaved, those who experience an apparition of their dead loved one.[202] New Testament scholar and atheist Gerd Lüdemann has famously argued that Peter's guilt led him to project an apparition of Jesus so he could forgive him.[203] Then afterward Peter convinced many of the others of Jesus' resurrection.

There are four main problems with this theory.

For one, how does this explain the other appearances? It is doubtful that Peter could have convinced the others like James or even the five hundred that the crucified Jesus was alive again. This is especially true of the appearance to Paul. Paul was not looking for forgiveness from Jesus; he was looking to destroy Jesus' movement, including Peter!

Second, Peter could have equally been enraged at Jesus for leading him and others astray. He had left his wife (and possibly children) for over three years to follow this man (see Mark

---

200. From an interview in Peter Jennings's *The Search for Jesus* (ABC News, July 2000).

201. See Habermas, "Explaining Away Jesus' Resurrection."

202. See, for example, Ehrman, *Jesus, Interrupted*, 177–79.

203. Lüdemann, *Resurrection of Christ*, 163–65, 174.

10:28–30), and now he was dead. Did he, like Paul, believe at this point that Jesus was cursed by God? How does Lüdemann know this was not Peter's state of mind after the crucifixion? If it was, Peter was not sad and looking for forgiveness; he was looking for revenge.

Third, hallucinations were not unknown in the ancient world, and a hallucinatory experience of a ghost or apparition would not have led to the claim that Jesus had risen from the dead. Dale Allison rightly challenges this theory: "Even if, however, we accept Lüdemann's suppositions, we are still left with the question why a hallucination led a first-century Jew to confess that Jesus had been 'raised from the dead.' "[204]

Last, why did the disciples of any of the other failed messianic movements not have hallucinations of their dead leader? Were they not also sad and lonely? Did they not also possess an imagination? We do not have a shred of evidence that any of them had hallucinations. Instead, the overwhelming evidence from these other movements suggests Jewish disciples were not the types to have hallucinations of a failed, dead messianic leader. Could Jesus' band of followers be the exception? Of course, but what is the evidence they were indeed hallucinating?

Again, why would they have claimed Jesus was raised from the dead? Why would hallucinations or visions of Jesus lead to this threefold, unparalleled innovation among his earliest Jewish followers? Hallucinations and visions of Jesus may have convinced his followers that he had been exalted to heaven like Elijah and had gained eternal life like the Maccabean martyrs, but it defies all the evidence to suggest this would have led to the unique claim that he was raised on the third day. As Wright notes well, "Indeed, such visions meant precisely, as people in

---

204. Allison, *Resurrecting Jesus*, 243.

the ancient and modern worlds have discovered, that the person was dead, not that they were alive."[205]

If Jesus' resurrection appearances were hallucinations, particularly like the well documented hallucinations of the bereaved, then they were unlike any hallucinations we have on record. The authors of the Gospels are at least aware of apparitions or ghosts appearing to loved ones and make clear this is not what happened in the case of Jesus:

> "See My hands and My feet, that it is I Myself; touch Me and see, for a spirit does not have flesh and bones as you see that I have." And when He had said this, He showed them His hands and His feet. While they still could not believe it because of their joy and amazement, He said to them, "Have you anything here to eat?" They gave Him a piece of a broiled fish; and He took it and ate it before them. (Luke 24:39–43)

In his book *Resurrecting Jesus*,[206] Dale Allison surveys the scientific studies and literature on hallucinations and finds that four things do not happen or very rarely happen in the case of a hallucination(s) of a dead loved one:

- Hallucinations are rarely, if ever, experienced numerous times by both individuals and groups over an extended amount of time.

---

205. Wright, *Resurrection of the Son of God*, 690–91.
206. See Allison, *Resurrecting Jesus*, 269–85.

- Hallucinations of apparitions are not usually seen by large groups, as Jesus is seen by the Twelve or even more than five hundred![207]

- Hallucinations have never led to the claim that a dead person had been resurrected.[208]

- Hallucinations do not involve the person's enemy.

All of these almost unheard-of phenomena in the literature on hallucinations happened in the case of the resurrection appearances of Jesus.[209] Allison summarizes,

These appear to be the facts, and they raise the question of how we should explain them. The apologists for the faith say that the sightings of Jesus must, given the reports, have been objective. One person can hallucinate, but twelve at the same time? And dozens over an extended period of time? These are legitimate questions, and waving the magical wand of "mass hysteria" will not make them vanish.[210]

---

207. Allison, *Resurrecting Jesus*, 283. Green and McCreery write, "There are reports of groups numbering from two up to about eight people seeing the same apparition at the same time, but there are no well authenticated cases of groups much larger than this doing so" (*Apparitions*, 41).

208. As philosopher and Christian apologist Blaise Pascal said in the seventeenth century, "It is not possible to imagine that a man has risen from the dead" (*Pensées*, 802).

209. If we bring in the Gospels and Acts, there are reports of Jesus' empty tomb, and empty burial places are nowhere in the literature on hallucinations. In addition, Allison says, "Apparitions do not, furthermore, typically eat or drink," but the risen Jesus is reported to have eaten and drank with his disciples (Matt 28:9-10; Luke 24:39-43; John 20:20, 24-29; Acts 1:4; 10:41).

210. Allison, *Resurrecting Jesus*, 269.

One possible exception to the first two of Allison's claims above is that Mary the mother of Jesus is said to have appeared to individuals and large crowds over the past five hundred years. However, it should be pointed out that the first Marian apparition on record (in 1531) was to one person, Juan Diego, and the more one looks at the evidence for this claim, the more questionable it becomes. For one, there is no written evidence of this appearance until over a hundred years after the event. Second, Archbishop Juan de Zumarraga was said to be a part of the event, but in his prolific writings he never mentions it. Third, this is nothing like the evidence we have for Jesus' appearances. We have bedrock documentation of multiple individuals and groups seeing the risen Jesus, within a decade of the event, and all the appearances of Jesus were over a span of no more than two years.

Finally, and most importantly, Marian appearances lack the innovation and *unexpectedness* of Jesus' resurrection appearances. There are many examples of Christians throughout church history claiming to have visions or dreams of saints and angels. It is not surprising, then, that eventually some Christians would claim Mary the mother of Jesus appeared to them. In the case of Mary or other saints, we can see why Christians over the millennia would expect them to appear to them. In contrast, after Jesus' crucifixion, there was no expectation of Jesus appearing to anyone. Wright explains,

> Nobody was expecting this kind of thing; no kind of conversion-experience would have generated such ideas; nobody would have invented it, no matter how guilty (or how forgiven) they felt, no matter how many hours they pored over the scriptures. To suggest otherwise is

to stop doing history and to enter into a fantasy world of our own.[211]

If Jesus' followers had hallucinations, they were unlike any type of hallucinations we have on record. The resurrection appearances of Jesus and what resulted from them, for instance, the founding of the largest religion in the world, are truly without analogy. They were completely unexpected. In a word, Jesus' resurrection appearances are unique.[212]

CEPHAS/PETER AND THE TWELVE

Now that I have argued that the people listed in our creedal tradition truly believed what they saw was not a hallucination, let us now ask what else we can learn about the resurrection appearances to individuals and groups recorded in 1 Corinthians 15:5–8.

It is a bedrock fact that soon after Jesus' crucifixion, Peter became convinced that Jesus appeared to him alive, raised from the dead. Ehrman suggests "that three or four people—though possibly more—had visions of Jesus sometime after he died. One of these was almost certainly Peter, since reports about his seeing Jesus are found everywhere in our sources, including our earliest record of Paul in 1 Corinthians 15:5."[213]

No one doubts the appearance to Peter.

One of the reasons for this is that we have at least two (1 Cor 15:5; Luke 24:34), possibly three (Mark 16:7), early and independent testimonies of Jesus' appearance to Peter.

---

211. Wright, *Resurrection of the Son of God*, 707.
212. See Allison, *Resurrecting Jesus*, 284–85.
213. Ehrman, *How Jesus Became God*, 192.

"He appeared to Cephas." (1 Cor 15:5)

"But go, tell His disciples and Peter." (Mark 16:7)

"The Lord has really risen and has appeared to Simon."
(Luke 24:34)

Luke agrees with Paul and the creedal tradition that Jesus'
appearance to Peter happened *before* the appearance to the
Twelve (Luke 24:36–49). Moreover, while Paul, Mark, and Luke
are aware of this appearance, none of them narrates an account
of it. This demonstrates some serious restraint on these authors'
part to not create a story *ex nihilo* to describe this most significant appearance to the Rock of the Church. The reason for this
restraint is that there must not have been a surviving account
of Jesus' appearance to Peter, and they certainly were not going
to make one up.

The next attested appearance of the risen Jesus in our creedal
tradition is "He appeared ... to the twelve" (1 Cor 15:5). That this
group of Jesus' followers believed Jesus appeared to them all
together is also a bedrock fact.[214] Paul nowhere else in all his
writings uses this title "the Twelve." He usually refers to others
who saw the risen Jesus or who were followers of Jesus before
his conversion as "apostles."[215] The Twelve, then, must have been
a specific group of followers of Jesus during his public ministry that had this title. Most scholars agree that "the Twelve," as

214. Thiessen and Merz: "There is no doubt that it really happened"
(*Historical Jesus*, 496). Catchpole says it is "the best attested of all the appearances" (*Resurrection People*, 210).

215. For example, Paul refers to James, the brother of Jesus (Gal 1:19), and
Adronicus and Junias (Rom 16:7) as "apostles" before he was (see 1 Cor 9:5).

attested in the four Gospels and Acts, are a group of followers Jesus gathered around him as his inner circle.[216]

This also might tell us something more about the historical Jesus' self-consciousness and the aims of his public ministry. "The Twelve" is a very significant number in the history of Israel. The twelve tribes of Israel would be the best candidate for a background here. Did Jesus believe his group of twelve followers symbolically represented the renewed Israel? One of the undisputed, bedrock sayings of Jesus from the Gospels testifies to this understanding: "And Jesus said to them, 'Truly I say to you, that you who have followed Me, in the regeneration when the Son of Man will sit on His glorious throne, you also shall sit upon twelve thrones, judging the twelve tribes of Israel' " (Matt 19:28).

What role, then, did Jesus believe he would play in the "regeneration"? Among the twelve tribes of Israel was only the God of Israel, guiding and leading them. Who did Jesus think he was? The Son of Man who would sit on his glorious throne? We can't be sure of Jesus' self-consciousness here just from his gathering of twelve followers, but this symbolically charged act and the saying above are certainly suggestive.

These twelve followers had an experience they interpreted as the risen Jesus appearing to them. It happened while they were all together, and even though it would have included Peter, it happened sometime after Jesus' individual appearance to Peter.

The Gospels of Luke and John also testify to this appearance to the Twelve (Luke 24:36–49; John 20:19–23; see also Mark 16:14).

---

216. "The Twelve" are multiply attested in the four Gospels, Acts, and Paul: Mark 3:13–19; Matt 19:28; Luke 8:1–3; John 6:67–71; Matthias replacing Judas in Acts 1 and 1 Cor 15:5. Ehrman writes, "One of the best attested traditions of our surviving sources is that Jesus chose twelve of his followers to form a kind of inner circle" (*Jesus: Apocalyptic Prophet*, 186). Meyer writes, "The historicity of the deliberate act of choosing twelve disciples to participate most intimately in his mission is beyond reasonable doubt" (*Aims of Jesus*, 154).

Unlike this early creedal tradition, the Gospels give the precise number "eleven" because Judas had died at this point (Luke 24:9, 33; Matt 28:16; Acts 1:26; 2:14; see also Mark 16:14). This further demonstrates the historicity of the Twelve because of the mathematical modifications in the later traditions. Those who composed this early creedal tradition (and Paul)[217] almost certainly knew it was only the Eleven who Jesus appeared to, but "the Twelve" must have become a well-known title by this time.

Furthermore, Luke and John agree on the precise wording of the risen Jesus when he appeared to the Twelve. Jesus said to them:

"Peace be with you [*eirēnē hymin*]." (Luke 24:36 NIV)

"Peace be with you [*eirēnē hymin*]." (John 20:19 NIV)

Even if the historicity of the Gospel accounts might be questioned, it is interesting to see this multiply attested memory of the exact words of the risen Jesus on this occasion: "Peace be with you."[218]

In my discussion of the extent of the creedal tradition in chapter 3, I agreed with the majority of scholars that the most primitive version of this tradition ended with verse 5: "and to the Twelve." Paul goes on to list three more resurrection appearances in 1 Corinthians 15:6–7 before including his own eyewitness appearance in 1 Corinthians 15:8. The appearances to Peter, to the Twelve,[219] to James, and to Paul are all bedrock

---

217. Paul seems to be aware of the Judas tradition: "The Lord Jesus in the night in which He was betrayed ..." (1 Cor 11:23).

218. Based on the Septuagint's translation of this phrase from Hebrew, it may well have been the single Hebrew word *Shalom* (1 Sam 25:6) or the phrase *Shalom aleikem* (Judg 19:20) that Jesus said to the Twelve. It is unlikely he spoke these words in Greek.

219. Even if the exact number might be doubted, that is beside the point. That a group of Jesus' followers believed Jesus appeared to them is bedrock.

appearances in that 99 percent of scholars agree that these three individuals (Peter, James, and Paul) and a group of Jesus' followers *believed* the risen Jesus appeared to them.[220] The other appearances do not pass the same 99 percent threshold. No one doubts Paul *believed* they happened, but as we will see, some doubt whether Paul received a *historical*, rather than legendary, account when it comes to the appearances to the more than five hundred and to all the apostles (1 Cor 15:6–7).

I will argue below that this skepticism on the part of some scholars is unfounded. These other accounts of Jesus' appearances are built on the same historical bedrock as the others. If you believe the Twelve experienced a resurrection appearance, you should also believe the five hundred and the other apostles did. It seems that these other appearances are just too incredible, too good to be true. Therefore, some conclude they must be legendary. But this is not the right way to judge the historicity of these traditions. Each should be judged by its own merits. Remember the wish list of the historian? We will see below that these three resurrection appearances pass the same high bar of reliability as the others.

Let us then move now to a truly "remarkable appearance," as J. A. Bengel calls it:[221]

"He appeared to more than five hundred brethren at one time" (1 Cor 15:6).

THE FIVE HUNDRED (!)

The creedal tradition attests: "After that He appeared to more than five hundred brethren at one time," and Paul probably

---

220. We could add to this list of bedrock appearances Mary Magdalene, but since she is only mentioned in the four Gospels, discussing Jesus' appearance to her is beyond the scope of this book.

221. Bengel, *Gnomon of the New Testament*, on 1 Cor 15:6.

added these words to the tradition, "most of whom remain until now, but some have fallen asleep" (1 Cor 15:6). In John Wesley's commentary on the New Testament, his note on this appearance says: "A glorious and incontestable proof! The greater part remain alive."[222] If true, this is indeed a glorious proof.

If you did not know where this resurrection appearance was found, you might very well believe it must be legendary. Over five hundred men and women at one time believed they saw the risen Jesus. This is too good to be true. We expect to find such an incredible claim alongside other fanciful accounts of Jesus and his apostles from the second and third centuries AD. In the second century, the Gospel of Peter, for example, has a clearly legendary account of Jesus' resurrection. When Jesus' disciples arrive early Sunday morning, a cross bursts out of the tomb, hovering in the air, and even speaks to them! We can imagine that at the end of this legendary story, it says that the risen Jesus appeared to more than five hundred men and women at one time![223]

Yet this most incredible resurrection appearance is *not* found in a legendary account from the second or third century. It is not even from the latter part of the first century, where many of the New Testament writings can be dated. As we saw in chapter 3 above, this tradition goes back to within a decade of Jesus' death and probably earlier. Furthermore, Paul adds to this tradition for his Corinthian readers (or hearers) "most of whom remain until now," meaning most of these five hundred eyewitnesses are still alive. Paul is piling on the evidence for Jesus' resurrection here.

---

222. Wesley, *Explanatory Notes upon the New Testament*, 455.

223. In fact, this is one of the reasons mythicist Robert Price rejects this as an early eyewitness account: "I judge the very notion of a resurrection appearance to 500 at one time to be a late piece of apocrypha, reminiscent of the extravagances of the Acts of Pilate" ("Apocryphal Apparitions," 69–70).

Even scholars who do not believe this event really happened agree that Paul is appealing to these living eyewitnesses as proof that Jesus rose from the dead.[224] C. H. Dodd explains: "There can hardly be any purpose in mentioning the fact that most of the 500 are still alive, unless Paul is saying, in effect, 'the witnesses are there to be questioned.' "[225]

Paul is in a sense saying to the Corinthians in the mid-50s AD, "Go on your next holiday to Galilee or Jerusalem and meet some of these eyewitnesses. They will tell you what it was like to see the risen Jesus!"

We see other ancient historians using the same kind of argument Paul is using here. Josephus argues at one point the truthfulness of accounts of his own life because, even over two decades later, people are still alive who "can either prove what I say to be false, or can attest that it is true" (*Ant.* 20.266). Paul is also writing this Letter to the Corinthians roughly two decades after Jesus' resurrection appearances, including the appearance to more than five hundred. Paul and Josephus are both making appeals to living eyewitnesses who can "attest that it is true."[226]

---

224. Murphy O'Connor: "Why, then, did he need to emphasize this point? The most obvious explanation is that he intended to underline the objectivity of the experience. A small group of close acquaintances might be accused of self-deception, but this is a much less plausible hypothesis when it is the question of a very large crowd. In this perspective Paul's purpose was apologetic, and this interpretation is confirmed by *hoi pleiones menousin heos arti*, for the point of this clause can only be that some of the witnesses are still available for questioning by those who might have doubts" ("Tradition and Redaction," 586). Pannenberg writes, "The appearance to five hundred brethren at once cannot be a secondary construction to be explained by the development of the history of traditions, because Paul calls attention precisely here to the possibility of checking his assertion by saying that most of the five hundred are still alive" (*Jesus: God and Man*, 97).

225. Dodd, "Appearances of the Risen Christ," 128.

226. Other examples from the ancient world include Tacitus: "I have felt to repeat this account given by people who were still alive when I was young" (*Annals* 3.15). See also Plato: "For I believe he died about seventy years old, forty

Travel was quite common in the ancient Roman Empire.[227] Where, then, would the Corinthians have traveled to meet some of these eyewitnesses to hear firsthand accounts of Jesus' resurrection? Some were in Jerusalem, no doubt (Peter, James, and perhaps others of the Twelve), but this appearance to the five hundred most likely took place in Galilee.[228] Josephus tells us that Galilee contained many villages and the smallest of them contained over fifteen thousand inhabitants (*J.W.* 3.41–43). Josephus is notorious for exaggerating numbers, which he is probably doing here, but this still implies that a group of over five hundred gathering in the open somewhere in Galilee is possible.

This appearance to the more than five hundred may even be the Galilean appearance recounted in Matthew 28:16–20.[229] Jesus' "brethren" (the same Greek word is used in Matt 28:10 and 1 Cor 15:6) are told that he will appear on a "designated" mountain in Galilee (Matt 28:10, 16). We can imagine that when they gathered at this mountain, the word spread and hundreds of people,

---

of which he spent in the practice of his art; and he retains undiminished to this day the high reputation he has enjoyed all that time—and not only Protagoras, but a multitude of others too: some who lived before him, and others still living" (*Meno* 92A).

227. Stark writes, "Anyone could cross the empire from one end to the other in a summer, and travel was common. Meeks (1983:17) reports a merchant's grave inscription found in Phrygia that attests to his having traveled to Rome seventy-two times, a distance of well over a thousand miles, and Ronald Hock (1980) estimates that Paul covered nearly ten thousand miles on his missions" (*Rise of Christianity*, 135).

228. See discussion in von Campenhausen, "Events of Easter and the Empty Tomb," 48.

229. The first to make this connection was John Chrysostom, *Homily* on 1 Cor 15:6. See also Robertson and Plummer: "The occasion of the appearance to the 500 is unknown; but it is probably to be identified with Matt. 28:16, where only the Eleven are mentioned, because only to them was the great commission (18–20) given, although the presence of others seems to be implied in 'some doubted'" (*1 Corinthians*, 336–37). For further discussion see Kearney, "He Appeared to 500 Brothers"; Gilmour, "Christophany to More Than Five Hundred Brethren"; Bishop, "Risen Christ."

men and women, followers and skeptics, gathered quickly to see this appearance of Jesus. Incredibly, Matthew even testifies that "some were doubtful" (Matt 28:17), which implies a larger gathering then Jesus' eleven followers.[230]

Whether this is the same event, I agree with William Lane Craig's conclusion: "Regardless of where the event occurred, Paul's tradition and personal comment attest to the fact that there were literally hundreds of people about who were known in the early church and who had been at an assembly where they experienced an appearance of Jesus and who were ready to testify to the fact. It is quite amazing."[231]

It is quite amazing.

Many scholars express unwarranted skepticism concerning this appearance to the more than five hundred. For instance, Ehrman accepts the historicity of the resurrection appearances to Peter, the Twelve, James and Paul, but he is skeptical about the five hundred. If it did happen, he admits "it defies belief that this could have been imagined by all five hundred at once. There is a certain force to this argument."[232] This is undoubtedly true. But he goes on to say, "It does need to be pointed out that Paul is the only one who mentions this event, and if it really happened—or even if it was widely believed to have happened—it is hard to explain why it never made its way into the Gospels, especially those later Gospels such as Luke and John that were so intent on 'proving' that Jesus was physically raised from the dead."[233]

Ehrman's argument, then, against the historicity of this appearance to the five hundred is ultimately an argument from

---

230. Paul may even show knowledge of this great commission delivered on this occasion in Rom 1:5-6.

231. Craig, *Assessing the New Testament Evidence*, 63.

232. Ehrman, *How Jesus Became God*, 202.

233. Ehrman, *How Jesus Became God*, 202.

silence: If this really happened, then why do we not see this appearance in the Gospels? For one thing, I have argued that it is found in the Gospels, in Matthew 28:16–20. But even if this is not the same event, this is not a sufficient reason to reject it.

We have already seen the incredible restraint of the authors of the Gospels. At least Luke and possibly Mark knew of an appearance of Jesus to Peter, yet we do not have it recounted in any of the Gospels. This is also true of the appearance to James mentioned in 1 Corinthians 15:7. Where is the account of Jesus' appearance to his own brother and the leader of the Jerusalem church (Acts 12:17; 15:13; 21:18)? If the Gospels are silent concerning the resurrection appearances to Peter and James (two appearances Ehrman accepts), why then not accept the historicity of the appearance to the five hundred?

Another argument Ehrman puts forward is that when Paul received it, it was already legend—that is, "made up."

> I am not saying that Paul necessarily made up the story of the five hundred himself; he may well have inherited it from an oral tradition. Moreover, there is no telling how traditions such as this come to be made up—but it happens all the time, even in our day and age. It is not always the result of someone "lying" about it. Sometimes stories just get exaggerated or invented.[234]

But this argument ignores how early this story was being circulated: sometime during the 30s AD, no later than a decade after Jesus' death. This was a period when surely such an incredible claim could have been checked and, if needed, refuted. In fact, we see this type of apostolic oversight when, for example, Peter and John travel to oversee the Samaritans who have received the

---

234. Ehrman, *How Jesus Became God*, 379.

gospel (Acts 8). Moreover, Paul mentions eyewitnesses among the five hundred that are *still* alive. It is reasonable to assume Paul himself had met some of them when he went to Jerusalem on his first (AD 37) or second (AD 46-47) visits. How else would he know that some of them are still alive? With his reputation on the line with the church in Corinth, it seems doubtful that Paul would have appealed to such hearsay. Through Paul's travels among the earliest Christians in the 30s and 40s AD, he was in a position to investigate such extraordinary claims and the living eyewitnesses themselves.

All in all, in spite of the large number, skepticism about this appearance to the more than five hundred is unwarranted. The tradition of this appearance is built on the same historical bedrock as the rest of the creedal tradition. It is very early, Paul appeals to those eyewitnesses who are still alive, and most importantly, Paul was in a position to investigate these claims to see whether they were true. According to this creedal tradition and Paul, this remarkable event happened in history. At a gathering, possibly in Galilee, more than five hundred men and women believed they saw the risen Jesus.

Yes, as Ehrman admits, "There is a certain force to this argument." And the historian is pressed to give an answer.

JAMES

What happened to James, Jesus' brother, after Jesus' death? All the Gospel traditions concerning Jesus' brothers are negative during his public ministry: "For not even his brothers were believing in Him" (John 7:5; see also Mark 3:31-35; 6:3-6; Matt 12:46-50; 13:55-58). Yet something changed. We see Jesus' brothers begin to follow Jesus after his resurrection (Acts 1:14), his brothers become traveling missionaries whom Paul knows (1 Cor 9:5), and when Paul meets with James, he considers him one of the "apostles" (Gal 1:19). In addition, Acts presents James as the leader of the Jerusalem church, even seeming to have higher authority on ecclesiastical decisions than Peter himself (Acts 12:17; 15:13; 21:18).

How do we historically account for this transformation? How did James become convinced that his brother Jesus, who had been crucified, was raised from the dead?

What would it take to convince *you* that your brother is the Son of God and Lord of the world? Possibly if after a gruesome and bloody death, your brother appeared to you again—alive! The creedal tradition testifies that this is what happened: "Then He appeared to James" (1 Cor 15:7).[235]

Even though not all scholars are convinced that James underwent a conversion due to Jesus appearing to him,[236] virtually everyone grants Jesus' appearance to James.[237] In other words, whether James was an unbeliever or already a follower of his brother Jesus, he *believed* Jesus appeared to him.[238]

---

235. While there were other people named James in the early church, no one disputes that this James is James, the brother of Jesus. Lüdemann admits: "Because of 1 Cor. 15.7 it is certain *that* James 'saw' his brother" (*Resurrection of Jesus*, 109). Dunn writes, "No one doubts that the James of 1 Cor. 15.7 is the James of Gal. 1.19 and 2.9, 12" (*Jesus Remembered*, 862n168). Conzelmann agrees: "James is of course the brother of Jesus (Gal 1:19). His status in the church was also grounded by 'his' appearance" (*1 Corinthians*, 258).

236. Allison: "This is far from certain" (*Resurrecting Jesus*, 262). Ehrman: "His brothers are said in a later source not to have believed in him (John 7:5), and it is striking that he had no relatives among his closest followers. Paul may imply that it was only after his resurrection that Jesus' brother James became a believer (1 Cor 15:7)" (*Jesus: Apocalyptic Prophet*, 201). Von Campenhausen: "It is possible, though not necessarily the case, that for James himself it meant a conversion; for, in the lifetime of his brother, he seems to have held apart from him" ("Events of Easter and the Empty Tomb," 52). See also Catchpole, *Resurrection People*, 157–58.

237. Mythicists and scholars who participated in the Jesus Seminar seem to be the only exception. See Funk and Hoover, *Five Gospels*, 454–55.

238. "Who would deny that James had a post-Easter Christophany even though the Gospels do not intimate such?" (Allison, *Resurrecting Jesus*, 306).

As with Jesus' appearance to Peter, we do not possess a narrative account of Jesus' appearance to James.[239] Again we see the restraint of the authors of the Gospels to not invent a story when they do not have one. As Reginald Fuller wisely notes: "It might be said that if there were no record of an appearance to James the Lord's brother in the New Testament we should have to invent one in order to account for his post-resurrection conversion and rapid advance."[240]

Jesus' appearance to his brother James is built on historical bedrock, even if we cannot know for certain James' attitude toward his brother Jesus before this appearance took place.

ALL THE APOSTLES

Let us now look at the final appearance in the creedal tradition Paul is quoting, 1 Corinthians 15:7b: "He appeared ... to all the apostles." Here we are left mostly in the dark. Who are "all the apostles"? Are they the same group as the Twelve or a larger group outside them? When and where did this appearance take place? We really do not know with any historical certainty the answer to these questions.

Since the testimony to this appearance is built on the same historical bedrock as the others, the bare minimum we can say is the risen Jesus appeared to a large group of apostles and that this group may have included but definitely exceeds the smaller group of the Twelve.[241]

Who then are these "apostles"?

---

239. It is not until over one hundred years later, in a clearly legendary account, that we find a narrative account of Jesus' appearance to James (*Gospel of the Hebrews* 7). See Elliott, *Apocryphal New Testament*.

240. Fuller, *Formation of the Resurrection Narratives*, 37.

241. Murphy-O'Connor: "There appears to be a consensus that the reference is to a group of missionaries more extensive than the Twelve" ("Tradition and Redaction," 587).

Paul does refer to other "apostles" throughout his letters. He seems to believe James the brother of Jesus is an apostle (Gal 1:19), possibly a husband-and-wife team, Andronicus and Junias (Rom 16:7), possibly Barnabas (Gal 2:9; see also Acts 14:14), and other unnamed traveling missionaries he refers to as "the rest of the apostles" (1 Cor 9:5). These are at least some of the individuals Paul had in mind when he quoted the creedal tradition: "He appeared … to all the apostles" (1 Cor 15:7).

Are the apostles restricted to only those who have seen the risen Jesus (see 1 Cor 9:1; Acts 1:21–22)? This seems to be what distinguishes "apostles"[242] from all the other followers of Jesus, but this is not certain.

If this appearance is also found in the later Gospels, the most likely candidate is Jesus' appearance to around 120 of his followers at his ascension in Jerusalem. "And He led them out as far as Bethany, and He lifted up His hands and blessed them. While He was blessing them, He parted from them and was carried up into heaven. And they, after worshiping Him, returned to Jerusalem with great joy, and were continually in the temple praising God" (Luke 24:50–53).

The parallel account in Acts also tells us that the Twelve (or Eleven) were there, along with "the women" (no doubt including Mary Magdalene), Mary, the mother of Jesus, and his brothers. This list includes only around twenty to thirty people, but it goes on to mention "the brethren" (Acts 1:15) Peter addresses. The entire group, then, that witnessed this postresurrection appearance and ascension was "a gathering of about one hundred and twenty persons" (Acts 1:15). Are these "about one hundred and

---

242. The Greek word *apostolos* means "sent one," and the apostles include the twelve sent out by Jesus, but are a larger group incorporating all who saw the risen Jesus (1 Cor 9:1; Acts 1:21–22).

twenty persons" the "all the apostles" referred to in this early creedal tradition (1 Cor 15:7)?

I think they are, but this is not certain.

THE APOSTLE PAUL

"Last of all ... He appeared to me" (1 Cor 15:8). That Paul the Pharisaic persecutor of the church became convinced that the crucified man Jesus appeared to him, raised from the dead, is a bedrock fact. I have already discussed Paul's background and conversion extensively in chapters 1 and 2 above. It is worth repeating that Paul's experience was completely different from Peter's. Peter was a devoted follower of Jesus, whereas Paul considered Jesus accursed and his followers as his enemies who needed to be destroyed. One could argue, as Lüdemann did above, that Peter had severe guilt for denying Jesus and *wanted* to believe he was still alive because he was looking for forgiveness. I showed why this does not work for even Peter, but no one could argue such a case with Paul. Paul did not have a guilty conscience; he was not looking for forgiveness, especially not from this crucified, accursed Nazarene.

Therefore, Paul's case is truly extraordinary. Not only was this the last appearance of the risen Jesus in recorded history, but the only appearance we know of to an enemy.[243]

What did Paul see near Damascus about a year or so after Jesus was crucified that not only transformed his life, but changed the course of human history? Paul was crystal clear on who he saw: "Have I not seen Jesus our Lord?" (1 Cor 9:1).

But did he *actually* see Jesus?

---

243. Even if James, Jesus' brother, did not believe in him before the resurrection appearance, one could hardly call James an enemy. It is interesting to note the progression here in the individual appearances listed. We go from the chief follower, Peter, to the more neutral James, to an outright enemy, Paul.

According to Ehrman,

> We obviously don't know what Paul actually saw. How can we possibly know? What he fervently claimed was that he saw Jesus himself, alive again. Believers would say that was because Jesus actually appeared to him. Unbelievers would say he imagined it. Either way, it is crystal clear that he believed he did see Jesus and that this radically changed his thinking.[244]

If he didn't really see the resurrected Jesus, this Pharisaic persecutor sure had quite the imagination!

He somehow imagined that the man he believed was cursed by God had appeared to him, raised from the dead. Remember, this was unparalleled innovation. Quite the imagination, indeed.

It seems that a better historical explanation than "imagination" needs to account for Paul's experience. Even if Paul saw something that was not in his imagination, some have wondered how Paul knew this "body of His glory" appearing to him was Jesus (Phil 3:21; 2 Cor 4:4–6),[245] especially since he had probably never met him and he did not know what he looked like. Paul's letters are no help here, but if the accounts of Paul's conversion in Acts are trustworthy, then we have our answer: Paul/Saul asks him, "Who are you, Lord?" (Acts 9:5; 22:8; 26:15), and he responds, "I am Jesus whom you are persecuting" (Acts 9:5; 22:8; 26:15). Paul knows this is the man Jesus who has been crucified, because this "body of His glory" identifies himself as "Jesus the Nazarene."

---

244. Ehrman, *Triumph of Christianity*, 52.

245. "Clearly the apostle thought of the risen Jesus as having a body of δόξα, one made of light (cf. 2 Cor 4:6)" (Allison, *Resurrecting Jesus*, 265). Second Corinthians 4:4, 6 "probably alludes to his great light experience on the Damascus road" (Dunn, *Jesus Remembered*, 857).

In spite of all the differences between the three accounts of Jesus' appearance to Saul in Acts, what the risen Jesus said to Saul in Greek is identical in all three accounts:

"Saul, Saul, why are you persecuting Me?" (*Saoul Saoul, ti me diōkeis*; Acts 9:4)

"Saul, Saul, why are you persecuting Me?" (*Saoul Saoul, ti me diōkeis*; Acts 22:7)

"Saul, Saul, why are you persecuting Me?" (*Saoul Saoul, ti me diōkeis*; Acts 26:14)

"Who are you, Lord?" (*tis ei, kyrie*; Acts 9:5)

"Who are you, Lord?" (*tis ei, kyrie*; Acts 22:8)

"Who are you, Lord?" (*tis ei, kyrie*; Acts 26:15)

"I am Jesus whom you are persecuting" (*egō eimi Iēsous hon sy diōkeis*; Acts 9:5)

"I am Jesus the Nazarene, whom you are persecuting" (*egō eimi Iēsous ho Nazōraios, hon sy diōkeis*; Acts 22:8)

"I am Jesus whom you are persecuting" (*egō eimi Iēsous hon sy diōkeis*; Acts 26:15)

This seems to reflect historical memory (from Paul himself?) concerning the words of the risen Jesus to him. Allison agrees: "So Paul's interpretation of his own calling is preserved in Acts. Again, it seems clear that Luke's source(s) for Paul's calling must stem ultimately from the apostle himself."[246]

This bedrock fact of Paul's conversion means that 99 percent of all scholars today and over the past two hundred years agree Paul *believed* Jesus appeared to him. They do not think Paul is lying or a fraud. Everyone agrees he was sincere in his belief.

---

246. Allison, *Resurrecting Jesus*, 265.

Another significant reason for this is that we know Paul shed his blood for his belief in Jesus (see Gal 6:17). In fact, even outside Acts and his letters, we know of many of the sufferings Paul experienced for the sake of Christ crucified and risen, culminating in his martyrdom under Nero in the mid-60s AD.

It is interesting to note that of all the earliest followers of Jesus, we only have solid, historical evidence for the martyrdoms of three of them: Peter, James,[247] and Paul. Paul (1 Clement 5.5–7; Polycarp, *To the Philippians* 9.1–2; Irenaeus, *Against Heresies* 3.1.1; Tertullian, *Scorpiace* 15) and Peter (1 Clement 5.2–4; John 21:18–22; Irenaeus, *Against Heresies* 3.1.1; Tertullian, *Scorpiace* 15) with the "highest probability"[248] died as martyrs under Nero's purge of Christians in the mid 60s AD (Tacitus, *Annals* 15.44; see also Suetonius, *Nero* 16). According to Josephus, James the brother of Jesus and "some others" were stoned to death for being "lawbreakers"[249] by the high priest in Jerusalem (*Ant.* 20.200).[250] Incredibly, these are the same three individuals (and the only individuals) listed in this ancient creedal tradition as witnesses to the risen Jesus (1 Cor 15:5–8).

---

247. I am speaking of James the brother of Jesus here. Though, if one accepts the historicity of Acts 12, which I do, then we also have the historical martyrdom of James the son of Zebedee (Acts 12:1–2).

248. Cullmann, *Peter*, 109. See also González: "It is also very likely that both Peter and Paul were among the Neronian martyrs" (*Story of Christianity*, 35). Jewett writes, "Paul was executed" sometime between "spring, 62, to August, 64" (*Chronology of Paul's Life*, 46). Marcus says: "Peter was probably martyred in Rome during the Neronian persecution around 64" (*Mark 1–8*, 30).

249. "What Law was it James broke, given his reputation within Christian circles as a Jewish-Christian leader who was careful about keeping the Law? It would seem likely that the Law had to relate to his Christological allegiances and a charge of blasphemy" (Bock, *Blasphemy and Exaltation*, 196n30).

250. Feldman writes: "Unlike the passage on Jesus (*Ant.* xviii.63–64), few have doubted the genuineness of this passage on James. ... If it had been a Christian interpolation it would, in all probability, have been more laudatory of James" (*Josephus: Jewish Antiquities*, 496 note a).

Therefore, the historical evidence does not only confirm that these three men were convinced the risen Jesus appeared to them, but that they also went to their deaths believing it.

Whatever these three men saw, it was worth giving their lives for.

THE FOOL'S SPEECH

Paul's trustworthiness and genuine belief that Jesus appeared to him is further confirmed by what he endured and suffered for the gospel throughout his little over thirty-year ministry. We have already looked at Paul's primary bedrock autobiography in Galatians 1–2, but there is another bedrock autobiography concerning some of Paul's life found in 2 Corinthians 11.[251] Some have called this Paul's "fool's speech," where in defense of his apostleship he "outboasts the boasters," that is, the false teachers in Corinth. As in Galatians, Paul takes a solemn oath before "the God and Father of the Lord Jesus" that he is not lying (2 Cor 11:31). Two thousand years later, 99 percent of scholars of all different backgrounds and worldviews agree.[252]

Instead of recounting to the Corinthians his apostolic victories, wonders, and miracles (as in Gal 3:5; 2 Cor 12:12; and Rom 15:19), Paul recounts all the sufferings and humiliations he has endured for the sake of Christ.

Here is only a sample of the great apostle's adventures:

---

251. Plummer writes: "In these twenty-one verses we have a summary of his career as an Apostle which, as an autobiographical sketch, has no equal in the NT" (*Critical and Exegetical Commentary*, 318).

252. As we saw above, 99 percent of scholars have always affirmed Paul's *Hauptbriefe*, his four undisputed letters, which includes 2 Corinthians. See Neill and Wright, *Interpretation of the New Testament, 1861–1986*, 362; Ehrman, *New Testament*, 308.

> Are they servants of Christ?—I speak as if insane—I
> more so; in far more labors, in far more imprisonments,
> beaten times without number, often in danger of death.
> Five times I received from the Jews thirty-nine lashes.
> Three times I was beaten with rods, once I was stoned,
> three times I was shipwrecked, a night and a day I have
> spent in the deep. I have been on frequent journeys, in
> dangers from rivers, dangers from robbers, dangers from
> my countrymen, dangers from the Gentiles, dangers in
> the city, dangers in the wilderness, dangers on the sea,
> dangers among false brethren; I have been in labor and
> hardship, through many sleepless nights, in hunger and
> thirst, often without food, in cold and exposure. (2 Cor
> 11:23–27)

What a boring life Paul had!

In the cult-classic movie *Fight Club*, Tyler Durden persuades his disciples to intentionally crash their car at high speed in order to have a "near-life experience." Not many humans have had more "near-life experiences" than the apostle Paul!

What is also incredible about this list of Paul's sufferings is that most of them are absent from the book of Acts. The author of Acts has only given us a glimpse into Paul's adventures following Christ. One might even say with Raymond Brown that "Acts might lead us to underestimate the apostle's extraordinary career."[253] Pauline scholar Ernest Best says further:

> If Acts amazes us with what Paul endured, then this
> list shows how inadequate its account really is and how
> much more Paul suffered than we can ever know. ... It

---

253. Brown, *Introduction to the New Testament*, 557.

is an amazing picture of Paul that emerges. How little we really know about him! How many untold stories of courage, compassion, and endurance lie behind this list! And it all must have taken place in the space of a mere dozen years![254]

Paul's missionary journeys in Acts alone are incredible, but 2 Corinthians 11 demonstrates that there are so many more untold stories of Paul's courage, sufferings, and herculean labors for Christ.

What can we learn from this fool's speech? That by the mid-50s AD Paul had already been imprisoned and beaten many times.[255] Death was Paul's daily companion. He had received the forty lashes minus one in Jewish synagogues five times. We know that in this case, Paul would have been stripped and bound to a pillar. One-third of the stripes were administered on Paul's front and the rest on his back while someone repeatedly recited Deuteronomy 28:58–59.[256] Paul himself had inflicted such punishment on followers of Jesus before his conversion (Gal 1:13; Acts 26:11), which surely must have come into Paul's mind as he was punished this way.

Roman magistrates beat Paul with rods three times, and "once" he was stoned. Do not read over that too quickly. To survive being stoned to death is miraculous itself. According to Acts, after they prayed over Paul, he got right back up and went back into the very city where they stoned him! William Barclay captures Paul's courage here well: "There could be no braver thing

---

254. Best, *Second Corinthians*, 113–14.

255. Acts records only one imprisonment before the time 2 Cor 11 was written, in Philippi (Acts 16:19–40). Paul also references this in 1 Thess 2:2: "after we had already suffered and been mistreated treated in Philippi."

256. Mishnah Makkot 3:10; see also Josephus, *Ant.* 4.238.

than Paul's going straight back amongst those who had tried to murder him. A deed like that would have more effect than a hundred sermons. Men were bound to ask themselves where a man got the courage to act in such a way."[257] This is another of many examples where we have an independent verification of Paul's letters in Acts. Both Paul and Acts testify that he was stoned only "once" (2 Cor 11:25; Acts 14:19; see also 2 Tim 3:11; 1 Clement 5.6).

Three times Paul was shipwrecked, and probably the most recent shipwreck was vividly in his memory as he wrote.[258] Paul says "a night and a day I have spent in the deep" (2 Cor 11:25). The way Paul writes this implies that he vividly remembers this nightmare as he was lost at sea, at the mercy of the waves and the wreckage he was clinging to for his very life.[259]

Paul continues his list of sufferings by mentioning eight different kinds of "dangers" he regularly faced on his journeys (2 Cor 11:26). It is no accident that "dangers among false brethren" concludes the list, since these false teachers are the primary problem facing the Corinthian church.

The climactic and closing story of Paul's fool's speech is one that has already been discussed in chapter 2. When in Damascus, Paul was hidden in a basket and let down the wall to escape King Aretas (2 Cor 11:32–33). We may not have a detailed account of

---

257. Barclay, *Acts of the Apostles*, 110. "The martyr dies once for all: but that blessed saint in his one body and one soul endured so many perils as were enough to disturb even a soul of adamant; and what things all the saints together have suffered in so many bodies, those all he himself endured in one" (John Chrysostom, *Homily* on 2 Corinthians 25.3).

258. At this point in Paul's ministry, Acts has mentioned the following voyages: Seleucia to Cyprus (Acts 13:4); Paphos to Attalia (Acts 13:13); Attalia to Antioch (Acts 14:26); Troas to Samothrace (Acts 16:11); Berea to Athens (Acts 17:15); and Corinth to Syria, calling at Ephesus (Acts 18:18); also, the journeys of Acts 9:30; 11:26 could have been made partly by sea. The three shipwrecks could have occurred among these voyages on the sea. The famous shipwreck in Acts 27 occurred years after the writing of 2 Cor 11.

259. See Moulton, *Grammar of New Testament Greek*, 144.

Paul's martyrdom under Nero, but this list of sufferings should give us good reason to believe that he endured it with boldness and courage, and the proclamation that "Jesus is Lord" must have been one of the last words on his lips.

Why did Paul endure the life of suffering he recounts in 2 Corinthians 11? At any point, he could have left it all and spent his life in comfort and safety as a tentmaker. Like his former associate Demas, Paul could have given it all up and enjoyed worldly pleasures in Thessalonica (see 2 Tim 4:10).

But Paul endured it all and died a martyr because he was absolutely convinced that the crucified man Jesus appeared to him, commissioned him that he should "no longer live for [himself], but for Him who died and rose again on [his] behalf" (2 Cor 5:15).

F. F. Bruce summarizes the power of Paul's conversion in his biography of the apostle:

> No single event, apart from the Christ-event itself, has proved so determinant for the course of Christian history as the conversion and commissioning of Paul. For anyone who accepts Paul's own explanation of his Damascus-road experience, it would be difficult to disagree with the observation of an eighteenth-century writer that "the conversion and apostleship of St. Paul alone, duly considered, was of itself a demonstration sufficient to prove Christianity to be a divine revelation."[260]

All the evidence suggests, and scholars agree, that Paul was not lying. He was no imposter or fraud. He sincerely believed what he proclaimed throughout the Roman Empire concerning Jesus' death, resurrection, and lordship over all creation (see

---

260. Bruce, *Paul*, 75.

Rom 8:34-39). Was he then deceived, or was he telling the truth? The historian is faced with these two options when it comes to the extraordinary transformation of the apostle Paul.

In addition to Paul, we can add Peter, the Twelve, and even the five hundred, James, and Mary Magdalene. Today, no one to my knowledge seriously entertains the option they were lying about seeing Jesus risen from the dead. Were they all deceived, then? If they did not have hallucinations, then what did they see that led them to launch the largest and most influential religious movement the world has ever seen?

As I quoted Fredriksen as saying above, "I do know as a historian they must have seen something."

What (or who) did they see?

———

Now that we have finished our multichapter discussion of the bedrock source, 1 Corinthians 15:3–8, we have one last bedrock fact to examine in the next chapter: the fact that, soon after Jesus' crucifixion and these resurrection appearances, his followers launched an indestructible movement that went on to overtake the Roman Empire and is to this day the largest religion in the world.

So now we turn to the question, How do we account historically for the rise of the Nazarenes?

7: The Rise of the Nazarenes
"Fighting against God"

So in the present case, I say to you, stay away from these men and let them alone, for if this plan or action is of men, it will be overthrown; but if it is of God, you will not be able to overthrow them; or else you may even be found fighting against God.

Acts 5:38–39

The tyrant dies and his rule is over, the martyr dies and his rule begins.

Søren Kierkegaard, *The Journals of Kierkegaard*

L et us get back in our phone booth one last time and time travel to Jerusalem in AD 135. We are arriving directly after the massacre of the last Jewish messianic movement, the Bar Kochba Revolt (AD 132–135). Only three years before, Simon Bar Kochba had been hailed by the famous Rabbi Akiba as the Messiah, the "son of the star" (what *bar kochba* means in Hebrew) based on Balaam's prophecy in Numbers 24:17: "a star shall come forth from Jacob." Simon must have taken this messianic claim very seriously. He tried to revive Hebrew as the official language of his newfound kingdom. He began issuing coins (which archaeologists have found) inscribed in Hebrew with his name, "Shimon," on one side and on the other, "Year One of the Redemption of Israel." Later coins had "Year Two of the Freedom of Israel." Simon attempted to restart the calendar to the beginning of his messianic reign in Jerusalem.

Incredibly, in 1961, archaeologists discovered in a cave near the Dead Sea letters written by Simon Bar Kochba himself! In what has become known as the Cave of Letters, in the same area the Dead Sea Scrolls were discovered, at least fifteen letters have been unearthed written by Simon to his subordinates. These letters even reveal his birth name, Simon ben Kosiba.

We also know the Christians living under Bar Kochba's control were heavily persecuted. Some were even tortured, trying to force them to curse Jesus' name. Early church father Justin Martyr was writing just a few decades after the revolt and details the atrocities done to the Christians under this false messiah in his *First Apology* 31.6 and *Dialogue with Trypho* 11.3; 133.6.

As you can imagine, none of this was looked on positively by the Romans, especially the emperor Hadrian (AD 117–138). By AD 134, Hadrian had sent his general Julius and his six legions to crush this messianic pretender, which he did. Imagine Julius as Maximus from *Gladiator* killing 580,000 followers of Bar Kochba and afterward saying to the cheering crowds: "Are you not entertained?"[261]

Hadrian did all he could after this revolt to remove the Jews and even Jewish history from the land of Judea.[262] He renamed Judea "Syria-Palaestina" and Jerusalem "Aelia Capitolina." He even set up a temple to Zeus in the middle of Jerusalem. From then on, few Jews lived in Jerusalem for many years, and no more messianic movements arose. The Jews went back to their Scriptures, and Rabbinic Judaism began to arise, with little emphasis on a coming Messiah.

---

261. For details of this war see Cassius Dio, *Roman History* 69.12–14.
262. See Ben-Sasson, *History of the Jewish People*, 334.

What happened to Bar Kochba and Rabbi Akiba after the war is legend, not history. Some accounts say Bar Kochba disappeared; others say Julius brought his severed head to Hadrian. Whether they disappeared or were tortured and killed by the Romans, one thing is crystal clear: they failed. Simon Bar Kochba was not the Messiah. In fact, later rabbis even called him a deceiver and false messiah.[263]

As with Simon bar Giora, or any of the dozen or so other Jewish movements we discussed above, none of their disciples claimed their messianic leader had risen from the dead and appeared to them. In the case of the many disciples of Simon Bar Kochba, they even had this as an option, since the Christian claims about Jesus would have been well known by this time. Yet not one of them did.

Since we have time traveled to this time, imagine asking one of Simon's disciples: "Why not say he rose from the dead like the Christians did of their leader?" This bloody, beaten disciple would likely respond: "Simon is no messiah. He failed. The Romans won. He deceived us all. I'd kill him myself if I could find him."

As we saw in chapter 5, a dead or failed messiah was no messiah at all.

The story of Simon Bar Kochba is not just fascinating history. We have a reason for beginning this chapter time traveling to the last failed Jewish messianic movement. This messianic pretender hailed by tens of thousands of Jews, who tried to restart the human calendar, does not have *one* follower today. In fact, the evidence suggests he did not even have one follower in AD 136.

---

263. See Lamentations Rabbah 2.5; Ta'anit 4.5 (24b).

Where are the followers today of Judas the Galilean, Theudas, Simon Bar Kochba, or even Apollonius of Tyana? Why is there not a religion today called Bar Kochbianity or Bar Kochbianism?

In contrast, there is a religion called Christianity today, the largest religion in the world, and this crucified Messiah Jesus just happens to have around 2.4 billion followers, about a third of the world's population.

This is the bedrock fact we are focusing on in this chapter.

HOW CAN WE ACCOUNT FOR THE RISE OF THE NAZARENES?

Jesus' movement, known first as the Nazarenes, survived his crucifixion, which defies all parallels to any movements of the time. Yet Jesus' movement did not just survive for a while and then perish centuries later. Nor did it continue to this day as a small group of followers of the Nazarene scattered throughout the Middle East. No. This fringe Jewish movement, proclaiming a crucified and risen Messiah, went on to become the dominant religion of the Roman Empire. Then, after Rome fell, Christianity continued its dominance in the East, in what is now Turkey and Russia and surrounding areas. It went on in the West to dominate even farther, all throughout what is now Europe, parts of Africa, and later the British Empire and America. Beginning in the last century, Christianity is growing the fastest in Africa, Latin America, South Korea, and more recently China. To this day, Christianity has more adherents than any other world religion. There are people all over the world becoming followers of this crucified Nazarene right now. An estimated seven people every minute are converting to Christianity; a number will confess Jesus as Lord even as you finish reading the words of this sentence.[264]

Furthermore, Jesus of Nazareth is considered by virtually everyone to be the most influential human being who ever walked the face of the earth.[265] How many people on earth daily think about Judas the Galilean or Simon Bar Kochba? How many daily think about, worship, and pray to Jesus of Nazareth?

How can we account for this?

E. P. Sanders writes,

> What is unquestionably unique about Jesus is the result of his life and work. They culminated in the resurrection and the foundation of a movement which endured. I have no special explanation or rationalization of the resurrection experiences of the disciples. Their vividness and importance are best seen in the letters of Paul. They are, to my knowledge, unique in their effect. ... That is as far as I can go in looking for an explanation of the one thing which sets Christianity apart from other "renewal movements." The disciples were prepared for *something*. *What* they received inspired them and empowered them. It is the *what* that is unique.[266]

What, then, is "the *what*"? According to N. T. Wright, "The resurrection, however we understand it, was the only reason

---

264. It is estimated that sixty-five million people annually identify as Christian and 3.8 million of that number become Christians due to conversion. When you break this down, an estimated 122 people identify as Christian every minute, seven every minute due to conversion. See Rambo and Farhadian, *Oxford Handbook of Religious Conversion*, 59.

265. See the list in *Time* magazine, http://ideas.time.com/2013/12/10/whos-biggest-the-100-significant-figures-in-history/, and see "25 Most Influential People in History by Attribute," List25, http://list25.com/25-most-influen-tial-people-in-history-by-attribute/5/, as just two examples of many.

266. Sanders, *Jesus and Judaism*, 320.

they came up with for supposing that Jesus stood for anything other than a dream that might have come true but didn't. It was the only reason why his life and words possessed any relevance two weeks, let alone two millennia, after his death."[267]

The *what* is the resurrection. There is no doubt about this. Believers and nonbelievers agree. Jesus' earliest followers (and Paul), in unparalleled fashion and with pure innovation, argued that Jesus rose from the dead and appeared to them. This brings us back to the ultimate question of this book and, I would argue, of human history: Did the historical Jesus rise from the dead? I will explore and finally answer this question in the concluding chapter, but let us first ask another question: If Jesus did in fact rise from the dead, if he is still alive to this day, would we expect his movement (the church) to have overwhelming influence in the world or to ultimately fail like Simon Bar Kochba's?

Of course, the rise of the Nazarenes shortly after Jesus' crucifixion and Christianity's success throughout the world could all be due to various accidents of history. Or it could be due to their leader rising from the dead and his continuing triumphal influence over his movement and the nations.

One possible reason that this movement endured and triumphed as it has is that its "purpose or activity" is not of human origin, but "it is of God" (Acts 5:38).

RABBI GAMALIEL'S PROPHECY

According to the book of Acts, Rabbi Gamaliel was presented with this young, rising movement of the Nazarenes, and he gave his fellow Jewish leaders in Jerusalem some wise counsel. After comparing the new Jesus movement to some of these other failed messianic movements, he says: "So in the present case, I say to

---

267. Wright, *Jesus and the Victory of God*, 658–59.

you, stay away from these men and let them alone, for if this plan or action is of men, it will be overthrown; but if it is of God, you will not be able to overthrow them; or else you may even be found fighting against God" (Acts 5:38–39).

Some scholars question the historicity of this account. They would argue that this speech is not historical and the author of Acts is putting these words on Rabbi Gamaliel's lips. Whether this account is historical or not, the argument, or even prophecy, remains. I believe this account is true to what Rabbi Gamaliel said on this occasion, but even if Gamaliel did not say these words, the author of Acts is saying that, if this Jesus movement ends like the other movements of this time, you can be sure it is "of men." But if it continues and its overwhelming influence and power prove to be indestructible, its origin is "of God."

When the author of Acts wrote these words in the second half of the first century, the followers of Jesus of Nazareth were infinitesimal within the empire, making up less than 1 percent of its population. Therefore, this was quite the claim to make. It was also falsifiable; as we saw in chapter five, a dozen or so movements just like them did fail. We could add to these failed movements the Essenes and the Sadducees, which were wiped out when Rome destroyed Jerusalem in AD 70. The origin of those other movements was indeed "of men."

Furthermore, there is no way the author of Acts could have known that one day Christians would make up well over 90 percent of the empire and that the Caesars would be baptized in the name of the crucified carpenter and worship him as Lord of the world. As St. Augustine, bishop of Hippo in North Africa, later said, "The Cross went from the place of execution to the foreheads of emperors."[268]

---

268. Augustine, *Expositions on the Book of Psalms*, on Ps 37:9–10.

The author of Acts could also not have known that within the next four hundred years, the gods of Egypt, Greece, and Rome who had been worshiped for thousands of years would be replaced by the worship of this crucified man, Jesus. John O'Meara writes, "The collapse of polytheism was in the end sudden, universal within the Empire, and practically absolute. ... Truly the gods had lost, and Christ had won."[269] It is as if Jesus said through his followers to the gods of Rome: "Come out of it and never enter it again!"[270]

This extraordinary conquest of the empire and its gods is why Bart Ehrman wrote *The Triumph of Christianity*. Twenty years before he wrote it, he was standing in the Areopagus in Athens, where Paul preached his famous sermon on Jesus and his resurrection to the Epicurean and Stoic philosophers, as recorded in Acts 17. Ehrman gives us his thoughtful recollection of that moment:

> Then the realization struck me. In the end, Paul won. What Paul preached that day on the Areopagus eventually triumphed over everything that stood below me in the Agora and above me on the Acropolis. It overwhelmed both the Temple of Hephaestus and the Parthenon. No one except, probably, Paul himself would have predicted it. Yet it happened: Christianity eventually took over Western Civilization.[271]

I agree that Paul himself would have predicted it. Like the author of Acts (if not Gamaliel himself) is saying, Paul knew that until Jesus returns, this movement proclaiming his death

---

269. John O'Meara, introduction to Augustine, *City of God*, xiii.
270. Paraphrasing Mark 9:25.
271. Ehrman, *Triumph of Christianity*, 282.

and resurrection would endure. It is indestructible. Its origin is "of God," not "of men."

To be clear, just because a movement endures and even becomes the largest religion in the world does not prove it is true. The handful of other world religions today have also survived from the ancient world and, with all their contradictory claims, they cannot all be true. Either one is true or none of them are. If the latter, then atheism is our tragic and hopeless reality. Yet, if one of these world religions is true, then Christianity's incredible origins, survival, and dominance in the world surely makes it a competitive candidate for the one true religion.

CHRISTIANITY'S UNIQUE ORIGINS

The historical origins of the handful of world religions that survive to this day are also significant here.[272] For example, when Muhammad died in AD 632, he had already conquered many nations and had tens of thousands of followers. It should be no greater surprise to the historian that the Islamic movement endured and continued conquering any more than that Genghis Khan's movement continued conquering after his death. If Genghis Khan had declared his movement as a new religion, had dictated certain scriptures from heaven, it very likely would have survived in some form to this day. Even Joseph Smith, the founder of Mormonism, already had thousands of followers at his death in 1844.[273]

---

272. A world religion by definition has more than 100 million adherents. Under that definition, there are only four world religions: Christianity (2.4 billion), Islam (1.8 billion), Hinduism (1 billion), and Buddhism (500 million).

273. It should also be pointed out that, while Mormonism is still experiencing rapid growth, its supernatural claims and the Book of Mormon itself have been tried and found wanting in the public square of ideas. To illustrate, you will not see on college campuses public debates such as "Do the Mormon gods

In contrast, how many cities and nations had Jesus and his followers conquered before he was crucified? In fact, how many nations did Jesus' followers conquer for the first 280 years after his death in AD 33? Not one. Instead the small tribe of Christians, within the mighty Roman Empire, advanced and converted masses of Greeks, Romans, and barbarians to their cause through the proclamation of Jesus' death and resurrection and lordship over all things, through the humanitarian services they created, through their exaltation of women, children, and the family, through their boldness in the face of martyrdom, and most of all, because they loved like Jesus did.[274] As Tertullian recorded the pagans saying in the third century: " 'See,' they say, 'how they love one another,' see how they are ready even to die for one another" (*Apology* 39).

Additionally, how many followers did Jesus have when he hung on that cross and died? Maybe over a hundred? Possibly as low as twenty, if we include only some of his women followers and possibly some of his twelve disciples.[275] This is assuming they were not enraged at him if after the crucifixion they became convinced he was a false prophet. Jesus' movement should have ended before it began. How did it begin if Jesus stayed dead? It is very difficult to get your movement going when you are dead.

Try it sometime.

Therefore, it is the extraordinary nature of the historical origins of Christianity *and* its continued success and triumph

---

exist?" or "Is the Book of Mormon reliable?" That would be a suicide mission for a Mormon to try to defend!

274. See Stark's *Rise of Christianity* for many powerful examples of this.

275. This is Ehrman's estimate in *Triumph of Christianity*, 294.

throughout the world that separates it from all other religions today.[276]

For these reasons, Christianity is truly unique.

CONTINUING INFLUENCE

Christianity's dominant influence did not end with the Roman Empire, the British Empire, or even with its present decline in Europe and America. The ideas of nobility in suffering, humility as a virtue, human rights, focus on the poor and the outcast, and the equality of all human beings are still taken for granted by billions of people across the world to this day. These ideas do not find their foundation in Hinduism, Buddhism, or Islam, but predominantly in Judaism and Christianity. As historian and agnostic Tom Holland says:

> Today, even as belief in God fades across the West, the countries that were once collectively known as Christendom continue to bear the stamp of the two-millennia-old revolution that Christianity represents. It is the principal reason why, by and large, most of us who live in post-Christian societies still take for granted that it is nobler to suffer than to inflict suffering. It is why we generally assume that every human life is of equal value. In my morals and ethics, I have learned to accept that I am

---

276. I cannot discuss the origins of Hinduism and Buddhism because, as we saw above, the sources are so incredibly late in the case of the life and death of Buddha. Moreover, we do not even know the name of the person who originated the ideas behind Hinduism. It might also be argued that neither of these two religions are actually *world* religions because they have largely remained in the part of the world where they originated. The vast majority of adherents to Hinduism have always lived in India and Buddhists in Asia. Specifically, Hinduism has been around for over three thousand years, yet for whatever reason it has failed to capture the hearts and the imaginations of cultures and nations beyond India.

not Greek or Roman at all, but thoroughly and proudly Christian.[277]

According to Pew Research, Christianity will still be the largest religion in the world in 2050, with Islam a close second. Although atheism and agnosticism are rising in America and Europe, they "will make up a declining share of the world's population."[278]

In spite of growing secularism in the West, the future of the world is religious, and all the evidence suggests that around a third of the world will still be followers of the crucified Nazarene for rest of this century and beyond. In fact, as Tim Keller says regularly, Christians today on average are "non-Western and non-white." Most live in Africa, Latin America, and Asia. In 1900, Christians made up 9 percent of Africa's population. Now Christianity comprises around half of the continent of Africa. This same explosive growth is happening in China. China is on course to have more Christians than any other nation, and we might even see a Chinese Constantine arise one day soon.[279]

According to a 2011 Pew Forum report,

277. Tom Holland, "Why I Was Wrong about Christianity," *New Statesman*, September 14, 2016, https://www.newstatesman.com/politics/religion/2016/09/tom-holland-why-i-was-wrong-about-christianity.

278. Raziye Akkoc, "Mapped: What the World's Religious Landscape Will Look like in 2050," *The Telegraph*, April 8, 2015, http://www.telegraph.co.uk/news/worldnews/11518702/Mapped-What-the-worlds-religious-lanscape-will-look-like-in-2050.html. Currently, Christianity has an estimated 2.4 billion adherents and Islam 1.8 billion. In 2050, Christianity is estimated to have 3 billion and Islam 2.8 billion.

279. Tom Phillips, "China on Course to Become 'World's Most Christian Nation' within 15 Years," *The Telegraph*, April 19, 2014, http://www.telegraph.co.uk/news/worldnews/asia/china/10776023/China-on-course-to-become-worlds-most-Christian-nation-within-15-years.html.

Mainland China has roughly 67 million Christians, representing about 5% of the country's total population. ... The general consensus among scholars of religion in China is that Christianity has grown substantially during the past three decades. It is too soon to know, however, whether Christianity's growth has peaked or will continue in the years ahead. Whichever turns out to be the case, the religious future of the world's most populous country will have a major impact not only on Christianity but on other religious traditions as well.[280]

If the growth of Christianity does remain the same, by 2050 China could have five hundred million Christians! How will a half a billion Chinese Christians change the course of human history? Other, smaller religions in China, such as Taoism and Confucianism, may follow the same path as the gods of Egypt, Greece, and Rome: they may disappear.

It is undeniable that this movement of the Nazarenes is still influencing nations and the world globally, but what about on the individual level? If Jesus rose from the dead and is still alive, it seems reasonable to expect him to be transforming lives throughout history and across the world. The daily experience of billions in our world involve the crucified Nazarene, not only those who are already following him, but also skeptics and even enemies.

---

280. Pew Research Center, "Global Distribution of Christians," December 19, 2011, https://www.pewforum.org/2011/12/19/global-christianity-regions. See also Keller, *Reason for God*, 6.

SKEPTICAL MEN AND WOMEN

The reason Paul's conversion is so powerful and resonates with so many is that he started out as an enemy of Jesus. When we survey conversions to Christianity over the past two thousand years, we find many Pauls: many enemies and skeptics becoming followers of Jesus. For example, A. N. Wilson, a journalist and intellectual atheist, converted to Christianity in the 2000s. The resurrection of Jesus was a key element in his conversion. He wrote:

> The Resurrection, which proclaims that matter and spirit are mysteriously conjoined, is the ultimate key to who we are. It confronts us with an extraordinarily haunting story. J. S. Bach believed the story, and set it to music. Most of the greatest writers and thinkers of the past 1,500 years have believed it. But an even stronger argument is the way that Christian faith transforms individual lives.[281]

In his lecture "On Fairy Stories," Tolkien noted: "There is no tale ever told that men would rather find was true, and none which so many skeptical men have accepted as true on its own merits."[282] Many skeptical men and women have been convinced that Jesus rose from the dead and is Lord of the world, and the cumulative influence of these individual stories has shaped the world.

It is beyond the scope of this book (or any book) to survey all the people throughout the past two thousand years who have been transformed by the risen Jesus. But if I had the time, I would begin with Justin Martyr (*Dialogue with Trypho* 8) and

---

281. A. N. Wilson, "Religion of Hatred: Why We Should No Longer Be Cowed by the Chattering Classes Ruling Britain Who Sneer at Christianity," *Daily Mail*, April 10, 2009, http://www.dailymail.co.uk/news/article-1169145/Religion-hatred-Why-longer-cowed-secular-zealots.html See also https://www.new-statesman.com/religion/2009/04/conversion-experience-atheism.

282. J. R. R. Tolkien, "On Fairy Stories."

Augustine of Hippo (*Confessions* 8.12.29) of the first millennium and finish with C. S. Lewis and biologist Francis Collins at the end of the second millennium, walking through century after century reading the profound testimonies of famous intellectuals who had an experience with the risen Christ.[283] I could even survey some of the thousands of converted Muslims throughout Africa and the Middle East who have in the twenty-first century claimed to have had dreams or visions of the risen Jesus.[284] Some I have myself met and questioned.

I wish I could survey all the art (Leonardo da Vinci's *The Last Supper*, Rembrandt's *Prodigal Son*), literature (Dante's *The Divine Comedy*, John Milton's *Paradise Lost*, John Bunyan's *The Pilgrim's Progress*, Fyodor Dostoyevsky's *The Brothers Karamazov*), philosophy (Augustine, Thomas Aquinas, Francis Bacon, Blaise Pascal, Frederick Copleston), music (Handel's *Messiah*, Bach's *St Matthew Passion*, Johnny Cash), and even films (*The Lord of the Rings*, Mel Gibson's *The Passion of the Christ*,[285] *The Chronicles of Narnia*) that were inspired by Jesus' resurrection and have brought such goodness, truth, and beauty into our dark world.

I wish I could further survey all the testimonies just in our own day, of people claiming the power of the risen Jesus freeing

---

283. See Lewis, *Surprised by Joy*; Collins, *Language of God*. Charles Colson writes: "It all began for me one evening in the home of Tom Phillips, a business colleague. Tom read a passage on pride from Lewis' *Mere Christianity*. Though I didn't let on, it was as if Lewis had written the words just for me. They pierced my heart, exposing my sin. That night, sitting in my car in Tom's driveway, I broke down in a flood of tears" (*We Remember C. S. Lewis*, 27).

284. See Doyle, *Dreams and Visions*, for over twenty personal testimonies. For a powerful individual story, see the testimony of Nabeel Qureshi, who had multiple visions of Jesus in *Seeking Allah, Finding Jesus*.

285. *The Passion of the Christ* is still the highest-grossing (in the United States) R-rated film in history. Jesus owns the R-rated market.

them from sexual addictions, alcohol and drug abuse,[286] occult activity, and depression and suicidal thoughts. For another example of an enemy, Sadhu Sundar Singh (1889–1929) grew up Hindu and even physically attacked Christians. Later he had a plan to kill himself, but then he had a vision of Jesus, and it transformed his life. He became one of the most inspiring missionaries of church history.[287]

It is enough to point out that billions today still *believe* they are experiencing that first-century crucified Nazarene in a number of ways. If Mithraism had taken over the Roman Empire in the fourth century, could it have done the same? Could Mithraism have inspired such art, philosophy, and literature? What about the philosophy of Apollonius of Tyana? What about Bar Kochbianism?

You will have to be the judge.

Let me close this chapter with the testimonies from three more "skeptical" men who had experiences of Jesus in the latter part of the twentieth century: Hugh Montefiore, Anthony Bloom, and Martin Luther King Jr. What makes their testimonies especially interesting is they were highly educated modern men who *believed* they had an encounter with the risen Jesus. They did not claim it was a resurrection appearance on the order of 1 Corinthians 15:5–8, but they were absolutely convinced that the same Jesus who appeared to Peter, the Twelve, James, and Paul appeared and/or spoke to them. They were also, like the earliest followers of Jesus, completely transformed after these experiences.

---

286. For example, see the testimony of Brian "Head" Welch, lead guitarist of the band Korn, http://www.youtube.com/watch?v=Fs7i_ckEHVA.

287. See Singh, *At the Master's Feet*.

Hugh Montefiore was Jewish, and while in college had a radical conversion to Christianity after he had a vision of Jesus. He spent the rest of his life as an Anglican bishop and lecturer of theology at Cambridge. He died in 2005 after having written over twenty books, mainly about Jesus and Christianity.

He recounted his meeting with the risen Christ in his book *The Paranormal: A Bishop Investigates*:

> I was sitting in my study ... when a figure in white approached and said "Follow me." I had no knowledge of Christianity whatsoever. ... It was certainly not caused by stress: I was in good health, a happy schoolboy with good friends, leading an enthusiastic life and keen on sport as well as work. I do not recall any need to suppress erotic fantasies! I am equally sure that it had nothing to do with my memories, for I had no memories about Jesus. Again, I am sure it was not wish fulfillment, for I was (and still am) proud to be Jewish. I am at a loss to know how it could be psychogenic, although I accept that my brain was the channel through which the experience came about. My sensory input at the time was not at a low ebb. I think it unlikely that the collective unconscious, if it manifested itself in a hallucination, would have taken what for me would have been an alien form. I cannot believe that I was in contact with a ghost, for the figure I saw was alive and life giving. I cannot account for my vision of Jesus by any of the psychological or neurophysiological explanations on offer.[288]

Anthony Bloom, also known as Metropolitan Anthony of Sourozh, was a famous monk and bishop of the Russian

---

288. Montefiore, *Paranormal*, 234–35.

Orthodox Church. Before his service to the church he studied at the University of Paris and was part of the French resistance against the Nazis during World War II. He died in 2003 after over forty years of serving the Lord as an Orthodox archbishop.

Bloom believes the risen Christ appeared to him as a teenager. He recounts his experience with the risen Christ this way:

> I do not know how to tell you of what happened. I will put it quite simply and those of you who have gone through a similar experience will know what came to pass. While I was reading the beginning of St. Mark's gospel, before I reached the third chapter, I became aware of a presence. I saw nothing. I heard nothing. It was no hallucination. It was a simple certainty that the Lord was standing there and that I was in the presence of him whose life I had begun to read with such revulsion and such ill-will, this was my basic and essential meeting with the Lord. From then I knew that Christ did exist. I knew that he was *thou*, in other words that he was the Risen Christ. I met with the core of the Christian message, that message which St Paul formulated so sharply and clearly when he said, "If Christ is not risen we are the most miserable of all men." Christ *was* the Risen Christ for me, because if the One Who had died nearly 2000 years before was there alive, he was the *Risen* Christ.[289]

I think for most, at least in America, Martin Luther King Jr. needs no introduction. King was a Baptist minister who was the heroic leader of the civil rights movement in America and he was assassinated in 1968. He did not claim to see the risen

---

289. Metropolitan Anthony of Sourozh, "I Believe in God," https://web.archive.org/web/20041204183831/http://www.metropolit-anthony.orc.ru:80/eng/eng_04.htm.

Christ the way Montefiore and Bloom did, but King believed he heard the voice of the risen Jesus at a most crucial time in his life.

He tells the story in his *Autobiography*. Late one night in January, in the early days of his work on civil rights, he received a phone call from someone who threatened his life and the life of his family. He could not sleep afterwards, he went into the kitchen and about midnight, and began to pray:

> "Lord, I'm down here trying to do what's right. I think I'm right. I am here taking a stand for what I believe is right. But Lord, I must confess that I'm weak now, I'm faltering. I'm losing my courage. Now, I am afraid. And I can't let the people see me like this because if they see me weak and losing my courage, they will begin to get weak. The people are looking to me for leadership, and if I stand before them without strength and courage, they too will falter. I am at the end of my powers. I have nothing left. I've come to the point where I can't face it alone."

> It seemed as though I could hear the quiet assurance of an inner voice saying: "Martin Luther, stand up for righteousness. Stand up for justice. Stand up for truth. And lo, I will be with you. Even until the end of the world."

> I tell you I've seen the lightning flash. I've heard the thunder roar. I've felt sin breakers dashing trying to conquer my soul. But I heard the voice of Jesus saying still to fight on. He promised never to leave me alone. At that moment I experienced the presence of the Divine as I had never experienced Him before. Almost at once my fears began to go. My uncertainty disappeared. I was ready to face anything.[290]

---

290. King, *Autobiography of Martin Luther King Jr*, 76–78.

Incredibly, Martin Luther King Jr. believed he heard "the voice of Jesus," the crucified Nazarene, and was then "ready to face anything." I doubt anyone would say King was lying about this experience, but did he imagine it? Or did he really hear the voice of Jesus of Nazareth?

You will have to be the judge.

What is undeniably true is that after this experience, he went on to become one of the greatest and most influential figures of the twentieth century.

———

Examples could be multiplied to infinity of people who believe the risen Jesus is still transforming their lives today. Despite having the odds stacked against it, the movement of the Nazarenes survived. Rabbi Gamaliel's (or at least the author of Acts) prophecy was proven true. Further, this movement has continued to overwhelmingly influence empires, nations, all of Western civilization, and billions of individuals right up to this present day. Moreover, Pew Research studies say it will continue. People all over the world, from different cultures and backgrounds, skeptics and even enemies, say they have experienced the risen Jesus and were utterly transformed from that moment forward.

This is the final bedrock fact of this book, and it is irrefutable.

Now we have to ask one more question in light of all the bedrock facts we have discussed. It is arguably the most important question of human history: Did this crucified man Jesus rise from the dead?

Conclusion

"This Is Wondrous Strange"

Why should any of you consider it incredible that God raises the dead?

Acts 26:8 NIV

The most incredible thing about miracles is that they happen.

G. K. Chesterton, "The Blue Cross"

The apostles were either deceived or deceivers if Jesus didn't really rise. Either supposition has difficulties. ... While Jesus was with them he could sustain them, but afterwards, if he did not appear to them, who did make them act?

Blaise Pascal, *Pensées*

Proposing that Jesus of Nazareth was raised from the dead was just as controversial nineteen hundred years ago as it is today. The discovery that dead people stayed dead was not first made by the philosophers of the Enlightenment.

N. T. Wright, *The Resurrection of the Son of God*

Before a live audience, philosopher and atheist Sam Harris and his fellow panelists were asked by a questioner, if they had the DeLorean from the film *Back to the Future* and could time travel anywhere in the past (or future), "When would you go and why?" After a brief discussion on time traveling and people in history they would most like to visit, Rebecca Goldstein said: "I would love to go back and see who Jesus was and what the deal was." Harris also said he wanted to meet Jesus and added: "Strangely, Jesus is on the list, a very short list because of the mysterious sway he has over so much of humanity."[291]

Even after two thousand years, why does Jesus of Nazareth possess such a "mysterious sway" over humanity? In light of all the bedrock facts we have examined in this book, facts that both believing and nonbelieving scholars agree on, let me propose an answer: the historical Jesus rose from the dead. He is still alive and to this day, as Philip Schaff puts it, "rules a spiritual empire which embraces one-third of the inhabitants of the globe."[292]

I believe this is the best way to make sense of the bedrock facts, especially the fact discussed in the previous chapter. If Jesus did in fact rise from the dead, if he is Lord of the world, as the earliest Christians claimed, then we would expect him to have the overwhelming influence, "the mysterious sway" he does in fact have over humanity. We would expect leading atheists such as Sam Harris to wonder about him two thousand years later, just as the leading nonbelieving intellectuals of every century before us have wondered about and had to deal with the person and claims of Jesus of Nazareth.

HORATIO, AS A STRANGER
GIVE IT WELCOME

I chose as the epigraph to this book Hamlet's famous words to his friend Horatio: "There are more things in heaven and earth,

---

291. Waking Up with Sam Harris: "What Is and What Matters: A Conversation with Rebecca Goldstein and Max Tegmark," YouTube, https://www.youtube.com/watch?v=cypm7hkJ2lQ.

292. Schaff, *Person of Christ*, 29.

Horatio, than are dreamt of in your philosophy."[293] Every time I read this quote from Shakespeare's *Hamlet*, I am deeply moved. I love it because Hamlet is telling his Wittenberg-educated, skeptical friend Horatio: Expect the unexpected. Welcome the strange and extraordinary. It is indeed wondrous strange that Hamlet's father's ghost is appearing to people, but do not reject it for that reason alone. Your philosophy should be open and wide enough for the supernatural. Horatio, more things are happening in our wonderful world and beyond than you can imagine.

Reader, I leave you with this challenge. Do not reject Jesus' resurrection only because it is wondrous strange, outside your expectations and experience. Instead, as a stranger give it welcome. If your philosophy is not wide and open enough to include the miraculous, then you need a new philosophy.

Open your eyes and your heart.

DIVINE INTERVENTION

A modern-day example of this Hamlet-and-Horatio discussion of the supernatural is found in the film *Pulp Fiction*. Jules (Samuel L. Jackson) and Vincent (John Travolta) are hired hitmen who visit a group of men in an apartment early one morning. After killing all of them except the one that their boss Marsellus Wallace wanted alive, a man bursts out of the bathroom and unloads his .357 Magnum on Jules and Vincent. Every single bullet misses them, even though they are at close range. Jules and Vincent then shoot him.

They are both severely rattled after surviving this extraordinary event, but Vincent dismisses it as "luck." Jules, however, is not so sure:

---

293. Shakespeare, *Hamlet*, act 1, scene 5.

Jules: That was divine intervention. You know what divine intervention is?

Vincent: Yeah, I think so. That means God came down from Heaven and stopped the bullets.

Jules: Yeah, man, that's what it means. That's exactly what it means! God came down from Heaven and stopped the bullets.

Vincent: I think we should be going now.

Jules: Don't do that! Don't you do that! Don't blow this off! What just happened was a miracle!

Vincent: Chill out, Jules, this happens.

Jules: Wrong, wrong, this doesn't just happen.

Vincent: Do you want to continue this theological discussion in the car, or at the jailhouse with the cops?

Jules: We should be dead now, my friend! We just witnessed a miracle, and I want you to acknowledge it!

Vincent: Okay man, it was a miracle, can we leave now?

While they are driving, Vincent offers a naturalistic explanation by comparing what happened to them to another "freak occurrence" he had seen on a television show. Jules responds: "If you want to play blind man, then go walk with a shepherd. But me, my eyes are wide open."[294]

---

294. *Pulp Fiction*, screenplay by Quentin Tarantino and Roger Avary, http://www.dailyscript.com/scripts/pulp_fiction.html. The expletives in this discussion have been removed because I think they would distract from the main point.

As a result of Jules's decision to retire from being a hitman, he survives an event later in the film, but the skeptic Vincent is killed.

Jules's eyes are wide open. So are Hamlet's. I would argue so are Mary's and Peter's, the Twelve's, James' and Paul's.

Are your eyes open to the supernatural, like Hamlet and Jules, or are you like Vincent, always dismissing something unusual as a "freak occurrence," no matter how compelling the evidence is?

PHILOSOPHICAL PRESUPPOSITIONS

No matter how convincing the bedrock facts about Jesus' death and resurrection are, many will still not believe, because whether or not one believes in the supernatural largely depends on one's presuppositions about heaven and earth. As C. S. Lewis says: "If anything extraordinary seems to have happened, we can always say that we have been the victims of an illusion. If we hold a philosophy which excludes the supernatural, this is what we always shall say."[295]

Bart Ehrman represents many who are faced with the facts and claim that, at least as a historian, it is impossible to demonstrate a miracle happened in the past. He argues: "Historians can only establish what probably happened in the past, and by definition, miracles are the least probable occurrences."[296] Elsewhere he writes that "any other scenario—no matter how unlikely—is more likely than the one in which a great miracle occurred, since the miracle defies all probability (or else we wouldn't call it a miracle)."[297] If anyone emphatically maintains that, as a historian, they can never discover a miracle in history,

---

295. Lewis, *Miracles*, 9.
296. Ehrman, *Jesus, Interrupted*, 179.
297. Ehrman, *How Jesus Became God*, 173.

then let them take a day off as an historian. Surely even historians can believe in the supernatural on their off hours.

Ehrman is correct, though, that miracles defy all probability. They are rare indeed. Even if all the miracles that have been
recorded in history were true, they are still rare. But what if sta-
tistical probability is not the only factor in deciding whether a
miracle has happened in history?

As Lewis further explains:

> If ... miracles are not intrinsically improbable, then the
> existing evidence will be sufficient to convince us that
> quite a number of miracles have occurred. The result of
> our historical enquiries thus depends on the philosoph-
> ical views which we have been holding before we even
> began to look at the evidence. The philosophical question
> must therefore come first.[298]

We should, in other words, be aware of our philosophical
presuppositions and commit to following the evidence wherever it might lead, even to places that might burst through our
presuppositions and current worldview. If all the historical evidence leads to the miraculous and all naturalistic explanations
not only fail but are absurd, then we should "as a stranger" give
the miracle welcome.

James Dunn, a critical New Testament scholar, compares
the resurrection of Jesus with another extraordinary historical
event, the creation of the universe:

> The most obvious strong parallel is creation. As belief
> that the cosmos is created determines how one perceives
> the cosmos and the place of the human species within

---

298. Lewis, *Miracles*, 10.

it, so belief in the resurrection of Jesus determines how one perceives the significance of Jesus and the function of life and death. In short, the resurrection of Jesus is not so much a historical fact as a foundational fact or meta-fact, the interpretative insight into reality which enables discernment of the relative importance and unimportance of all other facts.[299]

The resurrection of Jesus is a "meta-fact."
The resurrection of Jesus is more than a fact of history; it is a meta-fact, a foundational fact. As N. T. Wright says, "Studying Jesus … might lead to a reappraisal of the theory of knowledge itself."[300]

Jesus' resurrection enlightens history, explains reality, and illuminates knowledge.

To improve on Descartes:

Jesus died and rose again; therefore, I am.

HISTORICAL MIRACLES

Historians who will not allow the unexpected and miraculous into their data could be missing 'what really happened' in history. As historian Ben Meyer succinctly puts it, the historian who is committed to interpreting the past in a way that ignores miracles "accordingly finds himself in a situation which does not allow him, as a historian, to come to grips with history, for he cannot know whether or not the possibility he dutifully omits to consider offers the best account of a given constellation of

---

299. Dunn, *Jesus Remembered*, 878.
300. Wright, *New Testament and the People of God*, 96.

data."[301] Historians in this field whose philosophies can include the extraordinary and the miraculous are better guides here.

When undertaken with presuppositions that allow for the unexpected, the historical sciences, far from being a hindrance to discovering miracles in history, can undergird, support, and even bolster the case for a miraculous claim. This is exactly the case with the historical events concerning the resurrection of Jesus. And at least on the bedrock facts, Ehrman agrees:

> As an agnostic, I personally do not believe Jesus was raised from the dead and so I do not believe he "appeared" to anyone. But what I have to say about the disciples' visions are things I could have said just as easily back in the days when I was a firm believer. Many discussions of the resurrection are focused on just this question of whether the visions were veridical or not. ... I do not think it would be a historical sin at all to leave the matter of external stimuli—were the visions veridical or not— undecided, so that believers and unbelievers can reach common ground on the *significance* of these experiences.[302]

Therefore, the scientific tools of the historical method have led us to the common-ground agreement that Jesus died on a cross, and soon after his followers, individuals and groups, claimed he appeared to them alive, raised from the dead. Furthermore, those individuals formed a movement that over-took the Roman Empire and became the most influential reli-gious movement the world has ever seen. At the bare minimum, then, we can say that these historical facts do not *contradict* the resurrection.

---

301. Meyer, *Aims of Jesus*, 102.
302. Ehrman, *How Jesus Became God*, 187–88.

Can the historian go further? I believe he can.

These bedrock facts weigh strongly *in favor* of Jesus' resurrection. They undergird, support, and bolster the case the earliest apostles made two thousand years ago:

"He was raised on the third day" (1 Cor 15:4).

Critical historians such as James Dunn, Dale Allison, Raymond Brown, and Wolfhart Pannenberg, just to name a few, agree, as they all accept the resurrection of Jesus as a historical event.[303]

Pannenberg summarizes this view well:

> As long as historiography does not begin dogmatically with a narrow concept of reality according to which "dead men do not rise," it is not clear why historiography should not in principle be able to speak about Jesus' resurrection as the explanation that is best established of such events as the disciples' experiences of the appearances and the discovery of the empty tomb. If, however, historical study declares itself unable to establish what "really" happened on Easter, then all the more, faith is not able to do so; for faith cannot ascertain anything certain about events of the past that would perhaps be inaccessible to the historian.[304]

The resurrection of Jesus is the best explanation of the facts. It is a foundational fact, a meta-fact.

---

303. The late Pinchas Lapide, a Jewish professor who taught at Hebrew University, actually argued that Jesus bodily rose from the dead in *Resurrection of Jesus*. Yet, strangely, Lapide never converted to Christianity.

304. Pannenberg, *Jesus: God and Man*, 109; see also 97–98.

Let us then remind ourselves of the bedrock facts that bolster the "grandest fact of all history,"[305] as Charles Spurgeon referred to it, before we conclude.

THE BEDROCK FACTS

After studying the historical Jesus for decades, Joachim Jeremias said: "If we apply the critical resources at our disposal to the study of the historical Jesus with utmost discipline and conscientiousness, the final result is always the same: we find ourselves confronted with God."[306] This is also true concerning Jesus' resurrection. If we apply the critical resources at our disposal to the study of the historical events surrounding Jesus' death and the extraordinary events that followed, the final result is always the same: we find ourselves confronted with the risen Christ.

The bedrock facts laid out in this book are these:

- Jesus' death by crucifixion in the early 30s AD

- The claim that Jesus was raised from the dead is an unparalleled, threefold innovation:

  1. A positive interpretation of a crucified Messiah

  2. A two-stage resurrection, Jesus raised now and the general resurrection still to come

  3. This crucified Messiah is claimed to be divine, even Lord of the world

- Soon after Jesus' death, his earliest followers, individuals and a group of them, and at least one enemy

---

305. Charles Spurgeon, "John's First Doxology," sermon no. 1737.
306. Jeremias, *Jesus and the Message of the New Testament*, 12.

became convinced he appeared to them alive, raised from the dead

- These individuals included Peter, James, Paul and at least one group, the Twelve

- Paul was a Pharisaic persecutor of the church who was transformed into Paul the apostle after becoming convinced Jesus appeared to him

- Paul spent two weeks as Peter's houseguest and also met with James, Jesus' brother

- Within a decade of Jesus' death, either after Paul's conversion or at this meeting with Peter and James in Jerusalem, Paul received traditions and hymns concerning the historical Jesus. The most significant of these was the creedal tradition quoted in 1 Corinthians 15:3–7, which could be multiple independent traditions, but even so they all date to within a decade of Jesus' death

- Last, these individuals who believed Jesus appeared to him formed a movement that, through love and sacrifice, went on to overtake the Roman Empire, built Western civilization, and continues to extend overwhelming influence over nations and billions of individuals across the world. This movement known as Christianity is still the largest religion in the world

I am absolutely convinced the best explanation of these bedrock facts is that Jesus did in fact rise from the dead and began appearing to his followers with "many convincing proofs" (Acts 1:3) that he was alive and Lord of the world.

THOUGHT EXPERIMENTS

To help you consider what to do with the bedrock facts presented in this book, I would like to present you with some thought experiments.

- If you knew God had performed *one* miracle in history, which of all the claims to the miraculous would you consider the most likely?

- If you do not already, assume for a moment that Jesus did *not* rise from the dead in the early 30s AD. Instead, he stayed dead, rotted, and dissolved into dust. All the bedrock facts we have discussed above, Jesus' resurrection appearances, the resulting worldwide movement, billions of lives transformed, would then all be due to one or multiple naturalistic explanations.

- Assuming that, now ask yourself, what if Jesus really *did* rise from the dead? How would our world look different than it does now? Would there have been more resurrection appearances, to more individuals and groups, than are already on record? Would his movement have not just overtaken the Roman Empire in the fourth century, but also China? Would there be, instead of 2.4 billion professing followers of Jesus today, 4 billion? Six billion? Would more books have been written, more paintings painted, songs composed, lives transformed?

As Theodore Parker wrote, "Measure Jesus by the shadow he has cast into the world; no, by the light he has shed upon it."[307]

The reason I am convinced Jesus rose from the dead in the early 30s AD is not only the bedrock facts undergirding it that we have discussed in this book, nor is it merely the dominant influence he and his movement has had and still has on the world. It is also the extraordinary Person who is claimed to have been resurrected. As Tim Keller says, "Why did Jesus succeed as the only person who ever claimed deity and also founded a major—indeed, the largest—movement and religious faith? The first answer is that his life must have been exquisitely beautiful."[308]

Jesus of Nazareth's teachings, the stories he told, his actions and deeds, his humility, and most of all his love for the leper, the outcast, "sinners," even for his enemies, still melt our hearts. At the end of the Sermon on the Mount, we are told that the crowds were amazed at him (Matt 7:28).

Two thousand years later, billions are still amazed.

The claim that an ordinary person has been raised from the dead is not that compelling. The claim that the most extraordinary, most influential, the most beautiful and compassionate human being who ever walked the face of the earth rose from the dead is something to look into.

This is what I hope to have accomplished in this book. We have together gone on a journey through history and looked into it. We have unearthed the bedrock facts and sources surrounding Jesus' death and the extraordinary events that followed. As a result, I am concluding my historical investigation agreeing with the earliest Christian testimony: "He was raised on the third day" (1 Cor 15:4).

---

307. Parker, *Discourse of Matters*, 330.
308. Keller, *Making Sense of God*, 241–42.

What *more* would Jesus have accomplished in our world if he had actually risen from the dead?

THE GREATEST OF MIRACLES

It is because of the bedrock facts but also for reasons such as the thought experiments above that I think, at least in the case of the miracle of the resurrection of Jesus, it passes even philosopher and skeptic David Hume's (by his own admission almost impossible) bar for accepting a miracle. Hume wrote in his famous essay *Of Miracles*: "That no testimony is sufficient to establish a miracle, unless the testimony be of such a kind, that its falsehood would be more miraculous, than the fact, which it endeavors to establish."[309]

If Jesus remained dead, in light of the bedrock facts and the overwhelming impact he and his movement have had on history, his staying dead would be *more* miraculous than his resurrection.

Early church father St. John Chrysostom anticipated and answered this argument from Hume thirteen hundred years earlier: "For if Jesus did not rise again, but remains dead, how did the Apostles perform miracles in His name? But you say they did not perform miracles. How then was our religion founded? … For this would be the greatest of miracles, that without any miracles, the whole world should have eagerly come to be taken in the nets of twelve poor and illiterate men."[310]

For this would be the greatest of miracles.

If Jesus stayed dead, then no miracles launched the movement of the Nazarenes, turned the Roman Empire and then the world upside down. That would be a greater miracle indeed!

---

309. Hume, *Of Miracles*, 112.

310. John Chrysostom, *Homily* on Acts 1:1–2. Interestingly, Augustine makes the same argument in *City of God* 22.5. Augustine wrote after John, so he may have gotten this from him, or possibly they made the same argument independently.

Let us think this through.

If Jesus stayed dead, then you must admit, Horatio, that someone among the sad, hiding disciples of Jesus on Good Friday evening or soon after originated the threefold innovation involved in Jesus rising from the dead. This person would have been completely deceived in thinking Jesus appeared to them. This person created Christianity. It all began in his or her mind.

Was it Peter? Was it Mary? Was it James? Who was it?

Christianity, the most influential religious movement in the history of the world, would then be, as Gerd Lüdemann says, "a worldwide hoax."[311] It would be no doubt the greatest deception and hoax the world has ever seen.

Jesus stayed dead, and his indestructible movement, his "mysterious sway" over so much of humanity and "light he has shed" over literature, art, music, morals, ethics, all find their origins in the mind of a weeping fisherman.

I find that *more* miraculous than that Jesus actually rose from the dead.

I am convinced Hume's criteria has been satisfied. A miracle, therefore, has occurred.

FINAL QUESTIONS

Reader, there is undeniably a resurrection-sized hole in history. As New Testament scholar C. F. D. Moule forcefully wrote: "If the coming into existence of the Nazarenes, a phenomenon undeniably attested by the New Testament, rips a great hole in history, a hole the size and shape of the Resurrection, what does the secular historian propose to stop it up with?"[312]

---

311. Lüdemann, *Resurrection of Christ*, 190.

312. Moule, *Phenomenon of the New Testament*, 3; see also 12–13.

If Jesus stayed dead, if he did not rise from the dead, then what do you propose to stop it up with?

If Jesus did not appear to them, "who did make them act?"

The challenge for the historian is either to accept what the earliest followers of Jesus claimed, that God raised Jesus from the dead, or come up with a better explanation for why Christianity began, made the claims it did, and went on to conquer the world.

As I have read virtually every alternative historical explanation to Jesus rising from the dead, I find them all, in light of the bedrock facts, absolutely absurd.

However, there is one view I do have respect for. It is the cautious agnostic approach mentioned in chapter 6. This is best represented in what E. P. Sanders says at the end of his discussion of all the historical facts surrounding the death of Jesus and appearances to his earliest followers: "That Jesus' followers (and later Paul) had resurrection experiences is, in my judgement, a fact. What the reality was that gave rise to the experiences I do not know."[313]

"I do not know." Fair enough.

I will, though, challenge this approach the way Jules challenged Vincent: "Don't do that! Don't you do that! Don't blow this off! What just happened was a miracle! We just witnessed a miracle, and I want you to acknowledge it!"

The earliest followers of Jesus, against all odds, believed Jesus rose from the dead and appeared to them. And at least three of them, Peter, Paul, and James, we know gave their lives for this belief.

As I quoted Tolkien and Wilson as saying above, so many skeptical men and women have believed: "Most of the greatest writers and thinkers of the past 1,500 years have believed it."

---

313. Sanders, *Historical Figure of Jesus*, 279–80.

Do not stop at agnosticism.

This is indeed wondrous strange! Open your eyes and the eyes of your heart.

As a stranger, give the risen Jesus welcome.

Epilogue: New Creation

*If Jesus Christ was really raised from the dead—if he is really
the Son of God and you believe in him—all these things that
you long for most desperately will come true at last. We will
escape time and death. We will know love without parting, we
will even communicate with non-human beings (think angels),
and we will see evil defeated forever. In fairy stories, especially the best and most well-told ones, we get a temporary
emotional reprieve from a "real world" in which our deepest
desires are all violently rebuffed. But if we believe the Gospel,
we are assured that all those longings will be fulfilled in real
time, space, and history.*

Tim Keller, *Making Sense of God*

In the introduction, I quoted C. S. Lewis explaining why
Christianity is the True Myth. It seems only fitting to end this
book considering some of the glorious implications, for us and
our world, if Jesus really did rise from the dead, if this is indeed
the one True Myth.

The earliest followers of Jesus did not just claim that Jesus
rose from the dead, but that his resurrection was the inaugu-
ration of God's new creation right in the middle of history:
"Therefore, if anyone is in Christ, he is a new creature; the old
things passed away; behold, new things have come!" (2 Cor 5:17).

The resurrection of Jesus has proven that God has not abandoned his good creation but has already redeemed part of it in

Jesus of Nazareth. This is indeed proof that he will redeem the whole cosmos one day (see Rom 8:18–25). As Dale Allison writes:

> Yet another reason that I should like to believe in the non-metaphorical resurrection of Jesus is that this makes a compelling statement for the goodness of creation. ... To transfigure a crucified corpse is another way of saying, with Gen 1, that the material world, despite all the evil we see in it, is nonetheless good. God does not abandon matter but redeems it. ... [The resurrection] says that, despite the ills and sins flesh is heir to, despite the burden our arthritic bones become as we progress into old age, Gen 1 has it right, so much so that the creator of matter must be the redeemer of matter.[314]

What so many in our world long for and dream of, perfect justice, the end of all sin, war, and death, the redemption of the entire cosmos, will come true if Jesus rose from the dead.

In addition, it speaks to our individual, bodily resurrection still to come. This was in fact Paul's primary argument in quoting in the creedal tradition in 1 Corinthians 15. Because Jesus has been raised, so shall all his followers when he returns (1 Cor 15:20–23). As he wrote elsewhere, in Romans: "But if the Spirit of Him who raised Jesus from the dead dwells in you, He who raised Christ Jesus from the dead will also give life to your mortal bodies through His Spirit who dwells in you" (Rom 8:11). Or again in Philippians: "For our citizenship is in heaven, from which also we eagerly wait for a Savior, the Lord Jesus Christ;

---

314. Allison, *Resurrecting Jesus*, 216–17. N. T. Wright says, "The resurrection, in the full Jewish and early Christian sense, is the ultimate affirmation that creation matters, that embodied human beings matter" (*Resurrection of the Son of God*, 730). See also Dunn, *Jesus Remembered*, 879.

who will transform the body of our humble state into conformity with the body of His glory" (Phil 3:20–21).

The hope of resurrection, or at least some kind of continued existence after death, seems to be a universal longing of human beings today and throughout history. We can still see how the imagination and hearts of so many are inspired by Jesus' death and resurrection in literature and film, such as Shakespeare's Hermione from *The Winter's Tale*, Tolkien's Gandalf, Lewis's Aslan, the Wachowskis' Neo, Bryan Singer's Superman, and even J. K. Rowling's Harry Potter.[315]

Whether we are looking at the worship of the gods and mythological heroes in the ancient world or the quasi-worship of superheroes in films and stories in our present day, there seems to have always been this universal longing for a Savior. Someone who would rescue us from our ultimate enemy: death. Gilgamesh went on an epic quest to conquer death and achieve immortality in humanity's most ancient story in literature. He discovered, as Shakespeare says through Hamlet, that death is "the undiscovered country from whose bourn no traveler returns."[316]

If in the case of Jesus, we do have a "traveler" who has returned, and not just returned but conquered death for us all, then all the hopes and dreams of humanity, beginning with Gilgamesh, would be fulfilled in Christ.

This is how *you* fit in to the story of Jesus. Do you want this to be true?

---

315. See Rowling's discussion of the Christian allegory in the final book: Elena Garcia, "Harry Potter Author Reveals Books' Christian Allegory, Her Struggling Faith," Christian Today, https://www.christiantoday.com/article/harry.potter.author.reveals.books.christian.allegory.her.struggling.faith/14052.htm.

316. Shakespeare, *Hamlet*, act 3, scene 1.

Philosopher and atheist Luc Ferry wrote an excellent book, *A Brief History of Thought*, surveying the history of ideas. He broke it into three stages: Greek philosophy, Christianity, and the more modern secular humanism. Even though Ferry aligns with an atheistic secular humanism, he admits in his discussion of Christianity that its promises are unsurpassed in the history of thought.

He wishes it were true.

He concludes his discussion of Christianity by saying:

If the promises made to me by Christ are genuine; and if divine providence takes me in hand as an individual, however humble, then my immortality will also, in turn, be personal. In which case, death itself is finally overcome, and not merely the fears it arouses in me. ... I find the Christian proposition infinitely more tempting—except for the fact that I do not believe in it. But were it to be true I would certainly be a taker.[317]

If it were true, *I would certainly be a taker*.

The conclusion of the historical investigation in this book argues: it is true![318] "This Jesus God raised up again, to which we are all witnesses" (Acts 2:32). Give the risen Jesus welcome.

———

I close with some immortal words from one of the greatest of these "skeptical men," who was an atheist who became convinced Jesus rose from the dead, G. K. Chesterton.

---

317. Ferry, *Brief History of Thought*, 90, 263.

318. I even emailed Ferry after reading this to tell him the glorious news that it is true! Alas, he never responded.

If [Christianity] were an error, it seems as if the error could hardly have lasted a day. If it were a mere ecstasy, it would seem that such an ecstasy could not endure for an hour. It has endured for nearly two thousand years; and the world within it has been more lucid, more level-headed, more reasonable in its hopes, more healthy in its instincts, more humorous and cheerful in the face of fate and death, than all the world outside. For it was the soul of Christendom that came forth from the incredible Christ; and the soul of it was common sense.[319]

Earlier in the same book, he wrote:

On the third day the friends of Christ coming at day-break to the place found the grave empty and the stone rolled away. In varying ways they realized a new wonder; but even they hardly realized that the world had died in the night. What they were looking at was the first day of a new creation, with a new heaven and a new earth; and in appearance as a gardener God walked again in the garden, in the cool not of the evening but the dawn.[320]

319. Chesterton, *Everlasting Man*, 270.
320. Chesterton, *Everlasting Man*, 213.

Bibliography

Abanes, R. *One Nation under the Gods: A History of the Mormon Church*. New York: Basic Books, 2003.

Abegg Jr., M., P. Flint, and E. Ulrich. *The Dead Sea Scrolls Bible: The Oldest Known Bible Translated for the First Time into English*. New York: HarperOne, 1999.

Allison, Dale C. *Resurrecting Jesus: The Earliest Christian Tradition and Its Interpreters*. New York: T&T Clark, 2005.

———. "The Resurrection of Jesus and Rational Apologetics." *Philosophia Christi* 10.2 (2008): 315–35.

Apollonius. *Apollonius of Tyana*. Vol. 1, *Life of Apollonius of Tyana, Books 1–4*. Edited and translated by Christopher P. Jones. LCL 16. Cambridge, MA: Harvard University Press, 2005.

Arndt, W., F. W. Danker, W. Bauer, and F. W. Gingrich. *A Greek-English Lexicon of the New Testament and Other Early Christian Literature*. Chicago: University of Chicago Press, 2000.

Augustine of Hippo. *Concerning the City of God against the Pagans*. Translated by Henry Bettenson. London: Penguin, 1984.

———. *Expositions on the Book of Psalms*. Edited by P. Schaff. Translated by A. C. Coxe. *NPNF* 8. New York: Christian Literature, 1888.

Barclay, William. *The Acts of the Apostles*. 3rd rev. ed. The New Daily Study Bible. Louisville, KY: Westminster John Knox, 2003.

Barth, K. *The Resurrection of the Dead*. London: Hodder & Stoughton, 1933.

Bengel, J. A. *Gnomon of the New Testament*. Vol. 3. Edited by M. E. Bengel and J. C. F. Steudel. Translated by J. Bryce. Edinburgh: T&T Clark, 1860.

Ben-Sasson, H. H. *A History of the Jewish People*. Cambridge, MA: Harvard University Press, 1976.

Best, Ernest. *Second Corinthians*. Atlanta: John Knox, 1987.

Betz, Hans Dieter. *Galatians: A Commentary on Paul's Letter to the Churches in Galatia*. Hermeneia. Philadelphia: Fortress, 1979.

Bishop, E. F. F. "The Risen Christ and the Five Hundred Brethren (1 Cor. 15:6)." *CBQ* 18 (1956): 341–44.

Bock, Darrell L. *Blasphemy and Exaltation in Judaism and the Final Examination of Jesus*. WUNT 2/106. Tübingen: Mohr Siebeck, 1998.

———. *Who is Jesus? Linking the Historical Jesus with the Christ of Faith*. New York: Howard Books, 2012.

Bockmuehl, Markus, ed. *The Cambridge Companion to Jesus*. Cambridge: Cambridge University Press, 2001.

Bornkamm, G. *Jesus of Nazareth*. London: Hodder & Stoughton, 1960.

Bousset, W. *Kyrios Christos*. Nashville: Abingdon, 1970.

Bovon, François, and Helmut Koester. *A Commentary on the Gospel of Luke 1:1–9:50*. Hermeneia. Minneapolis: Fortress, 2002.

Bowersock, G. W. *Roman Arabia*. Cambridge, MA: Harvard University Press, 1983.

Brown, Raymond E. *The Death of the Messiah*. Vol. 2. New York: Yale University Press, 1994.

———. *An Introduction to the New Testament*. New York: Doubleday, 1997.

———. *The Virginal Conception and Bodily Resurrection of Jesus.* New York: Paulist Press, 1973.

Brown, Raymond E., Karl P. Donfried, and John Reumann, eds. *Peter in the New Testament: A Collaborative Assessment by Protestant and Roman Catholic Scholars.* New York: Geoffrey Chapman, 1973.

Bruce, F. F. *The Epistle to the Galatians: A Commentary on the Greek Text.* NIGTC. Grand Rapids: Eerdmans, 1982.

———. *Paul: Apostle of the Heart Set Free.* Grand Rapids: Eerdmans, 2000.

Bultmann, Rudolf. *Jesus and the Word.* New York: Scribner, 1958.

———. *Theology of the New Testament.* Vol. 1. Translated by K. Grobel. Waco, TX: Baylor University Press, 2007.

Burridge, Richard, and Graham Gould. *Jesus Now and Then.* Grand Rapids: Eerdmans, 2004.

Caird, G. B., and D. E. Jenkins. *Jesus and God.* Manchester: Faith Press, 1965.

Calvin, John. *Commentaries on the Epistles of Paul the Apostle to the Corinthians.* Edinburgh: Oliver & Boyd and St. Andrew, 1960.

Campbell, Douglas A. "An Anchor for Pauline Chronology: Paul's Flight from 'the Ethnarch of King Aretas' (2 Corinthians 11:32–33)." *JBL* 121 (2002): 279–302.

Campenhausen, Hans von. "The Events of Easter and the Empty Tomb." Pages 42–54 in *Tradition and Life in the Church.* Translated by A. V. Littledale. Philadelphia: Fortress, 1968.

Carrier, Richard. *On the Historicity of Jesus: Why We May Have Reason for Doubt.* Sheffield: Sheffield Academic Press, 2014.

Carson, D. A., and Douglas J. Moo. *Introduction to the New Testament.* Grand Rapids: Zondervan, 2005.

Catchpole, David. *Resurrection People: Studies in the Resurrection Narratives of the Gospels.* Macon, GA: Smyth and Helwys, 2002.

Chesterton, G. K. "The Blue Cross." Pages 17-32 in *The Complete Father Brown Stories*. Hertfordshire, UK: Wordsworth, 1992.

———. *The Everlasting Man*. San Francisco: Ignatius, 2008.

Collins, Francis. *The Language of God: A Scientist Presents Evidence for Belief*. New York: Free Press, 2006.

Colson, Charles. *We Remember C. S. Lewis: Essays & Memoirs*. Nashville: Broadman and Holman, 2001.

Conzelmann, Hans. *1 Corinthians: A Commentary on the First Epistle to the Corinthians*. Hermeneia. Philadelphia: Fortress, 1975.

———. "On the Analysis of the Confessional Formula in I Corinthians 15:3-5." *Union Seminary Magazine* 20 (January 1966): 15-25.

Copleston, Frederick. *History of Philosophy*. Vol. 1, *Greece and Rome*. Westminster, MD: Newman, 1959.

Craig, William Lane. *Assessing the New Testament Evidence for the Historicity of the Resurrection of Jesus*. Lewiston, NY: Mellen, 1989.

———. *The Only Wise God: The Compatibility of Divine Foreknowledge and Human Freedom*. Eugene, OR: Wipf & Stock, 1999.

———. *The Son Rises: The Historical Evidence for the Resurrection of Jesus*. Eugene, OR: Wipf & Stock, 2001.

Crossan, John Dominic. *Jesus: A Revolutionary Biography*. San Francisco: HarperSanFrancisco, 1994.

Cullmann, Oscar. *Peter: Disciple, Apostle, Martyr*. London: SCM, 1962.

Deissmann, Adolf. *St. Paul: A Study in Social and Religious History*. New York: Hodder and Stoughton, 1912.

Dibelius, Martin. *From Tradition to Gospel*. New York: Scribner, 1958.

Diodorus Siculus. *The Library of Diodorus Siculus, Fragments of Book XXVI*. Translated by F. R. Walton. LCL 11. Cambridge, MA: Harvard University Press, 1957.

Dodd, C. H. *The Apostolic Preaching and Its Developments*. London: Hodder and Stoughton, 1936.

———. "The Appearances of the Risen Christ: A Study in Form-Criticism of the Gospels." Pages 102–33 in *More New Testament Studies*. Manchester: Manchester University Press, 1968.

———. *The Founder of Christianity*. London: Collins, 1971.

Doyle, Tom. *Dreams and Visions: Is Jesus Awakening the Muslim World?* Nashville: Thomas Nelson, 2012.

Dunn, James D. G. *Christology in the Making*. London: SCM, 1989.

———. *The Epistle to the Galatians*. Black's New Testament Commentary. London: Continuum, 1993.

———. *Jesus and the Spirit*. London: SCM, 1975.

———. *Jesus Remembered*. Christianity in the Making 1. Grand Rapids: Eerdmans, 2003.

———. *The Theology of Paul the Apostle*. Grand Rapids: Eerdmans, 1998.

Ehrman, Bart D. *Jesus: Apocalyptic Prophet of the New Millennium*. Oxford: Oxford University Press, 1999.

———. *Did Jesus Exist? The Historical Argument for Jesus of Nazareth*. New York: HarperOne, 2013.

———. *Forged: Writing in the Name of God—Why the Bible's Authors Are Not Who We Think They Are*. New York: HarperCollins, 2011.

———. *How Jesus Became God: The Exaltation of a Jewish Preacher from Galilee*. New York: HarperOne, 2014.

———. *Jesus, Interrupted: Revealing the Hidden Contradictions in the Bible (and Why We Don't Know about Them)*. New York: HarperOne, 2010.

———. *The New Testament: A Historical Introduction to the Early Christian Writings*. 5th ed. New York: Oxford University Press, 2012.

———. *The Triumph of Christianity*. New York: Simon & Schuster, 2017.

Elliott, J. K. *The Apocryphal New Testament: A Collection of Apocryphal Christian Literature in an English Translation Based on M. R. James*. New York: Oxford University Press, 1993.

Evans, Christopher F. *Resurrection and the New Testament*. London: SCM, 1970.

Fee, Gordon D. *The First Epistle to the Corinthians*. Rev. ed. New International Commentary on the New Testament. Grand Rapids: Eerdmans, 2014.

Ferry, Luc. *A Brief History of Thought: A Philosophical Guide to Living*. Translated by Theo Cuffe. New York: HarperCollins, 2011.

Fitzmyer, Joseph A. *First Corinthians: A New Translation with Introduction and Commentary*. AB 32. New Haven: Yale University Press, 2008.

———. *The Gospel according to Luke I–IX: Introduction, Translation, and Notes*. AB 28. New Haven: Yale University Press, 2008.

———. *The Gospel according to Luke X–XXIV: Introduction, Translation, and Notes*. AB 28A. New Haven: Yale University Press, 2008.

Fredriksen, Paula. *Jesus of Nazareth, King of the Jews: A Jewish Life and the Emergence of Christianity*. New York: Alfred A. Knopf, 1999.

Fuller, Reginald H. *The Formation of the Resurrection Narratives*. New York: Macmillan, 1971.

Funk, Robert W., and R. W. Hoover, eds. *The Five Gospels: What Did Jesus Really Say? The Search for the Authentic Words of Jesus*. New York: HarperCollins, 1997.

Gerhardsson, Birger. *Memory and Manuscript: Oral Tradition and Written Transmission in Rabbinic Judaism and Early Christianity*. Lund: Gleerup, 1998.

———. *The Reliability of the Gospel Tradition*. Peabody, MA: Hendrickson, 2001.

Gilmour, S. M. "The Christophany to More than Five Hundred Brethren." *JBL* 80 (1961): 248–52.

González, Justo. *The Story of Christianity*. Vol. 1. New York: HarperCollins, 1984.

Green, Celia, and Charles McCreery. *Apparitions*. Oxford: Institute of Psychophysical Research, 1977.

Habermas, Gary R. "Explaining Away Jesus' Resurrection: The Recent Revival of Hallucination Theories." *Christian Research Journal* 23.4 (2001).

———. *The Historical Jesus: Ancient Evidence for the Life of Christ*. Joplin, MO: College Press, 1996.

Hays, Richard B. *First Corinthians*. Louisville, KY: John Knox, 1997.

Hengel, Martin. *Crucifixion: In the Ancient World and the Folly of the Message of the Cross*. Translated by John Bowden. Philadelphia: Fortress, 1977.

———. *Studies in Early Christology*. New York: T&T Clark, 2004.

Héring, J. *The First Epistle of St Paul to the Corinthians*. London: Epworth, 1962.

Hoehner, Harold. *Chronological Aspects in the Life of Christ*. Grand Rapids: Zondervan, 1977.

Hoffman, R. Joseph, ed. *Celsus on the True Doctrine: A Discourse against the Christians*. New York: Oxford University Press, 1987.

Hume, David. *Of Miracles*. Cambridge: Hackett, 1998.

Hunter, A. M. *Paul and His Predecessors*. Philadelphia: Westminster, 1961.

Hurtado, Larry. *How on Earth Did Jesus Become God? Historical Questions about Earliest Devotion to Jesus*. Grand Rapids: Eerdmans, 2005.

Jeremias, Joachim. *The Eucharistic Words of Jesus*. London: SCM, 1966.

———. *Jesus and the Message of the New Testament*. Fortress Classics in Biblical Studies. Minneapolis: Augsburg Fortress, 2002.

———. *New Testament Theology*. Translated by John Bowden. London: SCM, 1971.

Jewett, Robert. *A Chronology of Paul's Life*. Philadelphia: Fortress, 1979.

John Chrysostom. *Commentary on the Epistle to the Galatians and Homilies in the Epistle to the Ephesians of S. John Chrysostom*. Oxford: John Henry Parker, 1840.

———. *Homilies on the Epistles of Paul to the Corinthians*. NPNF 12.

Josephus. *Josephus: Jewish Antiquities*. Translated by Louis H. Feldman. LCL 19. Cambridge: Harvard University Press, 1965.

Käsemann, Ernst. *Essays on New Testament Themes*. Philadelphia: Fortress, 1982.

Kearney, P. J. "He Appeared to 500 Brothers (I. Cor. XV 6)." *Novum Testamentum* 22 (1980): 264–84.

Keller, Tim. *Making Sense of God: An Invitation to the Skeptical*. New York: Penguin, 2018.

———. *The Reason for God: Belief in an Age of Skepticism*. New York: Penguin, 2008.

King, Martin Luther, Jr. *The Autobiography of Martin Luther King Jr.* Edited by Clayborne Carson. New York: Warner Books, 1998.

Kloppenborg, John S. "An Analysis of the Pre-Pauline Formula in 1 Cor 15:3b–5 in Light of Some Recent Literature." *CBQ* 40 (1978): 351–67.

Kraeling, Carl H. *John the Baptist*. New York: Scribner, 1951.

Kramer, W. *Christ, Lord, Son of God*. Edited by C. F. D. Moule et al. Translated by Brian Hardy. London: SCM, 1966.

Lapide, Pinchas. *The Resurrection of Jesus: A Jewish Perspective*. Eugene, OR: Wipf & Stock, 2002.

Lewis, C. S. *All My Road before Me: The Diary of C. S. Lewis, 1922–1927*. New York: HarperOne, 2017.

— — —. *Miracles: A Preliminary Study*. New York: HarperOne, 2001.

— — —. "Myth Became Fact." Pages 341–44 in *God in the Dock*, edited by Walter Hooper. New York: HarperOne, 1994.

— — —. *Surprised by Joy: The Shape of My Early Life*. New York: HarperOne, 1955.

Licona, Michael R. *The Resurrection of Jesus: A New Historiographical Approach*. Downers Grove, IL: InterVarsity Press, 2010.

Lüdemann, Gerd. *Paul, Apostle to the Gentiles: Studies in Chronology*. Philadelphia: Fortress, 1984.

— — —. *The Resurrection of Christ: A Historical Inquiry*. Amherst, NY: Prometheus, 2004.

— — —. *The Resurrection of Jesus: History, Experience, Theology*. Translated by J. Bowden. London: SCM, 1994.

Manen, W. C. van. "A Wave of Hypercriticism." *Expository Times* 9 (1897–1898): 205–11.

Marcus, Joel. *Mark 1–8: A New Translation with Introduction and Commentary*. AB 27. New Haven: Yale University Press, 2008.

Marsden, George. *C. S. Lewis's Mere Christianity: A Biography*. Princeton: Princeton University Press, 2016.

Martyn, J. Louis. *Galatians: A New Translation with Introduction and Commentary*. AB 33A. New Haven: Yale University Press, 2008.

Marxsen, W. *Jesus and Easter: Did God Raise the Historical Jesus from the Dead?* Translated by V. P. Furnish. Nashville: Abingdon, 1990.

Meier, John P. *A Marginal Jew: Rethinking the Historical Jesus*. Vol. 1, *The Roots of the Problem and the Person*. New Haven: Yale University Press, 1991.

Meyer, Ben F. *The Aims of Jesus*. Eugene, OR: Wipf & Stock, 2002.

Montefiore, Hugh. *The Paranormal: A Bishop Investigates*. Leicestershire, UK: Upfront, 2002.

Moule, C. F. D. *The Phenomenon of the New Testament*. London: SCM, 1967.

Moulton, J. H. *A Grammar of New Testament Greek*. Vol. 1, *Prolegomena*. Edinburgh: T&T Clark, 2006.

Mowinckel, Sigmund. *He That Cometh: The Messiah Concept in the Old Testament and Later Judaism*. Nashville: Abingdon, 1954.

Murphy-O'Connor, Jerome. "Tradition and Redaction in 1 Cor 15:3–7." *CBQ* 43 (1981): 582–89.

Neill, Stephen, and N. T. Wright. *The Interpretation of the New Testament, 1861–1986*. Oxford: Oxford University Press, 2003.

Neusner, Jacob, W. S. Green, and E. Frerichs, eds. *Judaisms and Their Messiahs at the Turn of the Christian Era*. Cambridge: Cambridge University Press, 1987.

Nickelsburg, G. W. E., Jr. *Resurrection, Immortality and Eternal Life in Intertestamental Judaism*. Cambridge, MA: Harvard University Press, 1972.

Olivelle, Patrick. *Life of the Buddha by Ashva-ghosha*. New York: New York University Press, 2008.

O'Neill, J. C. *The Recovery of Paul's Letter to the Galatians*. London: SPCK, 1972.

Pannenberg, Wolfhart. *Jesus: God and Man*. Translated by L. L. Wilkins and D. A. Priebe. Philadelphia: Westminster, 1977.

Parker, Theodore. *A Discourse of Matters Pertaining to Religion*. Edited by T. W. Higginson. Boston: American Unitarian Association, 1907.

Pascal, Blaise. *Pensées*. Edited by M. J. Adler and R. McHenry. Translated by W. F. Trotter. Great Books of the Western World 30. Chicago: Encyclopedia Britannica, 1990.

Perrin, Norman. *The Resurrection according to Matthew, Mark, and Luke*. Minneapolis: Augsburg Fortress, 2009.

Plummer, Alfred. *A Critical and Exegetical Commentary on the Second Epistle of St. Paul to the Corinthians*. ICC. New York: T&T Clark, 1915.

Price, Robert M. "Apocryphal Apparitions: 1 Cor 15:3–11 as a Post-Pauline Interpolation." *Journal of Higher Criticism* 2 (1995): 69–99.

Qureshi, Nabeel. *Seeking Allah, Finding Jesus*. Grand Rapids: Zondervan, 2016.

Rambo, L. R., and C. E. Farhadian, eds. *The Oxford Handbook of Religious Conversion*. Oxford: Oxford University Press, 2014.

Ramsay, W. *Pauline and Other Studies in Early Christian History*. London: Hodder and Stoughton, 1908.

Robertson, Archibald T., and Alfred Plummer. *A Critical and Exegetical Commentary on the First Epistle of St. Paul to the Corinthians*. ICC. New York: T&T Clark, 1911.

Robinson, J. A. T. *Redating the New Testament*. Eugene, OR: Wipf & Stock, 2000.

Rodorf, W. Sunday: *The History of the Day of Rest and Worship in the Earliest Centuries of the Christian Church*. London: SCM, 1968.

Sanders, E. P. *The Historical Figure of Jesus*. London: Penguin, 1993–1995.

———. *Jesus and Judaism*. London: SCM, 1985.

Schaff, Philip. *The Person of Christ: The Perfection of His Humanity Viewed as a Proof of His Divinity*. London: James Nisbet, 1880.

Schweizer, Eduard. "Resurrection: Fact or Illusion?" *Horizons of Biblical Theology* 1 (1979): 137–59.

Scobie, Charles H. *John the Baptist*. Philadelphia: Fortress, 1964.

Scott, Bernard Brandon. *The Resurrection of Jesus: A Sourcebook*. Jesus Seminar Guides 4. Salem, OR: Polebridge, 2009.

Seeberg, Alfred. *Der Katechismus der Urchristenheit*. Reprint, Munich: Christian Kaiser, 1966.

Shakespeare, William. *Hamlet*. Edited by G. R. Hibbard. Oxford World's Classics. Oxford: Oxford University Press, 1998.

———. *Henry V*. Edited by G. Taylor. Oxford World's Classics. Oxford: Oxford University Press, 1998.

Sherwin-White, A. N. *Roman Society and Roman Law in the New Testament*. Oxford: Clarendon, 1963.

Singh, Sadhu Sundar. *At the Master's Feet and the Visions of Sadhu Sundar Singh of India*. Somerville, TN: Bottom of the Hill, 2014.

Stark, Rodney. *The Rise of Christianity: How the Obscure, Marginal Jesus Movement Became the Dominant Religious Force in the Western World in a Few Centuries*. San Francisco: HarperSanFrancisco, 1997.

Stendahl, Krister. "The Apostle Paul and the Introspective Conscience of the West." *Harvard Theological Review* 56 (July 1963): 199–215.

Strauss, D. F. *The Life of Jesus Critically Examined*. Philadelphia: Fortress, 1972.

Tabor, J. D. *The Jesus Dynasty: The Hidden History of Jesus, His Royal Family, and the Birth of Christianity*. New York: Simon & Schuster, 2006.

Tatum, Barnes. *John the Baptist and Jesus: A Report of the Jesus Seminar*. Salem, OR: Polebridge, 1994.

Taylor, A. E. *Plato: The Man and His Work*. London: Methuen, 1949.

Theissen, Gerd, and A. Merz. *The Historical Jesus: A Comprehensive Guide*. Minneapolis: Fortress, 1998.

Thiselton, Anthony C. *The First Epistle to the Corinthians: A Commentary on the Greek Text*. NIGTC. Grand Rapids: Eerdmans, 2000.

Tolkien, Christopher, ed. *Letters of J. R. R. Tolkien*. New York: Houghton Mifflin Harcourt, 2000.

Tolkien, J. R. R. *The Hobbit*. New York: Houghton Mifflin Harcourt, 1995.

———. "On Fairy Stories." Pages 38–89 in *Essays Presented to Charles Williams*, edited by C. S. Lewis. Grand Rapids: Eerdmans, 1966.

Tzaferis, Vassillos. "Crucifixion—The Archaeological Evidence." *Biblical Archaeological Review* 11 (January/February 1985): 44–53.

Van Voorst, Robert E. *Jesus outside the New Testament*. Grand Rapids: Eerdmans, 2000.

Vermes, Geza. *The Dead Sea Scrolls in English*. Revised and extended 4th ed. Sheffield: Sheffield Academic Press, 1995.

———. *Jesus the Jew*. London: Collins, 1973.

———. *The Story of the Scrolls*. New York: Penguin, 2010.

Vlastos, Gregory. *Socrates: Ironist and Moral Philosopher*. Ithaca, NY: Cornell University Press, 1991.

Wedderburn, A. J. M. *Beyond Resurrection*. Peabody, MA: Hendrickson, 1999.

Wenham, Gordon. *Paul: Follower of Jesus or Founder of Christianity?* Grand Rapids: Eerdmans, 1995.

Wesley, John. *Explanatory Notes upon the New Testament*. 4th American ed. New York: J. Soule and T. Mason, 1818.

Wright, N. T. *Jesus and the Victory of God*. COQG 2. Minneapolis: Fortress, 1996.

———. *The New Testament and the People of God*. COQG 1. Minneapolis: Fortress, 1992.

———. *Paul: A Biography*. San Francisco: HarperOne, 2018.

———. *Paul: Fresh Perspectives*. London: SPCK, 2005.

———. *The Resurrection of the Son of God*. COQG 3. Minneapolis: Fortress, 2003.

———. *Who Was Jesus?* Grand Rapids: Eerdmans, 1992.

Scripture Index

Old Testament

New Testament

Ancient Sources Index